Lewis' School, Pengam

• A History •

Founded 1729

Ewart Smith

Old Bakehouse Publications

First published in October 2013

The right of the Ewart Smith
to be identified as author of this work has been asserted by him
in accordance with the
Copyright Designs and Patents Act 1993.

ISBN 978-1-905967-50-6

Published in the U.K. by
Old Bakehouse Publications
Church Street,
Abertillery, Gwent NP13 1EA
Telephone: 01495 212600 Fax: 01495 216222
Email: theoldbakeprint@btconnect.com
www: oldbakehouseprint.co.uk

Made and printed in the UK
by J.R. Davies (Printers) Ltd.

British Library Cataloguing in Publication Data: a catalogue
record for this book is available from the British Library.

To my mother
who sacrificed so much that I could have a
grammar school and university education.

Contents

Acknowledgements

During the time I have worked on this project I have received help and encouragement in abundance from very many people. Four in particular I would like to thank: John Watkins, Gethin Morgan, Keith James and Peter Downing. They have read and commented on each chapter as it has been written and without their help and keen interest it is quite likely that the book would not have been completed.

In addition other friends and associates have furnished me with information and sources that I could well have found difficult to locate: Greg Buick, Bryn Butcher (Acting Headmaster, Lewis Boys' Comprehensive School), Chris Howard (former Headmaster, Lewis Boys' Comprehensive School), Steve James (Bargoed Library), J Coslett Jones, Rhiannon Cory, Gil Levy and her staff at The Winding House, New Tredegar, David Mills, Enrico Minoli, Mike Oliver (Lewis Boys' Comprehensive School), John Park, Chris Parry (Headmaster, Lewis Boys' Comprehensive School), Brian Russell, Bryan Stephens, Bill Tippins, Arthur Thomas, Hetty Watkins, E David Williams, and the staff at Glamorgan Record Office. To all these I owe a sincere debt of gratitude.

While I have made every effort to check names, dates, facts and figures, it is inevitable that this book contains errors. For these I apologise and accept sole responsibility.

Finally I must thank my wife, Betty, for her unfailing love and support that made this project possible.

Foreword

Since Arthur Wright wrote his *History of Lewis' School Pengam* more than eighty years ago no-one else, as far as I know, has until now attempted to write a sequel. Given the complexity of the task this is not surprising. To start with, collecting together all necessary information is no mean feat in itself. If it is to be widely read, a narrative that encompasses so many years also requires very skilful editing, otherwise the end result becomes no more than a long and somewhat tedious catalogue in which the overall story is lost in endless tables and lists. Yet exactly what to omit can be very hard to determine. Also essential is a well-judged selection of key themes which can be sustained from beginning to end. This too can involve difficult decisions when faced with the many diverse aspects of school life.

It is a measure of how effectively Ewart Smith has dealt with these challenges that his own story of *Lewis' School*, which is presented here, is told so clearly and succinctly. The text is effectively enlivened throughout by inclusion of a well-judged selection of photographs and other illustrations. From beginning to end the day to day lives of both staff and pupils are made real through the use of extracts from key documents, quotes from speeches and the school magazine, as well as summaries of academic and sporting achievements. It is good to see that the slapstick schoolboy humour remained undiminished at all times. The end result is a really good read which will surely capture the interest of both the general reader who has no previous knowledge of the school as well as those of us who were pupils there.

Old Ludovicans like myself will undoubtedly find that the account resonates well with their personal experience. As I remember it, rough and tumble it certainly was, as one would expect in any boys' school, but this was always a good-natured part of day to day getting by and it was never vicious. The boys were remarkably tolerant and I remember no bullying of eccentric or vulnerable individuals. A sense of competition and rivalry invigorated our lives, not only on the rugby field and in athletics but also for many through class work too. Those of more academic bent were allowed to indulge their interests without hindrance or question. Such positive regard for learning amongst many Pengam boys no doubt reflected a deep respect for education which pervaded all elements of their home communities. School discipline regarding misbehaviour and academic laxity was firm but not unduly punitive. My years there were immediately after World War 2 at a time when many of the staff were older men, some even World War I veterans. We happily accepted their eccentricities, shredded academic gowns and quaint mannerisms. Thus it was, at least for me, in those early post-war days.

Eventually the excellence of *Lewis' School Pengam* was recognised far and wide; its academic achievements during the later years before its status as a grammar school ended were particularly brilliant. Perhaps the most striking part of Ewart Smith's narrative is the insight it provides into how the school achieved such high distinction, both academic and otherwise, during many years of its long life, given that it had so few material resources apart from the native wit of the boys themselves. For parents and staff alike every penny counted. Occasionally, when a boy's family hit upon hard times perhaps through parental illness or death, a boy might have to leave school prematurely even though he was academically able. Not many jobs were available to him, but one option would have been to 'go down the pit' to provide for the remainder of his family. Problems posed by inadequate and sometimes dangerous buildings, with the constant threat of subsidence due to coal mining below, are writ large from beginning to end in Ewart Smith's story. One of my own vivid school memories of the surrounding coal industry is of the white dust produced by industrial slag heaps that bordered our playing field. This covered our shoes as we walked in the grass. We weren't too bothered by it because it seemed no more than an inevitable consequence of the industrial scene. The problem was eventually resolved by the mining authority introducing large water sprays to dampen the dust, though the slag heaps themselves remained for quite a while.

It becomes clear as Ewart Smith's story unfolds that major factors which ensured the school's success in the face of such relentless deprivation were not only motivation and hard application on the part of the boys with close support and often major sacrifice from their families, but also the unselfish life-long commitment and dedication of the teachers and governors, who gave so much of themselves for little material reward. It wasn't until I left for medical school, and so became able to compare my own experience with that of others, that I eventually came to realise fully how much I owed to so many dedicated people, particulary those at *Lewis' School,* who had prepared me to meet the challenges that awaited me in the wider world. I am sure that countless other boys felt this way too.

Our grateful thanks are due to Ewart Smith for all his efforts in producing this welcome book. It will surely help us never to forget the great debt we owe to all who laboured hard at *Lewis' School Pengam* to ensure that it achieved so much, having been given so little.

HOWARD GETHIN MORGAN MD (Cantab.) FRCP FRCPsych DPM (Lond.)
Emeritus Norah Cooke-Hurle Professor of Mental Health, University of Bristol.

Preface

(Taken from a school magazine published in 1934)
EDWARD LEWIS, OF GILFACHFARGOED: 1691-1728

How abundant is the harvest from actions sown in the service of others! Some such thought - call it a platitude if you will - must surely occur to us when we recall Edward Lewis, the Founder of Lewis' School. Were you, by the way, aware that our School rejoices (?) in the title of the 'Gelligaer County Intermediate School for Boys'? But this is the tribute of officialdom to itself.

Perhaps it would be idle to speculate overmuch upon the intentions, material or otherwise, of Edward Lewis when constructing his will. He must have been imbued with the desire to create, to fill a gap, to do something that would outlive his own brief life. This had a physical span of thirty seven years, from 1691-1728. By what magic is it wrought that these few years have now passed their second century?

Of his life, as is so often the case with such men, our information is meagre. He died unmarried. His birthday we cannot celebrate. He just lived and died, and the memory of his spirit lives after him, forming one more link in the chain of the immortal hope. One extraordinary thing we know he did: he made his will at the age of twenty-four in 1715. Youth's call to youth?

Edward Lewis had no bee in his bonnet. His benefactions were not of a spectacular order; they were directed to embrace his own kin and the poor he knew; he dealt with things as he found them, realising that man does not live on air and that the human spirit is part and parcel of man. His watchword appears to have been 'The greatest good for the greatest number.'

Many people are of the opinion that too much is given for nothing these days. It is up to us to remove this reproach which is tantamount to a charge of base ingratitude. And nothing is more keenly felt nor more demoralising.

Edward Lewis was not a self-made man who had the personal gratification of looking on the fruit of his bounty after he had amassed wealth. Nevertheless, babies have been named after him, and numbers have blessed the giver whom they have never seen.

In remembering our Founder we must of necessity consider the succession of benefactors and administrators who, inspired by the force of his example, have helped to keep the torch he lit burning brightly. Such a tradition has proved to be of incalculable value, ennobling the donors no less than enriching the foundation. The dry bones of tradition are, by their deeds, clothed with living tissues, auguring well for the future progressive prosperity of the instinct to uplift within us all. When we see what has become of so small a seed, we can realise, in our search for standards by which to measure our own conduct, that there is in very truth a standard of no mean value in the tiniest act of human sympathy. We need never fear to set in motion our humanitarian sparks, for their inherent divinity will produce the conflagration. Not only sickness, but goodness is contagious.

'Nequeo monstrare et sentio tantum' - Juvenal : Satires: VII, 56.
I cannot depict such a man in words though he lives in my mind's-eye.

The Ludovican, Lent 1934.

The English translation of the Welsh motto, *Ni Ddychwel Doe,* on the school badge is *Yesterday Never Returns.*

CHAPTER I

Early History - Pre 1900

The Founder and his Will

Next to nothing is known of the life of Edward Lewis, the founder of the school. He was the great grandson of landowner Sir Edward Lewis of The Van, Caerphilly, and St Fagans, grandson of Sir William Lewis of Gilfach Fargoed, and son of Charles Lewis of Gelligaer. In his Will dated 19 March, 1715 he gave generously to his relatives and friends, and to the poor of the parishes of Gelligaer, Bedwellty and Mynyddislwyn. To finance this he bequeathed, for charitable purposes, an estate in Glamorgan of around 400 acres which produced an income of about £30 p.a. It is said that he died unmarried on 17 April 1728, aged 37. There is no record of his burial in the Gelligaer register, possibly because the rector at the time was the aged Robert Thomas who was feeble and had a poor memory. On the other hand some believe that Edward spent a considerable time with his cousin John Morris of Clifford's Inn, London. Perhaps he died in London? Again there is no record of his burial in the parish in which Clifford's Inn was situated. Edward's Will was admitted to probate at Llandaff on 9 August 1729. This was the effective date of the creation of the Trust which would include establishing a school, Lewis' School.

Due to certain clauses in his Will, Edward Lewis's wishes could not take effect until the death of his mother Elizabeth. She lived at Gilfach Fargoed and in 1734 she made a Will leaving all that she had inherited from Edward to her near relative John Morris. Elizabeth died in 1739 and John Morris proved the Will at Llandaff in the April. There now appeared to be no impediment to the Trust carrying forward the wishes of Pengam's founder, but up turned Edmund Lewis of Hendy, who was next of kin after Elizabeth. He claimed the whole estate. Edmund was poor and was ultimately bought off with relatively small payments which, due to his death, the Trust did not have to continue to pay for very long.

At last there's movement

Nothing happened to implement Edward Lewis's wishes until the affair came to the Court of Chancery on 22 November 1743. Some ten years later, on 24 July 1753, the Master in Chancery certified that a scheme had been laid before him, and approved, to build a school near the Church in Kelligare. The Trustees could spend up to £40 to buy or build a house there for use as a school; £10 a year to pay a Schoolmaster to teach fifteen boys, and up to £15 to provide them with coats and caps. The school began to function around 1760; some considerable time after the founder's death. The first part-time master was Rev. George Parry whose salary was to be funded out of the rents from Cros Faen Ycha Farm (sic). If the tenants failed to pay the rent the school master did not receive any income. In fact on one occasion George Parry had to wait two years to get paid.

The first school
It is unclear whether of not the two-storey house near the parish church in Gelligaer where the school opened on 1 August 1762 was erected by the Trust or acquired by them. What is certain is that the ground floor was a single room measuring 22' by 16' (c 6.75m x 5m) while the upper floor was the Master's residence. This arrangement was most unsatisfactory, for the only access to the living quarters for the master's wife and children was through the schoolroom. Accordingly in 1815 an outside staircase was constructed at a cost of £2.7s. (£2.35) and remained part of the property until it was removed c.1920. Throughout this period the curate and the school master were one and the same person. Though many objected to this arrangement there was some common sense in it for at least it meant that the schoolmaster had been educated. To the outside world the school at Gelligaer was described as a Blue Coat School since the boys' uniforms were made from blue cloth.

The School and the Lectureship separate
Things trundled along quietly for years but notes of a meeting of the Trustees dated 3 December 1793 show that it was now thought necessary to have local Trustees, a full-time master, far better attendance from the boys, and a school in a better state of repair. By 1801 there was a new Board of Trustees. Under the new scheme John Perrett, as the resident trustee, managed the School and the Charity Estates. However the School, where the Headmaster was now paid £10 p.a., and the Lectureship, or clergyman, parted company. There would henceforth be two separate posts. A recurrent entry in the school's accounts during the period 1806-14 raises a smile. A significant amount was spent on re-glazing, the excuse given being that the yard space available for the boys to play ball games was totally inadequate. During 1812 desks, made by the local carpenter, first appeared in the school and in that year the then Head, Rev. David Davies became ill and retired.

A Marine replaces a Reverend
In 1813 Henry Williams who had previously served as a Private of Marines on board *HMS Vanguard* was appointed as Schoolmaster. Williams was an old boy who had assisted Rev. Davies during his illness

2

and was highly thought of by the trustees. When Henry Williams was Master it was a frequent occurrence, so an old boy reminisced, for pupils to barricade the door of the school room in the morning, and keep the Master out until he had promised them a holiday, together with an amnesty for the ringleaders. Whether or not this is a statement of fact seems doubtful but it is a good story. I cannot imagine L Stanley Knight or Neville Richards, the Headmasters when I was at Pengam, submitting to such pressure. Apart from becoming Headmaster, Williams was appointed Vestry clerk for Gelligaer, and subsequently, for Llanfabon as well.

Numbers gradually increased. By 1825 the accounts show that there were twenty boys in the school. The cost of clothes for each boy was £2.18s.9d (£2.94), itemised as: cap 1/9 (9p), boots 7/- (35p), cloth and trimmings £1.9s.3d. (£1.46), making up the cloth 6/- (30p), shirt 3/2 (16p), stockings 1/1 (5p), handkerchief 6d (2¹/₂p), hat 4/6 (22¹/₂p) and shoes 5/6 (27¹/₂p). At this time (the mid 1820s) the Trustees became aware of the value of the coal that lay beneath the ground they owned. They sought the advice of the Court of Chancery, advice which would eventually allow them to build an impressive new school in the valley below.

Investigating Educational Charities
In 1818 the Tory Government, with the Earl of Liverpool as Prime Minister, set up a Commission under Lord Brougham, to investigate the terms and conditions of all Educational Charities. The following year the Government set up another Commission to look into Charities for the Poor. Both sat until 1835, their reports being completed by 1837. These reports listed the lands owned by the various trusts; the value of the coal beneath, and the rents received from properties that belonged to the trusts. For the Lewis' Charity there were three separate parts to the Trust: one for the school, one for the poor, and one for the Lectureship or clergy.

Meanwhile, by the early 1830s the Master was paid £30 a year plus an allowance of £5 for coals. He could also spend up to £44 to clothe twenty boys. At the same time £5 a year was available to pay for bread for twenty-three poor persons in the parish of Bedwellty not in receipt of parish relief, and £63 could be distributed among the poor of Gelligaer. The Lectureship (the third part of the Trust) provided £35.12s.9d (£35.64) annually for ministers to preach every three weeks in the parishes of Bedwellty and Mynyddislwyn. The school prospered.

By 1834 thirty boys were on the books. The Trustees could now increase the Master's salary to £40 a year and the amount spent on clothes up to £2.10s. (£2.50) per boy.

The School and Lectureship re-unite
In December 1836 the Court in Chancery suggested that the posts of Lecturer and Schoolmaster be combined in order to get a more highly qualified teacher. They also suggested that girls should be admitted. The annual salary for the combined post would be £90 but it would be a condition of appointment that the clergyman/master must reside in Gelligaer and travel to St Sannan's Church, Bedwellty, and St Tudor's Church, Mynyddislwyn, to perform his necessary curate's duties. This was a tough condition to impose, for the distances between the three places are significant, even on horseback. Today, riding a horse from Pengam to St Tudor's and back in inclement weather hardly bears thinking about. There was now a rapid succession of Heads. One, James Asher, was dismissed for unspecified misconduct, reinstated, but left soon after.

George Bushell as Headmaster
In 1847, when George Bushell was the 21-year old Headmaster, the school was examined by the Commission of Inquiry into the State of Education in Wales. Their report stated that the school *appeared to do the master much credit. Books used were sanctioned by the National Society and all pupils are allowed to attend the place of worship chosen by their parents. Children of parishioners, who are admitted on the written recommendation of two parishioners, must agree to stay for four years. Clothes are provided and, at the end of the four years boys are apprenticed to an acceptable craftsman with a premium of £8, a further £5 being given to the apprentice at the end of his time on his producing a certificate of good behaviour from his master.*

George Bushell was said to be a man of considerable stature. One day, so the story goes, several workman were strolling over Gelligaer Common when, some distance away, was Mr Bushell with four pupils. 'Who is over there?' asked one of the workmen. 'There', 'Oh! that's Mr Bushell with his four pecks.' (4 pecks = 1 bushel!). School numbers during the period varied between thirty and fifty; the age range was 5 to 14 and there were two monitors.

Relocating at Pengam
During the first half of the nineteenth century the Rhymney Valley became heavily industrialised. People were pouring into the area to

work in the coal mines. The income derived from the sale of coal that lay beneath the land owned by the Trust increased significantly the wealth available to the Trustees from the endowment. As a consequence, a meeting of the Trustees in April 1848 led them to express their intention to move, after 88 years, from the vicinity of St Catwg's Church, Gelligaer, *to the valley*, that is, to the present site. This would put the school closer to the rapidly increasing population that was being drawn into the area by the expanding coal industry. They wished to abandon the one-classroom school house and build *a commodious new school with a chapel for divine worship and a residence for the clergyman, near Pontaberpengam.* The Court of Chancery sanctioned the move but it took another five years for it to come to fruition.

The new school was to be for one hundred and fifty boys and one hundred girls, who would be taught by a master and a mistress. The Lecturer/clergyman was to be superintendent of the school. An architect and builder were engaged and contracted to build the new school on land belonging to Tir y Bont Farm, near the river bridge in Pengam. By May 1850 much of the preparatory work had been done and on the 28th of the month the Bishop of Llandaff, Dr Alfred Ollivant, laid the foundation stone. Included with the stone were coins of the realm for that year and a parchment. When the school was rebuilt beginning in 1902, nothing was found, but they surprisingly came to light when the school was demolished in 2002. They now reside in the care of the current Headmaster.

The new school building, for which the estimated cost was £3200, included a church measuring about eighty feet by forty, with a tower and tall spire at the north-east end. Though a landmark for miles around, the spire was always a risk partly, without doubt, due to the underground coal workings. The first Head at the new school was Henry Cox who took up residence in April 1853. In the school buildings proper lived the schoolmaster and his family, and the monitors who taught on week days. For their labours they were paid between 2/6 (12½p) and 3/6 (17½p) a week. Cox left in 1854 to be replaced by James Tomlinson. At the new school the Trustees employed a woodward. His duties had been to look after the trees and fences but now, in addition, he was asked to be responsible for hauling coal and ringing the chapel bell on Sundays. The tower contained two bells, the smaller bell, cast in 1850, was still in use in the 1940s/50s and was rung to indicate the beginning and end of the school day, and lesson times. The chapel, as impressive as many a rural church, had its own table linen, communion plate, reading desk and organ. The total cost of the school was £4150 (c. £400,000 in 2013), some £675 of which was given by Rev. G W G Thomas, a trustee and former curate of Gelligaer. The west porch was added in 1860 at a cost of £88.16s.7d.

Changing Headmasters

James Tomlinson left in 1860. David Mosely, a 22-year-old bachelor was now appointed Master, and his sister Hannah, Mistress. After four years she left and David's new wife, Mary Ann, took over the rôle. There were by 1863 girls as well as boys in the school. The difference in the cost of clothing for the two sexes is quite marked. Each boy was allowed 50/- (£2.50) which would cover a short frock coat, waistcoat and trousers, all made of dark blue broadcloth, lined, with plain brass buttons; cap, linen shirt, necktie, two pairs of worsted stockings and one pair of boots. For each girl the cost was a mere 20/. They received a gown and trimming made from linsey-woolsey (a thin rough fabric of linen warp and coarse wool or cotton weft) which was dark blue with a very narrow strip of white, a pinafore or apron of brown holland (a coarse linen cloth), two pairs of worsted stockings and one pair of boots. When the Moseleys left in 1867 there were 91 pupils on the books and the great enemy of the school buildings was damp. The Head for the next eight years would be Alfred T Pullin. Pullin was highly thought of by his pupils and whilst at Pengam took Holy Orders. Later, he entered the Church.

Effects of the Forster Education Act

Up to 1870 the School was a simple Charity School that taught little other than the three R's, but the 1870 Forster Education Act was about to change all that. The Act decreed that every district must have a School Board with instructions to build an elementary school in each parish. Accordingly the Lewis Trustees, who were members of the Church of England, came under fire from the Nonconformists who claimed that the Lewis Charity Schools furthered the interests of the Church of England and realistically benefited only their members. They wanted this changed but the Trustees pointed out the terms of the Edward Lewis' Will and nothing happened. By the end of 1871 a Memorandum was sent to the Endowed Schools Commissioners complaining about this state of affairs. The protestors wanted money from the Charity to help the School Board of Governors, the Board to be undenominational and they wanted an appropriate change of Governors. Again the Trustees re-stated Edward Lewis's Will reminding everybody that the Charity supported Pengam School (with 298 on the books), Gelligaer Village School (with 58 pupils) and six other schools in the Rhymney Valley. The Commissioners responded to the Trustees by making several suggestions. Elementary education, they said, is now provided under the 1870 Act so local endowments should be used for aspects of education beyond those linked to elementary schooling. Apart from the three R's they contemplated instruction in geography, history, English grammar, composition, French and/or Latin, elementary mathematics, vocal music and natural science. The school should be for boys aged eight to sixteen but girls should also be considered. The Trustees suggested Exhibitions or Scholarships tenable at the School and at places of Higher Education. Furthermore there should be provision for boarders, cheap rail fares, elected Governors, and the retention of the existing building but modification in the use of the chapel so that it was not exclusively for the Established Church.

Dividing the endowment

The Lewis Endowment would now divide into two separate and independent endowments:

a   The Church or Lectureship Endowment under the former Trustees.

b   The School Endowment which would include portions of the estate that had provided for the Poor of Gelligaer, the bread at Bedwellty and the Apprenticeship for boys of the school. This would be under new Trustees or Governors and had the effect of placating the nonconformist complainants.

At the meeting of the Trustees on 4 September 1874 the schools at Pengam and Gelligaer were restructured. The Headmaster could not henceforth be a clergyman. The incumbent Rev. A T Pullin, was given formal notice to quit. The first meeting of the new Board of Governors was held on 8 September, when it was agreed that the new Head would have a salary of £200 p.a. together with a house and garden rent free. He would also take boarders. There were eighty-three applicants for the post from which Rev. David Evans MA (London), Calvinistic Methodist Minister of Salem Chapel, Dolgelly, was appointed. A condition of the appointment was that he could not practice as a minister during term. The age range for pupils was nine to sixteen; the fees were ten shillings a quarter for pupils under thirteen, and fifteen shillings for the older pupils. Boarding cost £25 a year. Eight pupils could be accommodated in the Head's house - the former Parsonage - and at least twelve more in the School House i.e. where Rev. Pullin lived. Prior to 5 April 1875 Rev. Pullin was assisted by a Mistress, a Senior Monitor, five Junior Monitors and a Pupil Teacher.

Because the use of the chapel was changed a new Parsonage and Chapel of Ease was suggested which should be built in Fleur de Lis. It was. Quite independently St David's Church was built in 1897. The school was to provide secular instruction as listed above, with the addition of Geometry, Practical and Experimental Science, and Mechanical and Engineering Drawing. A separate school for girls was to be given consideration. This became the arrangement, with minor modifications due to the Welsh Intermediate Education Act of 1889, until 1896. With these changes, the school became a Grammar School.

Tom Symonds
Some young boys are quite fearless. During the school year 1870-71 a lad by the name of Tom Symonds, who lived in the bungalow opposite the school, was punished by the Headmaster for climbing the spire. Some lad!

The New School opens
The new school opened on 6 April 1875 as Lewis' Endowed School but soon became known as Gelligaer Endowed Grammar School. Records do not indicate that there were any entrance qualifications. Cheap rail fares had been arranged for day-boys and by 21 May there were eight boarders and thirty-six day boys. Roger W Jones, who had been second choice for the Headship, was appointed Second Master. He would live at the Upper or School House and would be a pillar of the school for the next forty-four years. The school year was divided into four terms:
> January to Easter, with a one week holiday at Easter
> April to June, followed by a seven week Summer holiday
> August to Michaelmas (29 September), and a one week holiday
> October to Christmas, concluding the year with three weeks holiday.

This arrangement survived until 1897 when it gave way to the three-term year.

Expanding the school
Expansion for boarders took place in 1876. At Lower House a large dining room and dormitories were built. There were now seventeen boarders, twenty-two paying day-boys and eleven Foundation Scholars. At the same time it was decided to limit the number of boarders to twenty-four and the number of day-boys to forty-seven. By the middle of the year the total number of pupils had increased to sixty-five and the governors were still talking about a school for girls. Somewhat different from modern times the long summer holiday ran from the middle of June

to 8 August. Problems still persisted with the status of the chapel so, in 1885 the Governors gave the font, reading desk, altar rails and parts of the organ to the Trustees for them to transfer elsewhere as they saw fit. Thus the Nonconformists were placated. The chapel was now the Assembly Hall, but sixty years later it would have pews, a brass lectern, organ and pulpit, and once again the building would be referred to as 'the chapel'. Punishments in school were severe; education was deemed a discipline, the chief aim being the development of a strong moral character. Boys of the time who did very well in later life included Thomas Jones of Rhymney who became Assistant Secretary to the Westminster Cabinet and author of *Rhymney Memories*, a book written while on holiday in Canada. It detailed life in a Welsh village for the fifty years up to 1932.

Reminiscences of an Old Boy
How good it would be to gain a glimpse of school life in the late 1880s when David Evans was Headmaster. Fortunately that is possible through an article written by Edgar Jenkins of Pontypridd which appeared in *The Ludovican* in the summer of 1951. The article is to be found in Appendix 1.

Examinations
In 1883 the numbers at Gelligaer Endowed Grammar School sitting examinations set by the Syndicate of Cambridge University were 12 in the Junior Class, 31 in the Middle Class and 27 in the Senior Class. These included five pupils who were candidates for the Cambridge Local examination. All the results were signed off by R W Shackell MA, St Catherine's College, Cambridge, who was examiner to the Syndicate. The numbers were similar for 1884, and in 1885 five pupils who sat for the Senior Certificate passed in Higher Latin and in Higher French.

There was a big two-fold problem in the 1880s: attendance and the age-range of the pupils in each group. For instance the 10 pupils who sat the Junior examinations in 1886 varied in age from 10 to 15 whilst the time they had been in the school varied from 6 months to two years. There were 23 pupils who sat the examinations at the Middle level. Their ages varied from 12 to 15 years and the time they had been in school from 3 months to 3 years. Such variations in the pupils' ages and the time they had been taught made it very difficult for their teachers.

In 1898 the records show that the name of the school was now Gelligaer County School and that the Governing Body was Glamorgan County

Council. Sixty-three boys sat the entry examination and nine passed with another six described as Proxime, that is they were on the reserve list. At the same time 104 girls sat the entry examination for the first intake to the new sister school which was being built at Hengoed and would take its first pupils the following year. Three passed with four Proxime. The following year twenty-one boys passed examinations set by the newly created Central Welsh Board. The results were signed off by Owen Owen, the Chief Inspector.

Roger Jones takes the helm

When David Evans left in 1887 Roger W Jones, who had been Second Master for several years, became Head. He had been educated at Trefecca and before coming to Pengam had taught at Crediton Grammar School, Devon. The new Head now had sole right to take boarders for both houses but had to provide accommodation for a Second and Third Master, one of whom had to live in the School House and be responsible for discipline there. At his first Governors' Meeting Roger Jones presented a long list of wants. They included chemistry laboratory, gymnasium,

Roger W Jones BA

fives court, a gas supply, playground, cricket field, football ground, new furniture and lavatories. Under his leadership many of these improvements were to be achieved, and in addition he and W Lewis BA, introduced manual instruction and woodwork long before these subjects were recognised by the educational authorities in either England or Wales. Games fees were first introduced in 1887. They were 1/- (5p) per quarter for under thirteens and 1/6 (7½p) for over thirteens. The school's first rugby match was against Tredegar in 1888; the records show that two footballs cost five shillings and eightpence (c. 28p) each. The school also had a fife band. There were now 36 day-boys and 8 boarders compared with a greater total of 65 in 1876.

To help boys to occupy their leisure time the Chairman of Governors donated two sets of draughts, 4 sets of dominoes, one chess set and two boards to the school. With great pride the Head stated that the boys have not only a splendid laboratory, but a Bachelor of Science as teacher. Of the ninety-three boys in the school in 1889 three only had been there for four years, three for three years, nine for two years, twelve for between one and two years, while sixty-six had been pupils for less than twelve months.

The Welsh Intermediate Education Act

The 1889 Welsh Intermediate Education Act required each Welsh county, including Monmouthshire, to set up a Joint Education Committee. Under Section III of the Act the Education Committee had the duty of drawing up a scheme for Intermediate and Technical Education and specifying the Educational Endowments within the county which in their opinion ought to be used for the purpose of such a scheme. However, there was strong opposition to placing absolute control of education and Welsh Educational Endowments in the hands of County Councils. Years passed before this matter was resolved but the Pengam governors ultimately thought it unwise to oppose the Glamorgan County Scheme. Subsequently the buildings, endowments, revenues and relevant documents were passed from the Governors to the County Governing Body of Glamorgan. The old gym now became a Manual Training Room for twenty-four boys. They worked around twelve double benches. From then until 1895 there was no gym, but the new one, built for £450, remained in use until 1961 when a larger, modern gymnasium was built to replace it. The old gym was duly converted into a Swimming Pool in the mid 1960s, much of the cost being met by donations from Old Boys.

Boyish pranks

An old boy who was a pupil during the last decade of the nineteenth century recollected that there were many holes in the classroom floor and that rats, some of which had become relatively tame, lived beneath it. It was commonplace for boys to hide bread, etc., and bait a plank or loose board with it, then remain quiet to watch what happened. On occasions a rat would appear and soon become totally occupied eating the bread when a foot quickly pressed on the other end of the board would jerk the unsuspecting rat into the air to fall among the assembled boys. What amuses young boys obviously changes according to what is available.

Further expansion

Every school needs to be examined and inspected. The first examiners/inspectors at Pengam were staff from University College, Aberystwyth, next came the Cambridge Examinations Syndicate followed by the Central Welsh Board, the new examining body for Wales. Under the 1889 Act Monmouthshire was divided into six Districts, and each was to have its own Intermediate School. However, this educational advance was to present the school with a new problem. Would these new schools take pupils who would otherwise have come to Pengam? Would a school operated by Glamorgan County Council be willing to accept pupils from another county even if the Founder's Will wished it? Important changes were on the horizon. June 1896 saw the last meeting of the old Board of Governors which had been overseeing the running of the school for twenty-two years. The school buildings were now adapted for one hundred and seventy scholars. There was a large main room, two classrooms, laboratory, library, manual training room, a commodious gym, outbuildings and a master's room with a room over it on the first floor.

On the books were fifty-seven boarders - forty from Glamorgan, nine from Monmouthshire and eight from Breconshire - and seventy-seven day-boys. Twenty of the boarders were in the Headmaster's house, the remainder in School House. From 1875 to the end of 1897 eleven hundred and forty scholars had entered the school, 166 as Foundation Scholars from Gelligaer; 67 from Bedwellty and Mynyddislwyn. For the year 1896-97 there were 141 boys on roll at the beginning of the year but 27 fewer by the end of it. This was the first year that pupils sat the Central Welsh Board examinations which were in June and it was this that led to the four-term year being replaced by three. The Central Welsh Board report recommended three more classrooms, a larger Chemistry laboratory, lecture and art rooms, a new cloak room and new sanitary accommodation - what a nice way of putting it. A dining room was also suggested for day-boys bringing their own lunch.

The scene was now set for major alterations. These took two years (1902-04) to complete and resulted in the elevated building familiar to everyone until the large new comprehensive school was built on the other side of the main road.

CHAPTER 2

Moving into the Twentieth Century
1900-1920

A new era

When the school re-opened in September 1904 only two staff remained who had taught in the old buildings. These were the Headmaster, Roger W Jones, and H B Pittway, the Second Master. Four new staff were appointed including Arthur Wright BSc. a Chemistry graduate of Kings' College, London, who was to write *The History of Lewis' School, Pengam* (published 1929). The number on roll was now 123. All the facilities at the new school were in use by March 1905 but it would be September before it was officially opened by David Lloyd George, MP. In his speech he stated that *'he wanted half a dozen schools in Wales of the Eton/Winchester type which produce ideal Welsh gentlemen, not dependent on rank, wealth, birth or blood, but upon character and attainments.'* By the end of the year the dining room was in full use for boys who brought their own lunch: boarders were already catered for and a few boys were within walking distance of home. Tea or cocoa was provided so that they could always have a hot drink. The room had been constructed to take sixty but by 1912 there were more than two hundred on the dinner list. Another facility that was totally inadequate was the hot water system. The single boiler circuit was soon upgraded to a double circuit.

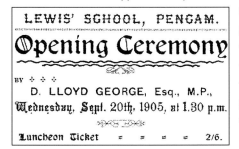

Buildings

Before the conversion of the old school the Manual Instruction Room - known as the 'Slojd Room' due to a Finnish system of teaching in vogue at the time - had been on the ground floor and backed on to the assembly hall. In the new building it was relocated on the first floor above the chemistry laboratory and behind the staff room. Here it would remain until a purpose-built workshop was erected to the north of the main building. The Slojd Room was then converted into two classrooms: Rooms 9 and 10, with a moveable partition separating them. The accommodation now correlated fairly well with the number of pupils on roll but this did not last long. As the numbers increased so did the pressure on teaching spaces, and at times even the gym was used as a part-time classroom.

During his time as Headmaster Roger Jones had, with the permission of the governors, erected at his own expense several wooden buildings. In 1919, as he was about to retire, he offered to sell them to the Governors. They were happy to agree.

Subsidence had long been a concern. It had been the reason that the tower and spire should not be rebuilt and would continue to be a problem until the large modern school was built on the other side of the road in the late 1990s/early 2000s. A particular difficulty in the school building in 1919 was that a supporting beam had moved. Representatives of the Powell Duffryn Company were called in to inspect the damage. They agreed to pay for the restoration.

Central Welsh Board

When the Central Welsh Board was created in May 1896, one of its most important functions was to set and administer examinations in Wales. The Board decided to offer four different examinations, each of which would lead to a certificate: a Junior Certificate two years into secondary education, a Senior Certificate after four years, followed by Higher and Honours Certificates two years after that. By 1907-09 the Senior Certificate was recognised, in various combinations of subjects, by numerous universities and professional bodies; it was the passport to a better world. However, the Board was luke-warm in its attitude to the teaching of vocational subjects and, surprisingly, to the teaching of Welsh, which presumably reflected a widespread feeling that Welsh did not lead to better career opportunities. Pengam's Governors and Headmaster were not entirely happy with the Board's attitude for they did have a Manual Training Room, but their attitude to Welsh was, for decades, luke-warm. Even in the mid 1940s the choice a new boy had to make on his first day was 'Welsh or French?' It was possible to spend eight years in the school and not attend a single Welsh lesson, and to leave having been taught La Marseillaise but not Mae Hen Wlad Fy Nhadau. Most parents however, endorsed the academic curriculum for this led to university and the professions, which in turn meant increased status and prospective earnings.

The Higher and Honours examinations were amalgamated in 1917. That year also saw the implementation of advanced courses - the precursors of A level. It was also laid down that pupils would sit the first School Certificate at the age of 16 and the second or 'Higher Certificate' at 18. The Junior certificate was phased out after the First World War and the Senior Certificate renamed School Certificate in 1923. A pupil who passed with credit in five specific subjects matriculated - a necessary qualification for university entry.

Prize Day

Prize Days have always been important days in the life of any school but the format of the event varies from school to school and even from year to year. At Pengam there were no prizes apart from being told that you were the best at this or that subject. From 1906 up to the outbreak of World War I the older boys at Pengam performed a Shakespearean play at Prize Day; *A Midsummer Night's Dream* that year, *Julius Caesar* the next. As the years rolled on it was the practice to include some of the highly successful items from the Annual Eisteddfod; for example a recitation or solo instrumentalist.

Old Boys' Reunions

Old Boys' reunion meetings were discontinued in 1906. No attempt was made to revive them until 1920.

Sport

Football and cricket had been played at the school since the 1870s but Athletic Sports' Days did not begin until 1899. Sport, and in particular gymnastics, had progressed so much by 1907 that the recently formed school Gymnastics team entertained Aberdare, Barry and Porth in a four-school competition held in the school hall, and won.

In June 1919 an Athletic Sports and Military Tournament was held at Pengam. It included rifle drill and physical drill. For the 80 yds sprint there were 36 competitors; for 100 yds 30 competitors; and for the 120 yds Junior Handicap 58 entrants were given handicaps of between 0 and 18 yds. There was also a shooting final and a 440 yds Open Handicap. Fifteen pairs competed in Fives in Junior and Senior competitions, while 51 entered for the Cross Country. These were given handicaps of up to 80 yds. The Caldwell Cup, presented by Mrs Hugh Caldwell in 1908, was awarded to D J Dando in 1909, I R Edwards in 1910, H C Phillips in 1912 and 1913, R Williams in 1914 but was not awarded from 1915 - 1917.

Clubs and Societies

The Central Welsh Board held their examinations in July. Unfortunately, this arrangement did not leave sufficient time for all the trials to take place to select those who would compete in the sports. In consequence it was decided to hold the annual school sports in June, a timing which remained for many years. Sporting activities thrived and the Literary and

Debating Society was also extremely active. In 1908 the Society, which met in the evening, held fortnightly meetings, alternating debates with lantern lectures given by members of staff and others. Topics included *Telescopes, Bridges, Nationalisation of the Railways, Notable Welshmen, Life of Mohammed, The Roman Camp at Gelligaer, Advantages of Education, South Africa,* and *Aeroplanes*. Though the Society was flourishing it was decided to discontinue it the following year because so many boys had to travel significant distances late in the day. An attempt was made at a revival in 1910 but it folded again at the end of the year for the same reason. That year the subjects for debate included *Is Commercial Supremacy Essential to maintain our position among Nations?* and an Old Boys' debate on *Socialism*. On each occasion two spoke for the motion and two against. Over the years many clubs were formed by enthusiastic staff and boys only to be wound up after a short time. In 1899/1900 a cycling club was formed which lasted two years. It was revived in 1912 but was abandoned after an accident in which a pupil was injured.

School Humour

For many years the room diagonally opposite the Headmaster's office was known as the Bell Room. Here hung the school clock. It was the duty of the class monitor, at the appropriate time, to leave the room to ring the electric bell outside the Headmaster's Office to indicate the change of lessons and the end of the school day. One afternoon in the middle of a maths lesson given by the Headmaster, he was called out to interview a visitor. Naturally the boys were thrilled but evil thoughts soon came into the minds of a few. One boy climbed up and moved the hands of the clock to 4.30, which signified the end of the school day. Another immediately nudged the monitor, a bit of a swot totally engrossed in his work and oblivious to what was going on around him, and pointed to the clock. The monitor rose and left the room to ring the bell but while he was out the hands of the clock were moved back to the correct time. On his return the monitor gathered his books together but while doing so the Headmaster arrived and demanded 'Who rang the bell?' 'I did, Sir' replied the monitor. 'Why?' asked the Head. 'It was half past four, Sir.' replied the boy who glanced at the clock to see that the time now stood at 4.10. As he was totally unable to give an explanation and too bewildered to realise what had happened he had to submit to a severe scolding.

Local Competition

In 1910 came news that alarmed everyone connected with the school. Monmouthshire County Council proposed building a Secondary School on the other side of the river in Fleur-de-lis. What effect would this school have on Monmouthshire boys who wanted to go to Pengam? Many parents didn't want to be denied sending their sons to such a prestigious school. Academic standards at the school were high, epitomised by E Bernard Fry of Blackwood gaining an Open Scholarship in Classics to Hertford College, Oxford, in 1911. The scholarship was worth £100 p.a. for five years. After some time these plans were revised. In their place the County proposed building at Abertysswg but this plan also fell by the wayside. Eventually it was decided to set up a Secondary School at Maesycwmmer in an existing building. This went ahead in 1921 and the building remained in use until 1937 when a new school with improved facilities was built at Britannia. The new school, known as Bedwellty Grammar School and later as Bedwellty Comprehensive School, thrived for decades but was closed early in the present century. Shortly afterwards its impressive buildings were dismantled. A new secondary school was also built at Rhymney.

Extra-curricular Activities
1913 was to see the first Annual St David's Day Eisteddfod, the main activity being a competition for the Best Original Play. In the years that followed, the annual Eisteddfod would be one of the highlights of the school year. Scores of boys would recite, sing, play instruments, write poetry and reveal their creative skills. Scouting was also popular and school camps thrived. During World War I several groups attended harvest camps: Fairford, Gloucestershire in 1917 and St Athan in 1918.

World War One
In July 1914 all, on the surface, seemed peaceful in Europe, but it was not to remain so for long. When the new term began on 15th September the war was in its sixth week. One of the first staff to leave was Physical Instructor Sgt. Charles Ward, VC who had gained the Victoria Cross for bravery in the Boer War. Appointed in 1904 Charles Ward was to return to the school after the war and remain until 1921. A school Cadet Corps was immediately formed with staff members Captain Frank Rees and Lieutenant R G Jones - senior master when the author arrived in 1944 - as officers. The idea was that they could give elementary military training to boys who were potential officers. Another possible offshoot of the war was the re-introduction, in November 1915, of a Prefect system. Years previously there had been prefects among the boarders but for no apparent reason the system had lapsed. The belief was that prefects acquired leadership skills and so influenced things for the better, but it should not pass unnoticed that it also made life a little easier for the staff.

Weather conditions in the mid 1910s were at times extreme. During the Great Blizzard of 28 March 1916 only seventy-six boys out of two hundred and twenty-six reached school - all were dismissed at mid-day. During this severe winter, and to help the war effort, a National Savings group was set up and War Savings Certificates issued. Over the period 1916-19 nearly £1000 was invested in War Savings by members of the school. The following year, the day before school was due to open for the winter term, our sister school at Hengoed, which had been opened in 1900, was destroyed by fire.

Correspondence between Arthur Wright and former pupils during the First World War and later years.

More than any other member of staff Arthur Wright seemed conscious of the needs of former students while they were away in the forces and was prepared to do something about it. For example he corresponded with W W Parsons RNVR of the Fleet Air Arm while he was a prisoner of war in Germany. Scores of letters were penned and sent by him, and it was not unusual for him to send parcels too. Several extracts follow which illustrate the relationship between this teacher and his former pupils.

1 In May 1914 **Cyril J Evans** wrote from 95 Sanitary Section, Sailors and Soldiers Institute, Alexandria, Egypt. He complained about the open sewers and filthy 'natives'.
In another letter an army lorry had hit him and he had a broken collar bone.
On 27.6.16 Cyril refers to collecting things for the school museum and to war stamps.
He writes that Galsworthy (a former teacher) has been promoted. Galsworthy was always bluff and genial with everybody. He queries Arthur Wright on chlorine in water, being concerned that where he is they put chloride of lime tablets into the water.

2 **Harold Lawrence** from Egypt on 27.5.1916. He is on the coast to sort out any trouble with the natives. E Bernard Fry is 100 miles along the coast. W W A Williams is in my tent. The Head's son is also in Egypt. Also J C Roberts, Abertysswg - his father is Baptist Minister there.
In another letter dated 27.6.1916 he encloses stamps.
On 8.7.1916 he writes that Vernwy Harris the architect's son is at Gallipoli.
20.10.1915 Now in the Dardanelles

No date: Gallipoli business is now over. Refers to E B Fry as being decidedly delicate looking in earlier years but now a picture of health and sporting a moustache. Both had been on the Peninsula.

3 Arthur Williams (letter 10.6.16) in the Field Ambulance of BEF. He sent Arthur Wright coins and records that there are worse smells than hydrogen sulphide.

4 R W Jones 29.3.16. At Portland, Dorset, in the Royal Fusiliers.
On 2.4.16. He is at Surbiton, his fifth place in five weeks.

5 J Llewellyn Roberts Good Friday 1916. 30 000 troops here.
Attested in February, called up April 3. I am now up at 5.30, on parade at 6.30. The Infantry Training has been brought down to 10 weeks.

6 R Ivor Davies 8.3.1916. In a Convalescent Camp at Rhyl.

7 Bert Ryan and **Herbert Ryan** c/o Colombo, Ceylon. They are on the *S S Purley* near Port Said on 14.2.16. They left Cardiff 11 days ago and are watching for submarines. They should put a searchlight on us to go through Suez. We lost the port lifeboat in rough weather - a wave knocked it. Radcliff's of Cardiff give a war bonus to their apprentices.

8 H T Jones 7.7.1916 He writes to say he'd joined the army.

9 Walter Wills. He was rejected but is now in YMCA Camp.

10 Tom C Jordan (aged 17) and **A E Roberts** (19) says that Eton boys are proud of their military record, Pengam boys appear to be ashamed of theirs. These two enlisted. Tom says that *Arthur Wright is the only master who showed the least interest in me.*

11 A E Roberts wrote that Tom had been invalided out. He'd met a boy who thought it a disgrace to fight for one's country. He'd had rheumatic fever and dysentery through wet and cold in the trenches. Back in the trenches of Ypres tonight.
Wrote again on 23.12.14 I allow 7/- (35p) per week from my pay for my widowed mother and my sister (aged 5). I'm in charge of lorries running supplies to the front. He refers to Pittway's accident.
15.1.1915 He refers to Pittway getting better. Not impressed with the Flemish people. They are mean and would rob you of your trousers.

Charged a franc for a bale of straw to sleep on and return it in the morning. The Belgians would sleep in the garden for you to have a room in their house. They are a healthy, vigorous, joke loving people and quite as good intellectually and physically as the best of British. The French are not. He thanks Arthur Wright for writing to him.
5.2.1915 Throughout life I have and will regard the Code of Honour taught me at Pengam.
Another letter 2.5.1915. Wrote to say he'd had a lovely parcel from Arthur Wright which included cakes and biscuits.

12 D J Jones 1.9.1916 Somewhere in France, 50 yards behind the lines. I would give my life rather than see my old school desecrated by the Germans as the buildings here have been. I thank all my tutors from the bottom of my heart for all they have done for me.

13 D A P Evans 21st Battalion HQ, Hatfield (no date) E R Morris is here with me.
Another letter - in the trenches.
22.6.15 Thanks for parcel. Just out of the trenches after four days. Near a large colliery about half the size of Bargoed. Our homes are among the pit props.
He was later killed in action.

14 J H Walters near the pyramids, Egypt.
20.2.1915 In Egypt with the Sydney YMCA Australian Imperial Forces. Enthused on a visit to Cairo museum. With very good Indian troops, also New Zealanders, Gurkhas and Sikhs.
In another letter he is with Australians.

15 Lewis J Watkins writes to say that he is looking after horses.

16 Arthur Ealsworthy writes from Llandudno to say that he is undergoing night training.

17 E R Morris wrote to say that D A P Evans had been killed in action.

18 Tom S Jones (Tirphil) 13.1.1916 France, two months after coming out. S Higgins of Blackwood has been awarded the DCM. There had been a gas attack on our lake positions. The area was flooded out, there are shell holes everywhere. On the trench boards the water is sometimes up to 3, 4 even 5 feet deep.
17.2.1916 France. Have done 16 days in the trenches: 4 front line, 4

support and 8 reserve i.e. (2F, 2S, 4R) X 2. He refers to Cpl Percy Morgan.

12.3.1916. From the trenches. Wrote to say that W Cliff Harris (former pupil) had died. There were many cases of trench foot and frostbite in the trenches.

19 From **Edith Evans**, sister of D A P Evans, on 16.11.15 to say that her brother had been killed by a shell whilst in the trenches.

20 Private E B Fry RAMCT, British Middle East Forces on 24.2.16. This is post-Oxford.
It is a surprise that he is a private and not an officer.

21 Jack Thomas Royal Flying Corps, Montrose. This is a miserable place - the people hate us. Would you like a piece of a propeller for the school museum?

22 H Trevor Jones he writes from the Royal Links Hotel, Cromer. Says he was treated too leniently in the physics classes. He also refers to the sad death of staff member Mr Matthews.

The House System
Over the years the House system operated in several different forms. In the early days there were two houses, Lower House and School House, but this arrangement lapsed in 1902. In May 1917 a new House System with six houses was created. (In 1921 it was reduced to five: Glyndwr, Picton, Islwyn, Caradoc and Tudor - all famous Welshman - and, because five was soon found to be inconvenient for competitions, to four in 1927).

The School in 1917
What follows are extracts from a handout to parents in 1917 showing what the school had to offer, the costs, and what was expected from the pupils and their parents.

Lewis' School, Pengam is a Public Endowed School, re-constituted by the Endowed Schools Commission in 1874, and placed under the control of the County Council of Glamorgan by Scheme of Charity Commission, dated 13th May, 1896.

Staff
Headmaster : ROGER W JONES, BA (London), London University Diploma in the Theory and Art of Teaching.

21

Assistant Masters: H B Pittway, MA (Victoria University) Second Master, Thomas Price, MA (An Oxford Honours Mathematician), Arthur Wright BSc. (London), Francis L Rees, BA, (Wales), R G Jones (Board of Education Certificated Teacher), T Matthews, MA (Wales), Stanley Edwards, BA (Wales), Dr Paul Diverres, D Litt (Rennes), MA (Liverpool) and Dr J A Pate MA, Ll.B (Cambridge), Ll.D. (Dublin).
Visiting Masters: F J Kerr (Art) and T Gabriel (Music).

History of the School

This School was originally established in Gellygaer Village on the foundation of EDWARD LEWIS of Gilfach Fargoed who, by Will dated 19th March, 1715, left property for the education of the Children of the Parish. It was afterwards removed to the present site at Pengam, and was re-constructed in 1874 by the Endowed Schools Commission as a Secondary School for Day Boys and Boarders. In 1896 it was included in the Glamorgan County Scheme; framed in accordance with the provisions of the Welsh Intermediate Education Act, and the School is now carried on under the inspection of the Central Welsh Board, with the object of providing such a course of Secondary Education as will fit Boys for Business, the Professions, or the University.

Subjects of Instruction

Scripture, English, Welsh, Latin, Greek, French, History, Arithmetic, Mathematics, Physics, Chemistry, Geography, Drawing, Woodwork, Cardboard Modelling, Vocal Music and Physical Exercises.

Inspection and Examination

The School is recognised as a Secondary School by the Board of Education, and is subject to their Inspection. It is also annually inspected and examined by the Central Welsh Board for whose Certificates Boys are prepared. These Certificates, which are of four grades - Junior, Senior, Higher and Honours, not only afford a guarantee of adequate training and knowledge, but also entitle the holders of them to exemption from nearly all the various examinations preliminary to entrance to the Professions.

Scholarships and Exhibitions

Boys from the School District, i.e. from the parishes of Gellygaer, Bedwellty and Mynyddislwyn, are eligible for Scholarships tenable at the School. These Scholarships cover cost of Tuition, Books, and (if required) Train fare. Usually, twelve Scholarships are offered for competition annually to boys from Elementary Schools, and three are awarded on the results of the previous year's work to boys already in the School.

All Boys in the School, resident in the Administrative Counties of Glamorgan and Monmouth are eligible to compete for the Exhibitions offered by their respective County Authorities. These County Exhibitions are of the value of £30 a year for three years, and are offered by the Counties for competition among pupils of the County Schools; they are awarded on the results of the Central Welsh Board Examination and are usually tenable at any place of higher education selected by the successful candidate.

Fees

Tuition - For Boys residing in the administrative County of Glamorgan, or in either of the two parishes of Bedwellty and Mynyddislwyn ... £4 a year. For Boys residing outside these limits £12 a year. The annual fee for boarders is £30.

If more than one child from the same family attend either Lewis' School, or Hengoed Girls' School, the fee for each child after the first shall be £3.

Boys should also subscribe one shilling and fourpence (almost 7p) a term to the Games and Library Fund but this payment is voluntary.

All Fees are to be paid to the Headmaster on or before first day of Term.

Notice of Leaving

A Half-Term's Notice will be required before the removal of a pupil; and the payment of half the fees for the term.

School Premises

The School Buildings, standing in their own grounds of 10 acres, are pleasantly situated on an eminence overlooking the Rhymney Valley. The site is remarkably healthy, as is attested by the almost unbroken immunity from sickness which the School has enjoyed for over 35 years. The premises comprise the Headmaster's house, School Hall, Class Rooms, Laboratories, Art Room, Woodwork Room, Gymnasium, Fives Court, Dining Hall, etc. The main block of buildings, with the exception of the School Hall, was erected in 1904, and was publicly opened on the 20th September, 1905, by Mr David Lloyd George, MP, now the Right Honourable David Lloyd George, MP, Minister of Munitions; and later Prime Minister.

Access to the School is easy. There are two Railway Stations at Pengam within five minutes walk of the School, one on the Rhymney Railway, and the other on the Brecon and Merthyr Railway; in direct communication with Cardiff and Newport respectively.

Admission

By the School Scheme it is provided that

(a) No pupil shall, without the special permission of the School Governors, be admitted to the School under the age of 11 years.

(b) No pupil shall remain in the School after the end of the School Year in which the age of eighteen is attained except with the permission of the School Governors, which in special cases, may be given upon the recommendation of the Head Master, until the end of the School Year in which the age of nineteen is attained.

Boarding Arrangements
Borders are lodged in the house of the Head Master, and are under his direct supervision. Each Boy is provided with a separate bed.

Clothes, etc - A list of Clothes, etc., required will be supplied by the Head Master. This list should be returned in the pupil's box, with particulars of clothes sent shown in the proper column. All clothes and boots must be sent back in good repair. No responsibility will be undertaken for any articles not properly marked. Each boy is required to have a black suit for Sunday wear. Dark clothes are recommended for ordinary wear. Every boy must wear the School cap, to be obtained of the Caretaker at the School, while going to and from school, and while in the School grounds.

Visits - Boarders may be visited by their friends on half-holidays when they will be allowed to spend the afternoon out if desired. It is especially requested, to avoid interruption of School work, that visits to pupils may be, if possible, confined to these days.
Sundays - St Margaret's Church and Chapels of various denominations where services are carried on both in Welsh and English, are within easy distance of the School. Boys are free to attend Morning Service at any place of worship desired by their parents; they all accompany the Headmaster to Evening Service.

Holidays
The Holidays are about seven weeks in Summer, four weeks at Christmas, and two weeks at Easter. At half-term one day's holiday is also granted.
Parents are strongly urged to see that their sons return to School on the first day of Term, as boys returning late hinder not only their own progress, but also the work of those who return punctually. Regular attendance is expected from all day-boys, and if any boy is unavoidably absent, the parent is requested to send immediate information to the Headmaster.
New boys may be received at any time, but should if possible, enter at the beginning of Term.

Thoughts Turn to Peace
Though the war was still being prosecuted in 1918 people's thoughts

were now turning to other things. Rhydderch E Williams of Bargoed became the first Chaired Bard, followed by J Stanley Jones of Bargoed - later Headmaster in New Tredegar - in 1919. With the end of the war in sight Roger Jones let it be known that he wished to retire. He had been Headmaster for thirty years, had seen the school rise from a small grammar school with about a hundred boys to a grammar school with two hundred and fifty pupils and a status second to none in the Principality. He thought that now, with the cessation of hostilities would be an appropriate time for a younger man with new ideas to take the helm. As we come to the end of an era it is a sobering thought that forty-five old Ludovicans died in the war.

Unfortunate Events

Epidemics were commonplace in the general population. In particular: influenza, whooping cough, chickenpox and tuberculosis. In 1904 there was an outbreak of an unspecified illness among the boarders at the school. The wife of the Headmaster Roger Jones nursed them but she became ill herself and died. They had celebrated their silver wedding the previous Christmas.

On 15 August 1912 Humphrey Owen Jones MA, DSc, FRS, together with his bride of fifteen days and their guide, were killed while ascending Arguilee Rouge de Peteret, Switzerland. He was 34. Owen Jones had been a boarder at the school from 1890 to 1894. He graduated from University College, Aberystwyth, in 1897 with a First in Chemistry, was elected to a Fellowship of Clare College, Cambridge, awarded a DSc. from London University in 1904 and had become a Fellow of the Royal Society earlier in the year - at that time the youngest ever. Between 1900 and 1912 Owen Jones was responsible for more than sixty scientific papers, discovered a new substance - carbon monosulphide - and, as a distinguished mountaineer, pioneered some of the most difficult climbs in Snowdonia before making the first ascent of Brouillard ridge to the summit of Mont Blanc.

Appointed in 1911 to teach Geography and Welsh, Thomas Matthews MA did much for the school. He was instrumental in publishing three volumes under the title *Dail y Gwanwyn* or *Leaves of Spring* which were collections of essays in Welsh written by the pupils. He also had two books published: *Welsh Records in Paris* and *Life of John Gibson, the Artist*, as well as numerous articles in Welsh periodicals. Sadly he died young in September 1916 after a long illness.

Background events linked to education

Around 1900 more than 1 in 3 boys and up to half of girls leaving Secondary Schools became teachers.

In 1910 women teachers were dismissed on marriage.

The poor medical condition of soldiers recruited for the Boer War created the climate for legislation on school meals and milk. 1910 saw the introduction of free milk.

The Arrival of D Vaughan Johnston MA

In March 1919 the Governors advertised for a new Head to replace Roger Jones MA who under a new scheme had to retire at 65. They were seeking a Headmaster who was to be under 40, have a Degree and speak Welsh. They offered a commencing salary of £500 p.a. rising by annual increments of £20 to £600 p.a. The Headship included a house rent free. Six applicants were short-listed. Three of these - Frank L Rees, Thomas Price and F T Williams were already on the staff. Ultimately John Morgan of Ystalfera narrowly lost out to D Vaughan Johnston MA.

Vaughan Johnston, a married man aged 36, took up the post of Headmaster on 4 June 1919. A former pupil of Swansea Grammar School, Vaughan Johnston had won a Mathematics Scholarship to St John's College, Cambridge, where he gained a First. For the six years prior to his arrival at Pengam he had been Head at Newtown Intermediate School. By the time Vaughan Johnston took up his post all the old staff had returned from war service except two. One had been killed when his ship went down, the other chose a new career. In July 1919 four staff left. Accordingly five new appointments were made to join the six staff who remained. September/October of the Head's first term gave him several problems he couldn't do much about. One of these was a two-week long railway strike which reduced average attendance from two hundred and forty to one hundred and fifty. During the strike some boys walked between ten and twelve miles a day to get to and from school. On 29 October, Alec Watkins, of Ystrad Mynach was killed by a train on his way to school. These events did not augur well for the new head.

Staff

During this period staff turnover was considerable, twenty-nine of those appointed leaving within three years. However there were a few long-term appointments: R G Jones (1907), Dr Pate (1915), H D Jones and T A Hughes (1919), and D Morris, W E Park and C M Harris (1920). R G Jones retired in 1945, C M Harris holds the record as the longest serving member of staff - more than forty years.

Teachers' pay in Wales was poor but things got much better after 1917. Now, Central Government was to pay 60 per cent of the salary costs compared with 40 per cent previously. New scales were implemented the following month bringing the Head's pay up to £500 p.a. The Second master was now paid £290, the highest teacher £260 and the lowest teacher £190 even though he was a graduate. Two increments were given for a First Class Honours degree and one for a Second Class Honours, Post Graduate or Teaching Diploma.

Pengam as other see us
It is always good to know how others see us, particularly people from abroad. What follows is a copy of a leading article that appeared in the Breton newspaper 'Ar Bobl', published at Carhaix, Cornouailles, on the 14 June,1913.

WHAT IS DONE ELSEWHERE
Far be it from us to think of saying that education in Brittany is not, broadly speaking, as satisfactory as it is in Wales. Indeed, we find schoolmasters who are devoted to youth and who do not spare their efforts to obtain good results in the schools of both countries. But there are many ways of doing a thing; and the ability to read and write, and the possession of a knowledge of geography and arithmetic, are not enough to enable one to boast of having a suitable education. I insist on the word 'suitable' (appropriée). In France, the uniform education, invariably the same, which is given in the primary schools of the 36,000 communes of the country, can, strictly speaking, turn out young people who are equipped with sufficient knowledge to enable them to get on in life and to attain the ideal of every good father of a French family, which is, the making of perfect functionaries of his children. But there is a great deal of difference between that and the claim that primary education with us is adequate for the mentality and the mind of our race.

We would neither like to offend anyone, nor to give the impression that we find what is done else-where better than what is done with us, but we are forced to establish a comparison to the disadvantage of our schoolmasters when we receive two volumes like 'Llen Gwerin' and 'Two Plays' from Wales. What are these little books? One of them is in Welsh, the other in English.

Both are the work of scholars between the ages of 12 and 15 years, who attend Lewis' School, Pengam, Glamorganshire, Wales, directed by Mr T Matthews, MA, Welsh master at the school. Mr Matthews is not satisfied with teaching his pupils the art of reading in a clear, intelligible voice, and how to write a page of dictation. He does better, though doubtlessly it is the large degree of freedom which prevails in the scholastic programmes in Great Britain which allows him this scope. He said to his pupils: 'You are young boys from a country which is different from England. You are Welsh boys. Consequently, in addition to English, you should know your mother tongue to perfection. I want to find out those of you who know Welsh best and who are best acquainted with the family traditions of your country and with the customs of your villages, and I am going to ask those boys to write a book!'

Do not be surprised. The young Welsh boys understood the thought of their good, patriotic master. Each one of them set to work. One of them wrote a page in Welsh dealing with such and such a custom of his village or parish; another wrote from memory the proverbs or recipes of which he had heard his grandmother speak; another, a ballad that he remembered. When the master gathered together all these varied productions, he sorted them out and kept enough of them to make a little bound volume of eighty pages, under the title of 'Llen Gwerin' (Folklore), which was illustrated with the portraits of the twenty-six 'authors,' who were between the ages of 12 and 15 years. 'This little book,' Mr Matthews writes to us, 'is now used as a reader in many schools in Glamorganshire'.

What noble desires of emulation the perusal of the work of their school-fellows at Pengam must arouse in the scholars of Glamorganshire. That is good work for a school, but there is better. Mr C Evans foresaw the arrival of the Anti-Welsh (these are the counterpart of the Anti-Breton). 'Pooh!' the Saxon will exclaim. 'Your pupils are good at Welsh, but they don't know my English! Mr C Evans forestalled this objection by arranging a competition among his older scholars (15 years) for a play written in English, the two best to be published as a booklet.

Two young boys, William Nash (later Assistant Medical Officer of Health, Mon C C) *and E N Williams,* (later Keeper of Archaeology at the National Museum of Wales) *carried off the palms of victory. Their two plays, gracefully dedicated 'To their mothers,' the one 'Paid Back' in Three Acts, the other 'The Knight,' also in Three Acts, had the honour of being printed in the form of a graceful booklet.*

And then you have young dramatists who already know glory and fame. What is possible in Great Britain is not possible in Little Brittany, our good tattlers will tell us with a smile. What is true here, is incorrect there. That may be! Nevertheless, truth is an indivisible whole, and if we honestly admit that the educational system employed in Wales gives better results from the point of view of regional culture than that employed by us, it would be no dishonour for us to borrow it. We have, indeed, taken the Boy Scouts from the English. Let us take from them, what would be far better, the School boys of Pengam.

A drawing of the front of the mansion Gilfach Fargoed, with its three floors (four for the porch) as it looked towards to end of the 17th century. Elizabeth Parkinson in *The Glamorgan Hearth Tax Assessments* lists Gilfach Fargoed, Llanbradach Fawr and Van, Caerphilly, as the only three houses in our area of upland Glamorgan with over 10 hearths. This was the home of Edward Lewis, the founder of Lewis' School, Pengam, from 1691 to 1728.

Gilfach Fargoed as it looked c. 1930.

The house adjacent to Gelligaer Church where the Edward Lewis' charity school, or Free School, was set up in 1762 on the ground floor. The Headmaster and his family lived on the upper floor, the outside staircase, shown here in 1907, being added in 1815 to provide access to the living quarters without walking through the schoolroom. The staircase was removed c. 1920 and the house demolished in 1970.

EDWARD LEWIS'
CHARITY.
THE SCHOOL LANDS
1. Two FARMS, Crossfane Isha   149a. 0r. 29p.
          "   Ucha   158a. 2r. 22p.
2. A FARM called Tir Trosnant   14a. 0r. 20p.
   subject to an annual payment of £5 for
   bread for the poor of Bedwellty.

THE POOR LANDS
1. A FARM called Waun yr Arglwys 55a. 2r. 10p.
2.   "   Gwerthonor Ucha 68a. 2r. 6p.
LECTURESHIP LANDS
1. A FARM called Gwerthonor Isha 43a. 3r. 24p.
2.   "   Tyr y Bont   47a. 1r. 29p.

The board used by Arthur Wright when he gave talks on the Edward Lewis' Charity. It shows the farms whose rents produced the finance for the setting up of Lewis' school; money to be distributed to the poor of Gelligaer and Bedwellty, and money to pay the clergyman at Gelligaer for his role as 'Lecturer' to the school, and for him to be able to preach at St Sannan's, Bedwellty and St Tudor's, Mynyddislwyn.

An early etching of the new enlarged school after the move from the small house adjacent to Gelligaer church to the site in Pengam. The spire houses two bells and rises above the east end of the chapel.

A photograph taken at about the same time as the etching but from the south-west. The room in the centre at right angles to the chapel is the chemistry laboratory; the room on the extreme right the masters' common room.

This photograph (the only one I have come across) taken in the late 1800s from the Monmouthshire side of the Rhymney river, shows both the school building and, on the extreme right through a gap in the trees, the Headmaster's residence.

Originally the Headmaster's residence, this building was used for boarders and, at a later date, became known as lower school. For many years in the '40s and '50s third year pupils were based here.

A school group in 1890 outside the west door. Headmaster Roger W Jones BA sits between M J Millett BSc. and William Price who was to 'die in harness' in 1902.

Science teacher M J Millett BSc. with a group of boys making up a soccer XI Was this the First XI and it included the teacher? Apart from the jersey, players wore what they had. A cap appears to be an essential part of the kit.

The school's cricketing fraternity in the 1890s. Science teacher M J Millett (with beard) is the teacher on which the school relies for its success in sport at this time.

An early group (the gym was built in 1895) with their teacher prepared for the exercises of the day. The shorter clubs (Indian clubs) with various swinging movements, were used to train for strength, but what were the long clubs used for? In almost every sporting or athletic activity the boys seem to be fully clothed.

Lewis' School had a thriving Cycling Club during 1899 and 1900. The team is shown here riding along in front of the main building. The room on the left is the chemistry laboratory, a very proud facility of the school at the time.

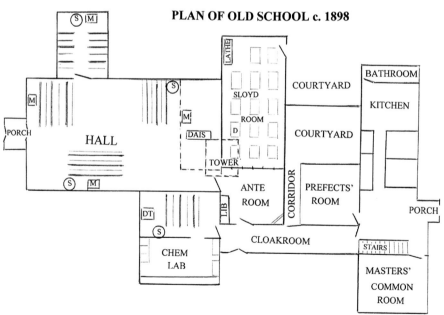

PLAN OF OLD SCHOOL c. 1898

A plan of the school as it was before the major rebuilding of 1902-04. The hall was used as the main teaching space with three teachers and their pupils based there.

The interior of the 19th century school showing the boys of Forms I and II at 'brushwork', while seated in their double desks in the hall.

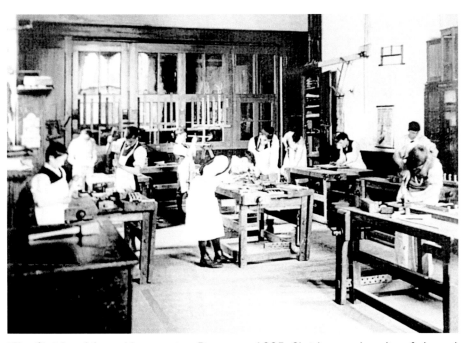

The Slojd or Manual Instruction Room, c. 1895. Slojd was a handicraft-based educational system which began in Finland in 1865. It involved woodwork and paper-folding and was thought to build character, encourage moral behaviour, increase intelligence and improve industriousness.

Headmaster Roger W Jones BA with his five staff c. 1895. The number of boys on roll at this time was about 140.

A member of staff with six boys seated outside the west door. The scene c. 1900, looks as though it could have been taken at many an English public school.

GELLIGAER ENDOWED SCHOOL
LEWIS' FOUNDATION.

Governors:
G. T. CLARK, Esq., Dowlais House, Chairman.

The Very Rev. Dr. VAUGHAN, Dean
OF LLANDAFF.
Rev. AARON DAVIES, Pontlottyn.
C. H. JAMES, Esq., Merthyr-Tydfil.
LEWIS D. REES, Esq., Cefn Hengoed.
WILLIAM LLEWELLYN, Esq., Wood-
field, Nr. Blackwood.

E. D. WILLIAMS, Esq., Maesyruddud,
Blackwood.
WILLIAM REES, Esq., Pengwaun,
Llanfabon.
JAMES LEWIS, Esq., Tydraw, Aberdare.
THOMAS WILLIAMS, Esq., Gwaelod-y-
garth, Merthyr Tydfil.

Headmaster:
REV. DAVID EVANS, M.A., (LOND.,)

Second Master:
R. W. JONES, ESQ., UNDERGRADUATE, LONDON UNIVERSITY.

THE object of this School is the provision of sound and liberal education for children between the ages of 9 and 16 years. The School will be conducted on the practice of the large Public Schools, as a Day and Boarding School.

The course of instruction comprises Latin, French, English Grammar, Composition, English History, Geography, Arithmetic, and various branches of Mathematics and Physical Science; many of which subjects bear directly upon the examinations for Managers of Collieries, now being conducted in the district under the Mines Inspection Act.

Tuition Fees—payable in advance :—

	Per Quarter.
	£ s. d.
Boys under 13 years of age...	0 10 0
Do. over do. do.	0 15 0

The Masters receive Boarders at the rate of £25 per annum in addition to the above fees.

The School Buildings are large and commodious; pleasantly situated in the Rhymney Valley, close to the two Pengam Stations, and about 1¼ miles above the Hengoed Viaduct.

Arrangements have been made with the Rhymney Railway Company, so that children may be conveyed to and from School at very low rates. Tickets issued only once a year—in August.

The next quarter begins on the   of   18

When it is intended to withdraw a boarder, at least a quarter's notice of withdrawal should be given to the Headmaster, such notice to terminate at the end of a quarter.

Application for admission, and for further particulars to be addressed to the HEADMASTER, Pengam School, Maesycwmmwr, via Cardiff.

This hand-out to parents c. 1878 tells us much about the workings of the school. The curriculum claims to be vocational as well as academic. Science is very low-key.

During the period 1902-04 major changes took place in the main building. The tower and spire were removed, extra rooms were added and the building was also extended upwards on its north-east side. The building in the foreground was temporary accommodation used while the re-building was in progress.

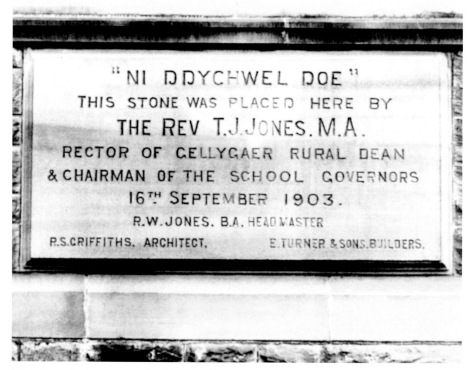

This foundation stone, laid by the Rector of Gelligaer Rev. T J Jones MA, was placed in the wall on the south side of the west door of the hall.

The front aspect of the school in 1909. The building looks very crisp and in good order, having been completed just a few years previously.

A view, at the same date, of the south-west corner of the school. The foundation stone can be seen set in the wall beneath the bank of windows.

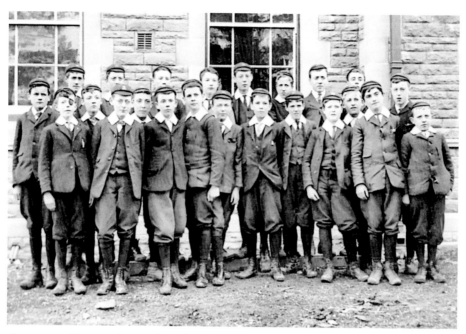

A group of boys, dressed in the uniform of the day, in front of the school c. 1908. School cap with an interwoven 𝕃 𝕊 as a badge; Eton collar, waistcoat, knee-length breeches and boots.

Two boys in the stocks in front of St Catwg's Church, Gelligaer. We assume they are posing for a photograph rather than suffering a penalty.

A gathering of parents and friends for the annual School Sports c. 1910. The ladies' hats suggest that the event is also a fashion parade.

The School Sports c. 1910. At this time one of the principal events was the tug-of-war.

Arthur Wright, chemistry teacher at the school 1904-44, and Second Master 1924-44. Dressed in style as he so often was and ready to cycle off, usually with a few boys as assistants, to take photographs of, and rubbings of the inscriptions on, bells in the parish churches of Glamorgan and Monmouthshire.

A corner of the chemistry laboratory, Arthur Wright's teaching base.

The hall c. 1910 with the board showing the scholarships awarded to former students. To the right, backing on to Room 1, are the display cabinets with exhibits of fossils and other items of general interest.

The set for a production of *The Merchant of Venice* in the hall.

A Galsworthy, who was to spend just two years on the staff, with the first-year pupils in 1913.

The school First XI in 1913. The staff are F T Williams BA on the left and R G Jones on the right. Before he retired in 1945 R G Jones would become Senior Master.

Roger W Jones with his staff in 1913. Standing from the left: T Matthews MA, R G Jones, A Galsworthy, F T Williams BA, S H Thomas BA. Seated: Frank L Rees, H B Pittway MA, Roger W Jones BA, JP, (Headmaster), T Price MA, Arthur Wright BSc.

A lesson in drawing a curved shape given in the Art Room by F T Williams BA in 1913. The glass doors in the centre lead to the corridor. The Staff Room is opposite and the stairs to the ground floor to the left. The doors on the right lead to a classroom, for a short period the Prefects' Room.

The Headmaster, Roger W Jones, addressing a group of boys in the school hall. The lighting is powered by gas, electricity being installed in 1931.

The view of the school that boys, alighting from the train at Pengam station, and probably including some of those in the above photograph, would have had as they walked to school.

A group of boys with one dressed as the *Mari Lwyd* (Grey Mare), a one-time Welsh midwinter tradition, possibly to celebrate the New Year. The participants accompanied a person disguised as a horse. The group travelled from house to house and sang at each one. Their expected reward was food and drink. The tradition declined with the advent of Nonconformism and was replaced by children carol singing who sought financial reward.

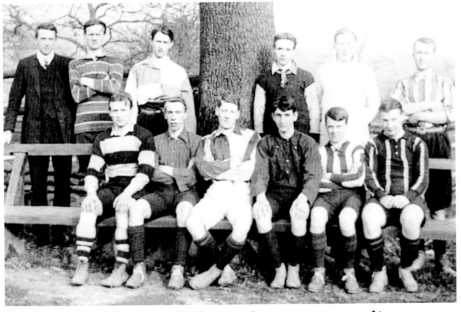

The school First XI c. 1910 arrayed in an assortment of jerseys.

The front cover of a copy of *Lorna Doone* by R D Blackmore. It was a Form Prize.

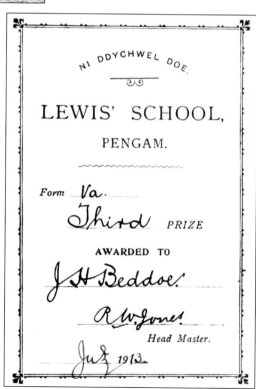

NI DDYCHWEL DOE.

LEWIS' SCHOOL,

PENGAM.

Form *Va.*

Third PRIZE

AWARDED TO

J H Beddoe

R W Jones

Head Master.

July 1913.

The presentation details on inside cover.

CHAPTER 3

Reorganisation and Expansion
The 1920s

In 1920 a Government Departmental Committee of the Board of Education recommended a national minimum pay scale for teachers. Glamorgan Education Committee were amenable to the suggestion and proposed to implement this scheme almost immediately in all their County Schools, but there was a problem with the two Lewis' schools. The funds at the disposal of the Governors could not possibly meet the increased costs. In spite of the mineral wealth that lay beneath the land that provided its finances, the Lewis' schools had always been relatively poor. If the Glamorgan Education Committee took over the responsibility for the increased salary costs in return for the money from the Lewis' Endowment which the governors had agreed should be transferred to them, who would pay the maintenance costs for the pupils who came from the adjoining county of Monmouthshire?

The proposed change generated two problems. In the first place what representation should the Glamorgan Education Committee have on the governing body in return for the money they were going to put into the two schools? In the second place how would the Monmouthshire pupils fit into the scheme? Following several meetings the School Governors agreed to four additional members, as nominated by Glamorgan Education Committee, being added to their governing body in return for the Committee becoming responsible for teachers' salaries. As part of the agreement the Committee made a not unreasonable suggestion: they would pay the extra running costs but only for Glamorgan pupils. Almost half the pupils at the two schools were Monmouthshire pupils: would the Monmouthshire County Education Committee pay for these? Not unreasonably Monmouthshire did not feel inclined to contribute to the upkeep of schools not in their county and not under their management. A decision had to be made by the end of the summer term otherwise all staff would be given notice to quit. This threat brought instant common sense to bear on the problem. Forthwith it was agreed that the revenues of the Lewis' Endowment in full would be paid to the schools' funds, the remainder of the maintenance cost would be divided each year between the two counties in proportion to the number of pupils from each county. This arrangement proved satisfactory and operated for as long as Monmouthshire pupils attended the two schools. Another part of the agreement was that Monmouthshire could build a new grammar school, Bedwellty Grammar School, on their side of the river. It did.

Possibly because there were boarders and it was a good way of occupying their time there was, up to 1920, school on Saturday mornings. This practice was very much in keeping with other public and boarding schools but ceased in January 1920. (Another suggested link with such schools appeared in an article in the *Daily Express* in October 1929. This claimed that Lewis' School was originally a Blue Coat Church School and that its pupils were still entitled to scholarships at the Horsham Institution in Sussex, but I can find no justification for this claim.)

Mutilation of the school grounds
One the most traumatic and far-reaching events in the history of the school at Pengam took place in 1921. A new and much needed road had been built from Ystrad Mynach to Glanynant, almost up to the school boundary. How could this new road be joined to Gilfach? The obvious and only reasonable route was straight thought the school grounds. From the school's point of view this was little short of an act of vandalism. Eventually an unsatisfactory compromise was reached. In return for this mutilation the school would gain a hard playground, a new fives court, a new tennis court and improved football and cricket pitches. In addition a high stone wall would be built to shield the Headmaster's house (later Lower School) from the road, and both sides of the road would be fenced. In September 1922 trenches were dug and pipes laid for the new road to go through the school grounds. The building of a Fives court was one of the few changes that was welcomed. Fives became a popular sport even generating House competitions. In February 1924 a low wall with railings along the southern boundary was agreed at a cost of £700.

By 1926 most of the project had been completed. However the resulting pitches were never adequately drained, always stoney and lacked the intended privacy. When the road was opened there was little traffic compared with today but crossing it was a hazard. It took several decades to make crossing safer but eventually a bridge was built in 1960. In 1928 two rows of saplings were planted along the main road in an attempt to win back privacy and to reduce the chance of soccer and rugby balls falling into the path of oncoming traffic. In 1923 a playing field was offered to the school for £50 and in the November Glamorgan County Council asked for details of land that was available for a cricket ground at £50 per acre. I find no record of the location of either plot of land - there was certainly no evidence of a cricket square in later years.

Changes at the top: D Vaughan Johnston

Vaughan Johnston's reign as Head-master covered the period 1919-1926. It was a period of reorganisation and expansion after World War I. He made several changes as soon as he took up the post including arranging that prefects, rather than the Headmaster, should read the lesson at morning assembly, and he introduced a new school cap. Vaughan Johnston's arrival also led to considerable improvement in science teaching in the school. In particular both physics and chemistry would be taught in the higher forms up to the level of the Central Welsh Board Honours Certificate. To make this possible David Morris BSc. was appointed. It was also a requirement of

D Vaughan Johnston MA

appointment at this time that staff lived within the school area which seemed to mean that they should be able to walk to school. While many lived in Gwerthonor Road (The Shant) others lived as far away as Blackwood.

Unlike today Vaughan Johnston could appoint his own staff. He was determined to promote science teaching and to this end appointed Philip J Davies and Neville Richards in 1924. P J Davies qualified with First Class Honours from Aberystwyth in 1923 and became a Qualified teacher the following year. His annual salary on appointment was £285. Neville Richards graduated from Cardiff in 1923. His annual pay on appointment was £277.10s. Strange to relate he was not a qualified teacher but proved convincingly that great teachers are born and not made. I doubt that a year spent training him would have improved his teaching skills or the examination successes of his pupils. Both teachers performed sterling work for the school, Neville Richards raising the standard of mathematical success such that it became equal to that attained anywhere else in the Principality. The Second Master was Tom Price MA who had been on the staff since 1904. Six months after being appointed to that role he left to take up the Headship of Rhymney Secondary School. Tom was known for being 'rather forgetful'.

An article by C M Harris, in the *Ludovican*, relates amusing circumstances in which J M Smith BA was appointed in 1922. Vaughan Johnston together with J D Thomas JP, the Chairman of Governors from 1909 to 1925, arranged to meet the applicant at a hotel in Cardiff.

Undoubtedly by what he had read in the returned application form and supplied testimonials, with reference to college soccer, cricket and rowing colours - particularly the latter I suppose - the Headmaster looked around the vestibule and elsewhere, I have no doubt - for a six foot athletic body. Eventually his gaze settles on somebody who could be a cricketer, though small as they come or go - a stumper perhaps. Yes! He could see a soccer player, undersized wing type. Stroke or number eight in a rowing crew? Never! Eventually contact was made (don't ask me how), and the usual inquisition followed, finishing up with something like this: 'We concede you your soccer and cricket colours, Mr Smith, but we are really puzzled about this rowing business'. A few of us can hear that reply, given in a soft Scotch brogue, and heralded by a wry smile and chuckle, 'Well, every rowing 'Eight' has its cox, you know.' 'Jock' got the job.

That the Headmaster D Vaughan Johnston was highly thought of over a wide area is epitomised by a letter in July 1924 from a Reverend gentleman in Seven Sisters. He asked Vaughan Johnston to sign his form seeking to become a Fellow of the Royal Astronomical Society (FRAS). Vaughan Johnston left in 1926 to become Chief Inspector at the Central Welsh Board. As a token of appreciation for all he had achieved during his stay at Pengam he was presented with a chiming grandfather clock by the staff and a fitted travelling case by the pupils.

School numbers
In the Summer of 1920 there were 286 pupils on roll, 134 from Glamorgan and 152 from Monmouthshire. They were taught by 12 staff and, apart from mathematics, almost exclusively Arts subjects - there was one science teacher. In the true traditions of a Grammar School every pupil up to and including Form V was taught Latin. Throughout the years pupil numbers gradually increased: to 369 by the Autumn of 1928. Of these 209 were Glamorgan pupils (107 of them claiming free entry) and 160 Monmouthshire pupils (78 with free entry). Such an increase was to bring severe pressure on the school's accommodation. By October 1929 there were 18 staff and 400 pupils.

Buildings
In 1922 it was resolved by the Governors to build three new classrooms. By November 1923 Glamorgan County Council, who now had to bear the cost, agreed to build just two. The following year the Governors

decided to divide the Handicraft Room, known as the Slojd Room, into two rooms. The Slojd room was on the first floor to the rear of the Staff Room. It was to be divided into two by a partition, part fixed, part folding, the result being classrooms that could each accommodate around thirty pupils. The Board of Education suggested that the changes be the other way around, that is that the new building be used as classrooms and the Slojd Room remain where it was. Ultimately, the original school suggestions were accepted. The Slojd Room would be moved to a new Handicraft Room to be built on the north side of the main block. It would be suitable for twenty boys and would cost about £730.

Accommodation problems at the two Lewis' schools involved a transfer of wooden huts. In July 1923 it was agreed to move a temporary hut from Hengoed to Pengam. This was achieved the following January but within two months the governors wanted the hut to go and sold it. In September 1924, huts, originally at Pengam, but then in Hengoed, were considered unfit to use as classrooms. Could they come back to Pengam? This was agreed at a cost of £100. One was placed near the gymnasium to be used for changing, the other would be a cricket pavilion.

Other smaller projects were: replacing defective and insanitary conveniences, reblocking the gym floor, building a new Fives Court and getting the Powell Duffryn Company to attend to subsidence problems in the cloakroom and elsewhere.

Finance
Some idea of the cost of operating the two Lewis' Schools can be gauged from the following income and expenditure figures.

Estimated expenditure for the year ending 31.3.1923.
Head's salary: Pengam £700 (worth c. £30 000 in 2013),
        Hengoed £600
Salaries for the full-time staff at Pengam £6015 (Hengoed £4233), Occasional teachers £72,
        Total (for both schools) £11620.

Additional costs were: Maintenance £776, Books £500, Stationery £1000, Chemicals (Cleaning, etc) £216,
Administration £250 (clerk £80, printing and postage £150), Rent of playing fields £10, Repayment of loans with interest £264.
        Grand total £14636.

Estimated income:
Grants from County Council under County Scheme:
      Fixed annual grant   £1650,
      Share of surplus revenue   £150,
      Fees   £1200.
Grants from Board of Education:
      Secondary grant   £4000,
      Examination grant   £150,
      Advanced courses   £400.
      Other monies received from County Council Education
      Committee   £448,
Grants from other Local Authorities (Monmouthshire) £500,
      Scholarship Funds   £250,
      Tack from horses   £2.
      Balance 31.3.1922   £703.

Estimated deficiency   £5183.
    (The Lewis' endowment money was now in the hands of
        Glamorgan Education Committee.)

Some, but not all pupils, paid the fees for tuition and books on the first day of term. Some also had to pay their own travelling expenses. In 1923 the additional fee to cover games and the library was two shillings (10p) per term. Because of the economic problems of the times there were many occasions when parents had problems with paying fees and other expenses. An example of this is a Bedlinog father who wrote to the Headmaster Vaughan Johnson to say that he was unable to pay for books. He says he is on short-time at the pit: *'I earned £2.2.9 (£2.14) for 6 days'.*

In the 1920s it cost a great deal to provide adequate heating and lighting in the school. This was before the days of double glazing and roof insulation. Schools were draughty places and young boys are not averse to leaving doors open. Coal in 1922 cost 49/4 (£2.47) per ton delivered, and in December 1924 the Powell Duffryn Co. quoted the price of large steam coal from Britannia colliery at 26/-per ton + 2/4 (£1.42) per ton delivered. Gas for lighting from Rhymney & Aber Gas Co. cost 4/6 (22^{1}/2p) per 1000 cubic feet giving a bill for the quarter of £5.4.5. (£5.22).

Furniture
Every pupil needs a place to sit and a surface on which to write. Until recent times the preferred furniture was the school desk, a heavy solid wooden structure fixed to an iron frame. A letter from the Headmaster,

D V Johnston, to the Education Supply Association in June 1924 includes pictures of single desks he purchased which were still in use forty years later. Single desks were called scholar desks. The record shows that in September 1926 there were 280 scholar desks. In addition four long desks would each sit six boys and there was one desk with three seats.

In 1920 the Governors bought a gas pendant for the hall (there was no electric light). In January 1924 the gymnasium required benches, beams, climbing ropes, mattresses and wall-bars: all these were secured for £57.

Governors

In spite of the severe financial constraints the governors were aware that the status of the school depended very much on the quality of the intake. Accordingly they continued to offer scholarships (20 in 1922) to enable boys they thought would profit from the education the school had to offer. They also agreed to pay for rail season tickets and books for deserving cases.

Complaints of the day to the Governors included a letter from Trelewis Trades & Labour Council protesting that the Governors had decided to discontinue entering pupils for the Junior Examination of the CWB. They thought the examination was of value in deciding who to employ from the group of pupils who did not stay on in school long enough to sit later examinations.

Another letter (in June 1924) from Edith Sumption of Fleur-de-lys threatened to withdraw her son from the school if there was no definite class for London Matriculation the following year. On a more pleasant note in October 1923 they received a letter from the National Eisteddfod Committee inquiring about the teaching of Welsh in their schools. They were pleased to reply that *there is every facility in both schools*.

Entry

Pupils who entered Pengam came from a broad geographical area which stretched from Ystrad Mynach and Abercarn in the south to Rhymney and Tredegar in the north. Any boy who lived in the parish of Gelligaer, Bedwellty or Mynyddislwyn was eligible for entry. But how were they financed? The answer is *from an almost unbelievable variety of sources*. In 1920 they could be financed in any of the following ways:

Governors' scholars - Glamorgan: Gelligaer,
                            Monmouthshire: Bedwellty & Mynyddislwyn.

Foundation bursars, excused fees: Gelligaer & Bedwellty.

Rhymney scholars under Rhymney District Education Fund.

Board of Education bursars (Former Glamorgan probationers who had to sign an undertaking to become Pupil Teachers).

Monmouthshire County Scholarships.

Glamorgan County Scholarships.

Monmouthshire Minor bursars
(Major bursaries are linked to Training Colleges).

Pupil teachers. (Pupil teachers in Glamorgan and Monmouthshire were under different regulations. They were pupils who attended school one day a week and spent the other days teaching in a Junior school.)

Student teachers (Full-time Student teachers in Glamorgan and Monmouthshire were under different regulations).

Higher Elementary Scholarships (transfers from an Elementary School with a grant for higher education).

Probationers from Glamorgan with 30/- (£1.50) p.a. allowance for books.

Bedwas Church Scholars under the Bedwas Church Charity.

The expectation was that all these pupils would progress and eventually sit the Junior and Senior Certificates of the Central Welsh Board.

Additional facts from the period that make interesting reading are:

In the 1920s pupils could legally leave school at 12, but parents of Pengam and Hengoed children were asked to sign forms agreeing to keep their children at the school for a minimum of four years.

To get the final entry mark 'Age marks' were to be added to the raw scores of those who sat the entrance examination. In 1921 this was one mark for each month below 12y 11m e.g. for a pupil who was 12y 11m nothing would be added but for one aged 11y 9 m, 14 was added to the raw score. For the Pengam entry of forty-two in 1922 the majority were in the 11-year age group, eleven were over 12 years with just one under 11 years of age. These prospective pupils were given 'age marks' which were slightly different from the previous year: 28 to the youngest (10y 7m) and 1 to the oldest (12y 10m). The top raw score was 228 out of a maximum of 325. The top score including the age weighting, 237.

In April 1923 in addition to the written test there was also an oral test. School Scholarships were awarded to 8 Monmouthshire boys and 12 from Glamorgan. In September 1924 a boy sat the scholarship entry but failed. The parents wrote to the Headmaster and wanted to know if they could pay for him to attend.

Two other letters from parents to the Headmaster written in 1924 illustrate typical problems. One refers to a boy who had passed for Maesycwmmer Secondary School (this would become Bedwellty Grammar School later) but whose parents would like him to go to a better school, for example Lewis' school. It asks '*Can I bring him to sit the entrance examination? He's 13.*'

Another from Cwmaber Council School, Penyrheol, refers to a boy who could not afford to come to Pengam but could now get help from the Royal Artillery Commemoration War Fund which could keep him at Lewis' School for four or more years. The letter says '*He's very good - has done a little algebra and geometry.*'

Curriculum
The school curriculum was determined by the needs of pupils studying for the Central Welsh Board examinations. The Senior certificate of the Central Welsh Board (renamed School Certificate in 1923) was taken after four years, the Junior Certificate which had been taken two years after entry was phased out after WWI. For School Certificate a pupil needed to pass with credit in five particular subjects to gain matriculation and this was essential for university entrance. The Higher Certificate was taken two years later as was the Honours Certificate which had disappeared during WWI.

Examinations
Examination entries for the years 1921, 1924 and 1934 show that candidates' names were not recorded on the entry forms. Each candidate was known only by a number so the inference must be that this was the case for all the intervening years. For the 17 boys who sat the CWB Higher papers in 1924 the numbers for each subject were: English 8, Latin 7, History 9, Pure and Applied Maths 6, Applied Maths 1, Physics 7, Chemistry 6, Welsh 6. Two years later there were 96 candidates for the Senior certificate. The subjects then were divided into five groups as follows:
(The numbers give the number of candidates, where known)
Group I: Scripture knowledge, English, Welsh Language and Literature, History, Geography.
Group II: Latin -16, Greek, Welsh - 36, French - 29, German - 0.

Group III:	Mathematics including arithmetic, mechanics - 9, Physics - 16, Chemistry 39, Geography, Botany, Biology, Geology, Agriculture, Domestic Science (including Elementary Physiology and Hygiene)
Group IV:	Music (theory) - 0, Music (theory and practical combined) - 6, Music (practical) - 0; Drawing- 27
Group V:	Woodwork, Metalwork, Woodwork and Metalwork (combined), Needlework and Garment Construction, Cookery, Laundry work, Book-keeping, Shorthand - there were no entries in this group.

For the Higher subjects in 1928 the numbers sitting were: English 5, Welsh 2, Latin 1, French 2, History 3, Pure and Applied Mathematics 4, Pure Maths 5, Applied Maths 3, Physics 7, Chemistry 4, with similar numbers in 1929. One boy did English, History and Pure Maths, another English, French and Pure Maths. In 1929 Edgar Lloyd Williams sat 6 papers for Advanced Mathematics. He got 3 As, 2 Good, 1 Credit.

Internal examinations were normally held twice a year; at Christmas and in July. How they were supervised is not recorded but things must have changed for the worst in December 1927 for an instruction was given to masters that they should remain with their Forms throughout the day. Spending the whole day supervising in the same room sans conversation with anyone hardly bears thinking about.

Music
There was no full-time music teacher at this time but Tom Gabriel GTSC was employed to teach the subject part-time until 1927 when D E Parry-Williams BSc., Mus. Bac., was appointed to take charge of the subject. For assembly Dr Pate, a learned and cultured man who was steeped in the classics and a master of the English language, played the harmonium (bought in 1892) and Frank Rees MA history (who was to die in a motor accident in 1928) played the piano. Stanley Knight, the newly appointed Headmaster, was desirous of developing the musical and cultural side of the school. Perhaps he thought that too much emphasis had been put on science during the Vaughan Johnston years. To this end a School Orchestra (the Greek word from which the word derives means 'dance') was formed in 1927.

To improve Morning Assembly copies of Milford's *Hymns of the Kingdom*, containing two hundred hymns and edited by Sir Walford Davies, were bought in 1923. They cost eight old pence a copy.

Prizes and Scholarships

The prestigious Caldwell medal was awarded each year to the boy who had attained the highest position in the school in the annual external examinations. In 1922-23 the recipient was Thomas Samuel Jones for results achieved in Chemistry, Physics and Mathematics.

There was little spare money in school funds to award prizes but a few organisations helped out. In October 1924 the secretary of the South Wales Branch Working Men's Club and Institute Union Ltd. wrote to the Headmaster to say that Patrick Collins was to receive a scholarship from them of £5 per annum. Would the school accept him? It went on to say that there were already two of their scholarship students in the school. At a lower but still most welcome level, The Cymmrodorion Society gave books to the value of one guinea to help the progress of the Welsh language.

At national level April 1924 saw the revival of State Scholarships awarded by the Board of Education. The regulations were the same as applied in 1920 and 1921.

Discipline

In October 1923 there were fairly serious problems at Hengoed Station including the smashing of a large window pane. At certain times pupils from four schools gathered on the platforms so it was inevitable that on occasion there would be friction between the different groups. It also appeared that station staff were too familiar with the pupils. The stationmaster suggested that there should school monitors on duty at the station but the Headteachers seemed reluctant to agree. Their reply was: *Tell your staff not to be over familiar with them. It's no good.*

Schoolboy gambling has always gone on whether it's playing cards and, at the same time having a smoke hidden in the bushes, or on the pool table. Occasionally some got caught. In October 1923 a boy was suspended for *'taking part in a betting transaction'*.

The system of Cs and Ns recorded in a pupil's diary seems to have originated at a Staff Meeting in December 1927. The minute records that:

> A 'C' (Conduct mark) will be cancelled if not covered one month later. (What did 'covered' mean?)
> Three Cs shall mean two hours in detention.
> Three Cs should not be given at one time.
> 'N' indicated 'neglect' in completing homework.

This was revised in October 1928. The master in charge should take detention in his own duty week and not the week after as was the practice previously. It was agreed that the system of 3 C s and Saturday detention be abolished. For a serious offence a 'D' should be given in the boy's diary and his name entered in the Detention book. *His name is to be read out in Assembly the following morning. This means one hour detention (from 4 to 5 pm) the day after. No master is to give more than 6 Ds in one day. D stands for disorder in class 'in absentia magistri'. It could be given for attempting to do the wrong subject in class, copying homework or other work. It was to be carried out on the evening after the name was entered in the book and should be held even if it was just for one boy.*

Illness and other problems

Two tragic events befell the school during the decade, one to a pupil and one to a member of staff. In September 1926 William Gwyn Jenkins of Hawthorns, Cefn Road, Blackwood, was drowned while swimming at Deri in the reservoir belonging to Groesfaen Colliery. He was a very clever boy with a bright future who had recently won a university scholarship. In his Higher Mathematics papers he scored 100% in one and 99% in the other. The other tragedy occurred in April 1928. Frank Rees MA, who taught history and English at the school, died on Sunday, 22 April. He was a former alumnus who had gained a First at University College, Aberystwyth. While on a family outing on Easter Wednesday his car skidded into a telegraph post near Hereford. His children, son John and daughter Lynn, were uninjured but his wife who was in hospital for three days with what was thought to be trivial bruising, developed blood poisoning from which she died; leaving two parentless children.

Infectious and contagious diseases such as scarlet fever, measles, mumps, whooping cough, tuberculosis and diphtheria were commonplace so it was not unusual to find a letter from a parent who asked if their son could return to school after his brother or sister had recovered from diphtheria and the house had been disinfected? A variation on this was a letter from a boy to the Headmaster explaining his absence which included two poignant facts: *Mother has been ill in bed for three weeks. I'm the only one to look after her.*

1926 is remembered for the General Strike. From 4 - 12 May there was a railway strike but seventy per cent of the boys made it to school, many of them walking several miles each way. During the strike the covered play area, later to become the dining hall, was used as a soup kitchen, primarily for the children from the village.

School Houses

New school houses with associated colours, were introduced in 1927 with the various members of staff attached to one of them as follows:

Lewis: red; A. Wright, T A Hughes, WE Park, W J Morris.
Llewellyn: orange; Frank Rees, H D Jones, D Morris, P J Davies.
Ifor: yellow; R G Jones, J M Williams, J W Perrett, N Richards.
Islwyn: green: Dr J A Pate, C M Harris, J M Smith, A A James.

Clubs and Societies

By June 1924 the Cadet Corps, which was formed in 1914 to train boys in readiness for the armed forces had become a scout troop. The record declares that they no longer have any rifles. There seems to be little evidence that there are any flourishing clubs or societies in the school.

Special events

Three events are worthy of mention.
1. The wedding of the Duke of York in 1923 which was seen as a valid reason to close the school for the day.
2. The Bicentenary Celebrations commemorating the founding of the school in 1729. A service was conducted by the Dean of Llandaff and took place at St Catwg's Church, Gelligaer, on Wednesday 29 May 1929.
3. In July 1929 a new church was built at Maesycwmmer. Dr Joyce, the Bishop of Monmouth, laid the foundation stone. Also present was school governor Lieut Col Lindsay CB JP.

In 1929 a minority Labour Government proposed to raise the school-leaving age to 15, but it did not happen until the Labour Government enacted it in 1947.

Sport

At the beginning of the decade the principal sport was soccer. By the end the school had moved firmly into the rugby camp. This change took place in 1924. When the last soccer matches were played in the 1923-24 season both the Senior and Junior XIs were undefeated. The Junior XI, who were coached by the Games master J W Perrett and went four years undefeated, played in the Nelson & District League. The school soccer XIs played in light and dark blue quartered pattern jerseys redolent of Oxbridge. Jack Perrett was appointed in 1920 and remained on the staff until the mid 1940s. He was fairly strict, beating his short stick against the wallbars as he organised his young troops. Always well dressed it was reputed that he could climb a rope using one arm, having lost the other in the retreat from Mons in World War I. On

63

Annual Sports' Days he was responsible for the impressive gymnastics displays.

Sports' Days were important occasions with guests of honour attending to present the prizes. From 1908 the ultimate prize was the Caldwell Cup which was awarded annually to Sports' Day's top athlete. It was known as the Victor Ludorum Cup. As a momento the winner received a bronze medal but in 1921 it was decided that the cup would be awarded to the most successful House. In place of the cup and the bronze medal, the Victor Ludorum was presented with a silver medal paid for by the Headmaster.

The Caldwell Cup

Cricket was always an important sport, the school even had a roped off cricket square and possessed a heavy-weight grass roller. The senior team played in the Schofield Shield Competition and won it in 1926. To give some idea of the costs involved, in April 1924, a Gun and Moore 'Canon' treble spring handle cricket bat cost £1.5s.0d (£1.25); six Challenger match balls 10/6 (52¹/₂p) each; composition balls 2/- (10p) each; a set of stumps of best ash with solid brass tops and steel shoes 10/6 (52¹/₂p); a score book (for 25 matches) 4/- (20p). Some Governors took a keen interest in the sport. For example, Colonel Lindsay, one of the local gentry who lived at Ystrad Fawr near Ystrad Mynach, wrote to the Headmaster asking if there were any Monmouthshire boys younger than 15 who could play cricket. He was looking for recruits to join another team of a higher standard.

At the Welsh Amateur Athletic Association meetings from 1923 to 1926 runners from the school won just about everything there was to win. In particular A E Powell won the Cross Brothers cup at Cardiff Arms Park in July 1923. The most impressive school rugby player of the time was Iorwerth Evans who later hooked for Wales at Senior level. However, there must have been problems with schools' rugby in general for a letter from Pontypridd Boys' School in 1924 stated that they were keen to keep the rugby flag flying.

The games master at any school cannot be expected to give up every Saturday morning to supervise a school team: if there is more than one team it is asking the impossible. The problem is solved by other staff being prepared to help. At a Staff Meeting in December 1927 it was agreed that *for Saturday sports' fixtures the master on that week's school duty shall attend and referee or umpire if able. There shall be no fixture on the first or last Saturday of term.*

Trips
School camps continued to be popular. Some camps operated for a month and a pupil could decide for how many weeks he attended. The charge was *one pound a week* (in addition pupils had to cover their own transport costs). Camps were held at Dawlish, Minehead, St Athan and Aberystwyth.

The most important school trip arranged during the 1920s was to the British Empire Exhibition at Wembley in 1924. Enquires revealed that what was termed a Camp hostel was available for pupils from the provinces who wanted to go to London. The cost was 5/- a day (25p). This charge covered accommodation, breakfast, sandwiches and a substantial evening meal. No pupil under 12 would be accepted and the teacher to pupil ratio had to be at least 1:20. Every pupil was required to present a medical certificate to confirm that they were free from infectious diseases.

With this information in mind details of the proposed visit were circulated among the boys in the February. Early numbers showed that 55 boys plus 3 or 4 members of staff would like to join the excursion during the second week of June. On 10 June the party left for London with history teacher Frank Rees in charge. They stayed at a Children's Hostel at Park Royal. The final size of the party is uncertain, one entry records that 73 boys wanted to go; an actual list records 36 boys' names. A letter from Glamorgan Education Committee to the school after the event refers to a grant of £35 to help with the costs for 25 to 30 boys. Two boys, George Griffiths and Wilfred Philpot, were awarded scholarships to go.

Non-teaching staff
For years the caretaker and his wife supplied the boys with tea or cocoa at a penny a cup during the morning break. This helped to supplement their pay of £12.8s.8d. (£12.43) a month. In addition in November 1921 the caretaker was paid 1/6 (7½p) per night for work connected with Evening Classes. By comparison a boy employed as a laboratory assistant who, so the advertisement requested should be *young and inexperienced,*

was paid 7/6 (37½p) a week on appointment to be increased to 8/6 (42½p) if he proved satisfactory.

Staff and their salaries
At the beginning of 1920 there were 23 staff including the Head. Staff were paid one-sixth of their annual salary every half a term. Annual salaries were: £625 for the Headmaster, £475 for H B Pittway, £450 for A Wright, Frank Rees and T Price, £447 for R G Jones, £420 for Dr Pate, £300 for J M Williams, T A Hughes and H D Jones, and £270 for C M Harris and W E Park.

By comparison the salaries of the staff at the sister school at Hengoed were considerably less. The highest paid teacher there was Miss Cameron who was paid £380 pa, Miss Macgrath (a non-graduate) was paid £145 but Miss Moore (also a non-graduate) was to see her annual salary rise from £165 to £260. All lady teachers at Hengoed were unmarried and referred to by the title of 'Miss'.

Total expenditure for Pengam and Hengoed for the half term was £2657.17s.7d.

When new salary scales were introduced any arrears were paid immediately. Under the new scales A E Larkman, a non-graduate who taught physics and stimulated great interest in wireless among the boys, was paid £300 p.a.

In February 1921 Dr J A Pate became unwell and sought time off. He was replaced, on a temporary basis, by Mr Jenkins BA, who was paid £5 per week, the payments to Mr Jenkins being deducted from Dr Pate's pay - how things have changed.

The number of staff employed in June 1922, when pupil teachers were withdrawn from both schools, was 15 at Pengam and 17 at Hengoed.

Two years later H B Pittway, the Second Master, was ordered to have three months rest. In the October the Governors agreed that H B Pittway could be on full salary for three months, surely a measure of the great esteem in which he was held by them. In the following February he resigned after 24 years service which included 22 as Senior Master.

R G Jones spent much of this early time at the school assisting the Headmaster with book-keeping and other clerical work but in 1925 taught Art and assisted with general subjects such as arithmetic to first year pupils. In March 1924 he agreed to £48.16s.10d (£48.84) - a significant amount in those days - being deducted from his pay since he had inadvertently been overpaid by this amount.

From 1925 staff were paid in nine equal amounts each year compared with six in the immediate past.

At a Staff Meeting in September 1928 a somewhat amusing question was raised. Why were boys not saluting masters when they passed on the street? How times have changed.

Many staff appointed to the school remained there for the whole of their teaching careers but some who did apply to move do not seem to be particularly concerned when they were unsuccessful. H D Jones was such a man. In October 1924, after five years at the school, he sought a reference from the Headmaster to support his application as an Assistant Inspector or Sub-inspector. D V Johnston's reply supported the application. It was unsuccessful but he was probably satisfied with his current lot. He was still there 20 years later.

Many staff lived near the school and this resulted in much social interaction. Whist drives and dances were held in the school hall until the installation of chapel pews made it impossible. There must have been a great number of staff and friends who objected to their installation - an act which certainly reduced social activity in the school.

L Stanley Knight

It is recalled that when Lewis Stanley Knight was appointed to the Headship three senior boys, as representatives of the whole school, came forward to meet him and welcome him to the school. He was 39, single, had been awarded a BA Hons Wales in 1912, an MA in 1914 and he was also a Fellow of the Royal Historical Society. In 1919 The Honourable Society of Cymmrodorian published a thirty-four page article by him entitled *Welsh Cathedral Schools to 1600 A.D.* During the war he had seen active service and had been wounded. He was a Welsh speaker who was proud of his roots.

L Stanley Knight MA

Old Boys

In 1924 J Ivor Griffiths won the Gold medal in surgery at University College, London. Subsequently he was awarded a Fellowship (FRCS) in 1929 and for 1933-35 became a research scholar at the Royal College of Surgeons. Two Old Boys who were pupils in the '20s who went on to make a name for themselves were Harold Davies of Ystrad Mynach and Hayden Davies of Rhymney. Both sought a career in politics and became Westminster MPs. Another old boy who became a politician was Morgan Jones MP, He was appointed Parliamentary Secretary to the Board of Education in 1924.

At this time Old Boys' reunions tended to be spasmodic. In 1923 they took the form of a Whist Drive and Dance in school with special rooms set apart for smoking and conversation, but in 1924 the Reunion was a Dinner at Cox's Cafe, 110 Queen Street, Cardiff, when Morgan Jones MP was the speaker. The evening cost 5/6 (27^{1}/2p) each. The park in Caerphilly is named after him.

Reminiscences by Arthur Thomas, Blackwood
(As related to the author in 2012)
How I remember that first day in September 1929. I had walked from Blackwood with Roy Bennett the only other boy from Blackwood to have passed. We carried our sandwiches and thermos flask in our satchels. We were assembled on the tennis court in front of the school and from here sent to our new Form Room. Mine was the Bell Room, Room 5, on the right as we walked towards the chapel. We had four forty-five minute lessons in the morning and three forty-minute lessons in the afternoon.

I was very impressed with the chapel. As you entered the Prefects pew was on the left. There were no other pews nor was there an organ - they would come later. At the rear was a raised platform with two rows of chairs. The Headmaster and staff took their places on the platform for morning service - all Welsh on Tuesdays and Thursdays, English on the other days. One of the prefects read the lesson. There was no school uniform, our parents couldn't have afforded that but we did all wear a school cap to which we had to sew an enamel badge depicting a white lion on a black background. The edges of the badges proved quite lethal in the occasional altercation between two boys. In the first year we were placed in Form 2. We wore short trousers until we got to Form 4 but even in Form 5 some boys were still in short trousers. You had to buy your own textbooks and pay a termly fee: one guinea (£1.05) to the school plus one shilling and seven pence (8p) for games.

Conclusion

To round off the decade Arthur Wright published his well researched book *The History of Lewis' School, Pengam*. It was another example of his total dedication to his adopted school. Meanwhile Stanley Knight could look back with satisfaction at the changes he had initiated since being appointed. As Head he began to restore a balance between Arts and Science subjects. However, with a national movement towards more science teaching and bearing in mind the staff he had inherited, it seemed inevitable that the school, with its record of successes in mathematics and science subjects, would become one of the best in Wales.

CHAPTER 4

Through the Years of Depression
The 1930s

School buildings

Major problems arose with the school buildings as the decade opened. Not only was there an increase in pupil numbers but there were also the difficulties caused by what was happening below ground - the very place that had caused the governors such joy when they realised the value of the coal beneath their feet a century earlier. There were in fact serious problems of subsidence for the Governors at the two Lewis' schools. Significant though these were at Pengam, at Hengoed they were so problematic that the Governors considered building a completely new school on a site off Gwerthonor Road on the New Road to the north side of Tiryberth. This did not happen but decades later the Mid-Glamorgan Education Committee moved Lewis' Girls School from Hengoed to Ystrad Mynach.

In December 1930, the laundry, the sole surviving part of the old school, was pulled down and the materials re-used to provide a changing shed near the pavilion. In the same year Lower House, originally the Headmaster's residence, was modified to suit the needs of a school for juniors. The Head was quite clear that he was not really in favour of this; he would have preferred to see a school all under one roof - something that did not happen until the comprehensive era in 2002. The Staff Meeting towards the end of the Summer Term 1931 agreed that from the forthcoming Autumn term Forms 2ABC and 3ABC would be housed in Lower House, soon to become known as Lower School. Six masters would be based there who would be responsible, in rotation, for its supervision. The remaining thirteen members of staff would carry out their supervisory duties in Upper School. Detention would be in Upper School and would include Lower School boys. The bell at Upper School, which could be heard throughout the village, would signify the times of the beginning and end of school, and the times of the change of lessons. Pegs in the covered area at Upper School, which became the larger Dining Hall some years later, would be where Lower School boys could leave their coats during assembly.

In October 1931 a major improvement occurred: electricity was installed throughout the school. It was first used on 2 October - and the gas fittings, other than those in the science laboratories, were removed. A year later new gas taps were installed in the laboratories, the chemistry storeroom cleared, and the physics laboratory rebuilt to include a storeroom. This storeroom took in part of the corridor and one-third of the lecture room, the remainder of the lecture room being converted into a laboratory for biology which was officially brought on stream in September 1933. In 1932 the prefects were allocated the room upstairs, opposite the staff room and next to the Art Room, as their very own Prefects' Room. Unfortunately, their capture of this private space did not last long as the room was soon needed to accommodate the ever increasing number of pupils - an increase due to the expanding population and the desire of the governors to give more pupils a better education. In the Autumn the shower baths, adjacent to the gymnasium dressing rooms were equipped with duckboards and towel rails that had been made by VI Science boys in their woodwork lessons.

In April 1933 a stained glass window given by John Herbert James in memory of Edward Lewis was placed in the Headmaster's office. Other improvements included removing the boot-lockers in the cloakrooms and replacing them with hat and coat hooks, fitting electric light in the workshop, electric clocks in the corridor, Head's office and gymnasium, and permanent wireless apparatus in the hall. The latter enabled the 1938 Armistice Service from the Cenotaph in Whitehall to be heard in school. The Honours Board, previously updated in 1919, was updated once more in 1936.

Records also show that decoration of the school had been completed by February 1935 and that it was the intention to go ahead with the building of a new dining hall, gymnasium and library - the library to be open to all in the Rhymney Valley. This rather over-generous and unrealistic suggestion never materialised.

In 1935 it was thought that the large number of absentees due to coughs and colds was partly due to the poor ventilation in several of the classrooms, particularly those in Lower School. The Chairman of Governors proposed providing better ventilation by perforating holes through the external walls, surely a procedure that would have made the rooms much colder. In addition the lighting and blackboards needed upgrading. A motion put to the staff read *the conditions in these rooms are not conducive to the best health and efficiency of pupils and staff.* Not unnaturally the motion was carried unanimously.

The chapel
During October Half-term 1930 the Powell Duffryn Company, the

company responsible for the underground mining, accepted liability for the damage caused to the hall and the four rooms off it, and agreed to carry out the necessary repairs. Doors were re-framed with three-inch timber and the walls replastered, but this was just tinkering with the problem. The company was forced to return in August 1931 to undertake major work. Room 2, the classroom at the south-west corner of the hall, was taken down and completely rebuilt. A major improvement to this room was the placing of a new double-window in the original blank south wall. In the same year, what had been known as the hall, gradually reverted to being called the chapel but this was not the official title until 1935. The gallery at the west end, designed and erected by H B Pittway and Arthur Wright in 1911, was pulled down and destroyed.

An organ, built by S F Dalladay of Hastings with two keyboards and nineteen stops, was presented by the Old Boys' Association in memory of those Old Boys who had died in the First World War. This beautiful instrument was accepted by Alderman Evan Thomas and Headmaster L Stanley Knight who, when he spoke, pleaded for the hall/chapel to be extended so that it would accommodate 400 boys. Unfortunately the new organ partially obstructed the Coat of Arms of the Lewis family which had been designed and painted by R G Jones high up on the east wall. The design had been taken from the leaden tank at St Fagan's Castle, the home of Sir Edward Lewis, great grandfather of our founder. The first quarter is said to derive from Golyddian, Lord of Cardigan, the other three are noted chieftains from whom Sir Edward claimed descent. On the ninth of May 1931, with Dr Rocyn Jones in the Chair, the organ was dedicated by the Bishop of Monmouth, following which a recital was given by Dr D Morgan Lloyd of Cardiff. The instrument was first used for Morning Service two days later, and was electrified at a cost of £20 in 1940.

Slowly the hall evolved once more into a chapel. Pews were installed, paid for by friends of the school, a carpet was laid on the stage and a new chair given for the exclusive use of the Second Master - at this time Arthur Wright. Because of the new pews, July 1932 was the last time Central Welsh Board examinations could be held in the hall. From then on they would be held in the four rooms off the hall/chapel, Room 5 (the geography room) and the two rooms on the first floor behind the staff room where the heavy partition separating them could be opened up. The chapel could now seat 260 boys on pews - the remainder would stand - and a Prefects' pew lay to the left on entry. To every plus there is a minus. The Science and Art teachers did not think these changes in the hall such a wonderful idea. Where could they site their exhibition cases? Subsequently they were found new homes in the corridors.

As the decade progressed many additions and improvements took place. A new window was placed in the chapel displaying the armorial bearings of the five bodies associated with the school: the Arms of Edward Lewis, the three parishes of Gelligaer, Bedwellty and Mynyddislwyn, and lastly the school. Two paintings by J E Hennah of Newport were also acquired to hang in the chapel - one, of the school and its surroundings as seen from near Pengam Pit, the other of a scene near Henllys, a typical Monmouthshire scene. The pews installed in the chapel in 1933 reduced the overall seating capacity but were considered in harmony with the rich old roof beams. G W Davies of Bargoed, very generously gave the panelling in front of the stage and paid for the staining of the timber around the organ to match it. But there was one big problem that would never be solved - the chapel was too small for the number of boys in the school. It needed extending.

As the decade closed the key stone above the west window began to move, repairs were needed to the floor, the chapel roof and the roof of the music room were damaged in a gale, and a large fissure appeared in the wall of Room 1. For this the Powell Duffryn Company would not accept responsibility but agreed to pay £9 (c. £500 in 2013) towards its repair; surely an expression of the measure of their guilt.

The Grounds
Improvements continued to be made outside the main building: the path from the gate on the main road to the front door was kerbed and laid with tarmac; two drinking fountains were installed; a lean-to bicycle shed was attached to the woodwork room; the covered playground and the areas around the east end were tarmaced, and the large ball-court used for fives was pulled down to provide the bricks for a new shower-bath building attached to the gym. While not the case today, would this early re-cycling be another example to illustrate the poverty of the school?

In the open spaces around the school buildings there were still many major problems areas: in particular an excessive amount of gravel on the field covered by an inordinate accumulation of mud. Looking on the brighter side of what the Governors were able to do for sport, they purchased a mower, coconut matting for cricket, sand for pits, agility mats, a Junior discus and shot, a toe and stop board, and bolts for hurdles which had been made in the school workshop. Newly planted trees and shrubs helped to beautify the surroundings.

In 1939 a request was made for a Belisha Crossing on the main road between Upper and Lower School. However, many people, including some Governors, thought this would prove more dangerous than leaving things as they were. Decades later when a crossing was finally decided upon it was a bridge. The same year a new school flag, a silver lion on a black background was designed and made by Cefn Fforest Sewing Guild. It was flown for the first time from the school flagpole, attached to the gable at the east end of the main block, on 18 May 1939.

A most unusual event occurred in December 1931. The Gelligaer and Rhigos Hunt released a 'bagman' fox near Bedlinog. The chase took place, the fox eventually being caught by the hounds and killed on the school field.

Non-teaching staff
Throughout the '30s the school caretaker was David Morgan. He left in 1934 after 46 years service to the school, 29 as caretaker. During his reign many a window was accidentally broken by over-active school boys. His offer to them was always the same: *you provide the glass and I'll provide the putty and restore the window*. His leaving present was a cheque for £15.15s. (£15.75) but unfortunately he did not enjoy a very long retirement: he died in May 1938. There were 242 applicants for David Morgan's replacement. A shortlist of 20 was drawn up which was reduced to 6, and then 3, from which Mr and Mrs Hester were chosen. The new caretaker was expected to provide hot water for the boys' hot drinks at lunchtime but the only source for this was his home. In 1936 the Governors solved this problem by agreeing to buy a small boiler for £2.10s. (£2.50).

In January 1937 thirty-seven men applied for the job of a shared groundsman between Pengam and Hengoed. The pay offered was £2.18s. (£2.90) for a 44 hour week. At the same time a clerical assistant's pay was £52 p.a. plus increments of £6.10s. (£6.50) up to a maximum of £104 p.a. The school also employed laboratory assistants who were to be aged between 14 and 17.

Trips
As in the 1920s an important extra-curricular activity during the '30s was the School Camp. In 1931 the fifteenth school camp went to Castletown

in the Isle of Man. The charge was £1 a week plus rail fare. W E Park, T B Price and J W Perrett took 18 boys. 'The big plus from the activity is that there is so much more understanding between the boys, and between the boys and the masters'. In 1932 W E Park, who appears to be group leader, assisted by J W Perrett and Brodest the cook, took 16 boys to Worthing. They spent two weeks in a camp 200 yards from the beach. The following year, W E Park, T B Price, N Richards and the cook took 16 boys to Clacton-on-Sea. They travelled by rail from Pengam to Clacton, via Cardiff, Paddington and Liverpool Street, then by lorry to the camp - a small site with other campers - a short distance from the beach. Some stayed for two weeks, others for three. Whilst there they played cricket on an Essex County Ground against a team of actors who were performing at the Ocean Theatre. School scored 126 and then dismissed the actors for 25. They must have been very proud of themselves that day. Other camps took school groups to such places as Dawlish, Llandogo and Shanklin, Isle of Wight. No camp was arranged for the summer of 1937 as a far more ambitious project was in the offing for the following Easter - a fifteen-day cruise to Gibraltar, the Canaries and the Azores at a cost of £14.

Trips to local industry are usually of great educational value. Groups of boys visited the British Oxygen Works at Cardiff, and the coal By-product works at Llanbradach. Eighteen boys were taken underground at Llanbradach Colliery where they saw 50-60 horses in their stables, and the pump room with its huge gleaming engines (3-4000 horsepower) used to raise thousands of gallons of water a day to the surface. Here the noise levels were surprisingly low. However, one disappointment was that they could not go to the coalface because shot-firing was taking place there. The great surprise of the visit was how clean and orderly everything was.

At the Cottage Hospital, Tredegar, the group were shown X-ray equipment and what it could do, and at Rhymney Brewery observed the whole process of beer-making from barley to bottling. Other groups visited the Western Mail and Echo facility at Cardiff to see how a newspaper is produced and the observatory at Penylan where Dan Jones, the Chief Astronomer gave a short talk before conducting them around.

In the summer of 1935 Arthur Wright took five boys to London on a four-day visit at a cost of £3.10s per boy. They were met at Parliament by Morgan Jones MP, a former pupil, who showed them around the

House of Lords and St Stephen's Hall. Apart from Parliament the group visited The Tower, Greenwich, and Woolwich Arsenal. For those with a classical interest the Latin Society visited Caerleon where Ludovican V E Nash-Williams, Keeper of Archaeology at the National Museum of Wales, spoke to them, and W J Morris's pet society Societas Apium Latina went to the Archeological Department at the National Museum of Wales. Here they were shown around by Nash-Williams's deputy. Geography teacher W E Park was obviously a keen traveller. In the summer of 1937 he travelled to America returning on the SS *Queen Elizabeth*, a journey about which he was to give several informative lectures.

Nearer home The Roger Williams Company brought Shakespeare to the pupils. In 1935 they staged *The Merchant of Venice* in the Parish Hall, Fleur-de-lys. The previous year their play was *Twelfth Night*.

Red-Letter Days

The School Eisteddfod produced more items in English as the years rolled by, but back in 1931 even the programme, which listed the prizes and scholarships awarded in the previous year, was in Welsh. Tea was available at 4 p.m., costing 1/- (5p). In 1933 no entries were received for which the award of 'Chaired Bard' could be given. Two years later pews had been installed in the chapel and this reduced the number of pupils who could be seated, and sadly there was no chaired bard. Arthur Wright chaired the proceedings in 1934 when two novel items were introduced, namely 'whistling' and 'mouth organ' solos. These extremely popular items continued for several years, but why did they cease?

At the 1935 School Eisteddfod the audience was informed by Rev. W R Lewis who conducted the proceedings that *St David lived in the 6C but his biography was not written until the 11C (by Rhygyfarch), his father was Sulien (a scholar), Dewi Sant was the only Welsh saint canonised by the pope; William I, a Norman Frenchman, gave us the Domesday Book; Henry II, a lawyer, the jury system; and Edward I (the imperialist) our first foreign Prince of Wales.* Items in 1936 included essays, elocution in English and Welsh, piano playing, solo singing, penillion, whistling party (6 in a group), mouth-organ solo, single chant, and Art: lettering, cartoons and pastel work. The suggested topics were, a man's head, a bull's head, a sailing ship or a bridge. In the 1938 copy of *The Ludovican* the editors pleaded for more pupils to take part in the Eisteddfod; some Forms, they said, submit next to nothing. To stimulate more interest they proposed a points system with an award for the winning house.

In previous years it had been the custom to distribute the prizes on St David's Day, when the Eisteddfod took place but, because of the increasing number of boys in school, attendance was restricted in 1934 to boys alone: there simply wasn't the room in the chapel for boys and visitors. In consequence a Speech Day was introduced later that year and every subsequent year. This was attended by boys who would receive prizes and certificates, together with their parents. The first guest speaker was Sir William Jenkins MP for Neath, former Chairman of Glamorgan C C and of Glamorgan Education Committee. Sixty-six boys were presented with Senior Certificates, half of whom were now exempted from matriculation - the basic qualification for university entry - while 15 out of 20 had passed the Higher Examination. Other notable guest speakers at Speech Day were Dr J Ivor Griffiths - a brilliant former student who became a Wimpole Street specialist, Mrs Parfitt who had been a pupil at Pengam from 1860 to 1869, Dr W Idris Jones, Head of Research at Powell Duffryn, Captain Elliot Seager MC, High Sheriff of Glamorgan and Dr Emlyn Stephens, Inspector of Higher Education in Glamorgan. Dr Stephens words of wisdom to each boy was that he should know: *Where he is; Where he is going; What he is going to do.*

Dr Idris Jones in his speech included these words:

> *For yesterday is but a dream*
> *And tomorrow is only a vision*
> *But today, well lived, makes*
> *Every yesterday a dream of happiness*
> *And every tomorrow a vision of hope.*
> *Look well, therefore, to this day!*
> *Such is the salutation of the dawn!*

He continued *We want to send forth from our schools the boy who can choose the better and reject the worse, who gives of his best always and fully, who has his decks always cleared for action, who has many interests, who doesn't cry for the moon nor over spilt milk, who realises that education ends neither in youth nor in middle age but continues through every year of his life and enables him to solve the many problems which confront him.*

Speech Day became another opportunity for the Headmaster to share his thoughts with a wider audience. Following Dr Idris Jones he commented that education is starved financially before moving on to an area close to his heart. *Educationists in Wales are slow to grasp the importance of music as a spiritual and mental force capable of moulding character, besides being one of the greatest joys on man's round of pleasure.*

Traditionally the Founder's Day service had been held in Gelligaer Church but in 1930 it was held for the first time in the School Hall. When the Rector of Bedwellty, Rev. Rhys Davies spoke, he suggested that every tenth year alternatively the service should be held in St Sannan's, Bedwellty and in St Tudor's, Mynyddislwyn, something which, as far as I can see, never happened. The advice of Rev. R D Edwards, the Founder's Day speaker in 1932 was: *If your privilege has given you education, it is your business to pass on the labour of an educated mind. Every privilege is a gift, every gift a trust for others who need it.* For the 1935 service, the BBC made preliminary arrangements to broadcast it but never carried the intention through. The Lord Bishop of Llandaff preached, and Rev. E Bernard Fry MA, a former student and Oxford graduate, presented every pupil with a copy of Bishop Ollivant's sermon of 1850. This was the year that the foundation stone of the school at Pengam was laid. A copy of John Buchan's *The King's Grace* was also given to every pupil. Two years later Rev. Gwillym Davies MA of the League of Nations told the assembled boys: *The secret of greatness is firmness in making up your mind.* He went on: *You are the generation that is going to see civilisation saved or are going to see it buried in its ruins.* He spoke of the forthcoming war that he said was inevitable but said that afterwards France will shake hands with Germany, Germany with Russia, Russia with Japan, and Japan with the United States. Rather prophetic, but not in the time-frame envisaged.

For the 210th anniversary of the founding of the school the service in 1939 was held at Gelligaer church. Rev. J O Williams, the rector took the service and the preacher was Venerable Archdeacon of Llandaff R V Jones.

Breaking Broadcasting Silence

To a young person today a world without television is unimaginable but it was not too long ago that a world without radio was the norm. What follows is a report by D V Roberts, a sixth form boy, that appeared in a copy of *The Ludovican* in 1937.

Armistice Day, 1937
November 11th! Another year has flown and again we commemorate the day sacred to the memory of those who gave their lives in the war to end war.

This year's ceremony was unique in that for the first time in the school's history, the service was broadcast. We have heard many voices in the Assembly Hall but never have we listened to the speakers without seeing them. This year, however, we were transported in mind to the heart of

England's mourning public - to the Cenotaph, Whitehall. If we could not see the proceedings, we could at least, through the able medium of Mr Howard Marshall, the BBC commentator, imagine the scene.

We enjoyed this privilege through the courtesy of Mr Camm, of Bargoed, and of Mr Rees and his colleague, who installed the apparatus in the hall.

Silence fell on the assembled group as His Majesty's Grenadier, Coldstream, Scots and Welsh Guards played several well known airs and the silence was unbroken until the end of the service which was conducted by the Right Reverend and Right Honorable the Lord Bishop of London. But immediately the service finished, many were the whispers that were heard. Our first broadcast was ended!

Now that we have tasted the first fruits of school broadcasts, does it seem too ambitious to anticipate the time when television will invade the 'school on the hill?'

Finance

It is interesting to look back to see how some of the school's capitation money was allocated and spent. In 1935 the 12-year-old Gestetner cyclostyle machine was giving trouble. It would cost £15 to repair so the governors agreed to buy a new one for £38. A blackboard on a stand cost £5, coke was 39/- (£1.95) a ton, to sharpen two saws cost 30/- (£1.50) and two javelins cost 16/- (80p). An electric saw costing £25 was asked for but the request was refused as being too dangerous a machine to have in a school. Departmental allowances were recorded as: Chemistry £100 for chemicals and apparatus, Biology £25, Woodwork and Metalwork £65, Geography £5, Dining Hall £2, towelling and dusters £5, mattresses for the gym £10, six music stands £2.2s. The groundsman could spend up to £2.5s. for tools. (By way of comparison £1 in 1935 has a purchasing power of about £55 in 2013.)

Pupil Numbers

The total number of pupils on roll each year changed little over the period. When the Autumn Term opened in September 1930 of the 406 on the registers, 238 came from Glamorganshire and 168 from Monmouthshire. New boys who were placed in one of three unstreamed forms, entered the school with one of several different forms of financial support. The returns for 1933 show that many pupils had been awarded scholarships from various sources - 231 are described as Government scholars, 22 as Glamorgan County Scholars and 26 as Rhymney Scholars while 131 were fee-paying. The staff complement that year was 18.

Academic Successes

Scholarships or Exhibitions were awarded to more than forty boys over the decade, the most prestigious of which were the Meyricke Scholarships awarded to Morgan G John, Ivor T Minhinnick and Edgar W Powell. A Meyricke Scholarship was highly esteemed as it was given to the best students in Wales sitting the Central Welsh Board examinations. Pengam gathered three in the short space of five years. Morgan John also won a State Scholarship, a Monmouthshire County Scholarship and passed the Intermediate Science examination for London while Edgar W Powell of Blackwood was awarded a State Scholarship and a National Science Exhibition Scholarship to Jesus College, Oxford.

Some of the others who distinguished themselves were:
Head Boy J Alec John: £100 p.a. Natural Science Scholarship at Jesus College, Oxford.
Clifford James: Faraday House Exhibition worth 50 guineas a year. Joseph Jacobs: Open McLoghlin Scholarship from the Royal College of Surgeons.
H G Jenkins: Glamorgan Music Scholarship.
K R Marchant: South Wales Institute of Engineers Scholarship.
Alun J Evans: Medical Scholarship. In January 1939 the school received notice that Alun, a former Head Boy and son of a miner, had gained a First in Geography at University College, Aberystwyth.
J R E Saunders: Older Universities Scholarship worth £110 plus fees and a County Scholarship worth £10 plus fees. The former was reduced to £10 plus fees because of his father's income. The boy opted for the Civil Service instead of the scholarship and incidentally, was the best batsman in the school.
Cyril Raymond Young: a Glamorgan Major Scholarship.
Douglas Vernon Roberts: Industrial Chemistry Scholarship at the Technical College, Cardiff.
J H Williams: Welsh Church Exhibition Scholarship to St David's College, Lampeter.
David Charles Jenkins: a Monmouthshire and a Glamorgan County Exhibition Scholarship.

At the end of the decade Leslie Minhinnick won a Gladstone studentship worth £100 plus board and lodge, tenable at St Deiniol's Library, Howarden. He graduated with a First in Theology and was awarded the Canon Hall Junior Greek Testament prize. Ivor and Leslie Minhinnicks' father was agent to the Powell Duffryn Company.

Moving to the CWB School Certificate examinations which were held each July, i.e much later than is the case for the equivalent examinations today, the records show that the numbers entered for the Higher School Certificate varied in the 1930s between 7 and 22. The subjects taken were English, French, Latin, History, Geography, Music, Pure and Applied Maths, Pure Maths, Applied Maths, Physics, Chemistry, and Biology; the most popular subjects being English and Maths. Almost all pupils studied three subjects. Each practical subject was allocated about 5½ hours teaching time a week; the other subjects 40 minutes less. Some of the classes were so small - often 1 or 2 in French, Welsh, Latin and Music - that attempts were made to save cash and staff by coordinating some of the teaching with Bargoed Grammar School, but the idea never bore fruit. For School Certificate (the equivalent of examinations taken today at the age of 16+), by the end of the period, the numbers hovered around the 70 mark, fewer than thirty gaining that all important matriculation.

The Coming War
It is easy to believe that the Second World War, which began in September 1939, came as a surprise but an article by Ronald David Lloyd, a first year pupil, in *The Ludovican* in the summer of 1937 makes it quite clear that most people knew what was going to happen. The question was: when? How many pupils thought about what was to come and the effect it would have on their lives? How many of them would not live to see the peace or would never be the same again after their war-time experiences? Student R D Lloyd's thoughts are reproduced here.

Hitler and Homer
What a lovely day, Herr Hitler.
Yes it is, where are you going?
Up on the side of a mountain, to write a poem on 'The Scenery of the Mountain.'
That is only wasting your time, why not come and see my Army, Navy, and Air Force Parade? And you can take information from my artillery, and we'll fight side by side with each other. And let Germany and Athens be united.
No! Your motto may be war, but my motto is peace, and no man on earth can make me change my mind. What good is fighting? Millions of men die at th e bayonet point, just for the sake of a couple of square miles of land.
Nonsense man, you don't have to fight, your men will fight for you. You just come along and see the men I have, and perhaps you will change your mind.
No, I am not going with you, and I am not going up the mountain. I am going home to write a poem on 'Peace,' so goodbye! Hitler.

One senses that this eleven-year-old had listened to conversations at home that had caused him to think, even worry. Perhaps his father had served in the First World War. What did the son's future hold?

Sport

Cricket had been played in school since 1876. There was even a cricket pitch laid out in 1897 but, as in many sports the fortunes of the teams depended on the enthusiasm and skills of the particular teacher and on the ever changing abilities of the boys who remained in the higher forms. 1930 provided a good start to the decade, the team winning 11 matches out of 14 that year and 8 out of 11 in 1931. That year, for the first time, two boys C Jones and E Davies, represented the school in the Glamorgan Secondary Schools XI. For the season the top batting average for the school was 52 over 10 innings and the top bowling 50 wickets at an average of 3.1 runs per wicket. Amongst others schools they beat Caerphilly, Howard Gardens, Quakers Yard and Canton. To conclude the season the match against the Masters shows a scoreboard of Masters 31, School 32 for 3, and the match against the Old Boys a scoreboard of School 99, Old Boys 28.

Significant unhappiness seems to have arisen early in 1935 for in February a staff meeting was called to decide whether or not the school should go back into the Schofield Shield competition from which they had withdrawn the previous year. Sixth Formers R Pearce (Captain) and J Saunders (Sec.) were called in to make the case for re-entry. Their well-reasoned case resulted in the staff voting 18 to 1 to re-enter. The decision to return proved well-founded; school won 9 out of their 10 matches. The big problem for home games was the poor quality of the school pitch. In 1938 the Governors agreed to hire the Welfare Ground, Fleur-de-lis, at a cost of 7/6 (37^1/2p) a match.

Two clubs that made sporadic appearances were the Tennis Club and the Badminton Club. A new Tennis Club was formed in 1934. Using ten players they won 3 of their 5 matches. As with most other sports supported by the school suitable facilities were non-existent. There were no school tennis courts but the Governors did approve a proposal to convert the hard surface area in front of the school into tennis courts. Over the remainder of the period, with Neville Richards in charge, the team of A J Evans, Cyril Evans, D Riden, G Hughes, H R Matthews and J C Tippet was reasonably successful.

During the nine years prior to 1938 there was no Sports' Day; the ground was never fit enough to hold such an event on it. One Headmaster's report in the mid-1930s stated that *it looks like a deserted battlefield.* Nonetheless, on 9 June 1938 the 33rd School Sports took place. There were 43 events. It was the first Sports since 1928. At that time different Houses were denoted by colours. Red House won with 120 points and were awarded the Caldwell Cup. They were followed by Purple House with 97 points and Black House with 82. This particular sports' day was very business like. Staff, Friends and Old Boys were asked for donations while pupils were asked to pay an entry fee of 2d per event, 6d being the fee for any number of entries. Every boy was expected to take part in at least one event i.e. pay 2d towards the expenses! A profit of £5.18.3 was made: £4.14.10 of which came from catering. The principal aim of the venture was achieved: the school wanted to buy a cup for Sports' Day. However, they must have thought that the gods were against them for the diary shows that during the three months April, May and June in 1938 the only day it rained was on Sports' Day. On the day, Mr David Badham of Ystrad Mynach presented the prizes. Around this time the staff subscribed 2/- each to buy four silver medals and four bronze medals which would be awarded to the First and Second teams in the forthcoming Inter-school Race.

Thirty schools took part in the 1938 Schools' Amateur Athletic Association Sports at Mountain Ash. Pengam student E M Lewis set a record for the Long Jump of 20 ft 3½ in. and Berwyn Jones a record of 5 ft 2 in. for the High Jump. In the Senior section Pengam were second and in the Middle Section third. A new sport that was to become extremely popular was the Cross Country - the first school Cross Country, held on 1 June 1938, was won by E B Jones. The Headmaster also agreed to another venture. He arranged for the use of the Swimming Pool at Bargoed. Tenders were invited to transport the pupils there. Gelligaer U D C agreed to do it for £2.8.0 per week.

After their school days several Old Ludovicans continued to be successful. In May 1931 H Aubrey, won the sprint at the Welsh A A A. He was also the only Welshman to win in the International Race v Achilles Club, at Swansea. G J Evans represented Wales at the Empire Games in London. He won the Hop, Step and Jump at the Welsh AAA with a jump of 44ft 4 in.

Rugby in Pengam was a comparatively new sport. It had ousted football during the previous decade, probably because of the increase in the number of boys from south Wales going up to Oxford and Cambridge where it was the preferred game. In 1930 school won all six matches beating Canton, Abertillery (twice) Barry, Penarth and West Mon. In 1931 they won 17 of the 18 matches played. Honours came to the school: K I Jones (captain) and C M Jones played in the Welsh trials and were taken as reserves for the game against Yorkshire.

In 1934 Old Ludovican Iorwerth Evans then of Bedford and London Welsh played for Wales against Scotland at Murrayfield. Wales won 13-6. And in 1936 H G Williams of Bargoed was awarded his Welsh Secondary School's international rugby cap. He was described as a big, hefty school pack leader. Throughout the season the weather was atrocious, the school winning just five matches out of the sixteen played. By today's fixtures some of the teams played were unusual. For example they lost to Barclays Bank, Cardiff, but beat Powell Duffryn Office staff.

Clubs and Societies
This was the age of stamp and coin collecting, and lantern lectures. The Philatelic and Numismatist Society re-started with about 40 members in 1931 under the guidance of Arthur Wright. It met every two weeks, alternating with the Music Society, and charged a membership fee of 3d. Apart from meeting to exchange and talk about stamps and coins, the group watched a Lantern Lecture entitled *Here and There in the Stamp Album* which had been loaned by Stanley Gibbons (the premier company in stamp collecting) and also visited a stamp exhibition in Cardiff.

The Geography Society, formed in February 1930 for boys in the Fifth and Sixth forms soon became very active. At the first meeting Dr Pate gave a Lantern Lecture on *Norway*. Other lectures which followed were entitled *Across Canada* by H G Burley, VI Arts, *History and Geography* by W J Morris, *The Historical Geography of France* by T A James, *My visit to the USA and Canada* by W E Park, *The World and the Universe* by Neville Richards, *Atlantis - the lost continent* by Rev. E B Fry, *The Gold Coast* by L J Lewis, *Our Neighbourhood* by Arthur Wright and *A Holiday in the Pyrenees* by Mr Evans of Bargoed Labour Exchange.

Another society was the Music Society, probably the one with the largest membership. Here boys were encouraged to listen and analyse the music played for them. Talks with such titles as *In Defence of Jazz* and *In Defence of Classical Music* stimulated much discussion, and the associated school orchestra was said to be invaluable for Morning Service. The League of Nations Union Society which met on a Friday often discussed the radio programme broadcast on the previous evening, but there were also lectures: One very spirited presentation entitled *Isolation* was given by

Neville Richards and W E Powell, another entitled *The Philosophy and Arcana of Communism* was given by W J Morris and Head Boy J A John.

So many societies depend for their strength on a particular member of staff and/or an industrious sixth former. For the Mathematics and Scientific Society sixth form student J Browning, with the support of Arthur Wright, who acted as chairman, was such a person. In 1935 he was the first boy to give a lecture to the society: his title *Einstein's Theory of Relativity*. Another science topic was *Blood* given by P E Goodman to about thirty boys. W J Morris ran a Classical Society.

The Urdd group went from strength to strength, as illustrated by the number of articles that appeared in the school magazine. Originally set up by Prof. W J Griffiths of Cardiff and Prof Miell Edwards of Brecon the group frequently attracted more than seventy boys to its meetings. It had a Savings Association, and much correspondence was exchanged with French pupils. L S Knight, always a strong supporter of Urdd, wanted the school to produce a *Welsh gentleman first and a Welsh scholar second*. The Urdd group was helping him to do just that.

Some societies blew hot and cold. For instance a Debating Society blossomed briefly in 1932. At its first meeting it debated *Whether the gramophone would ever replace the Teacher*. Later debates followed. Some of their topics were: *That the exam system should be abolished; That we should submit to the tyranny of convention* and *That we are too fond of Sport*. After a break of four years the society was re-formed with W J Morris, Handel Morgan, Harold Hoof and Neville Richards supporting it. The motion for the first debate this time was *That this house demands an immediate fusion for educational purposes, of a certain institution at Hengoed and this foundation of Lewis' School, Pengam*. The motion was defeated by 7 votes. The second debate had as its topic *That in the opinion of this house the school curriculum is not satisfactory, and the time for drastic alterations is overdue*. This time the motion was carried - by 5 votes, but I don't think the Headmaster took too much notice!

The Ludovican
Though not the intention at the time, the end of term staff meeting in the summer of 1930 was to prove extremely important in helping to preserve facts and thoughts concerning the history of the school. The meeting began with a discussion as to how much the Games fees should be set at for the following term. They agreed to raise them from 1/4 (c 7p) to 1/6 but two of those present looked towards more distant horizons. Arthur Wright (yes - it's that man again) and R G Jones proposed

that there should be a school magazine. It should be called *The Ludovican* and be published once a term. On a page size measuring 10 in by 6 in, it should have a light blue cover with dark blue printing. Were these colours suggested because, at the time, the school rugby colours were light and dark blue, possibly chosen with the Oxbridge colours in mind? The cover would include the coat of arms, motto and date of foundation (1729) in addition to date of issue. Could there be 32 or 40 pages?

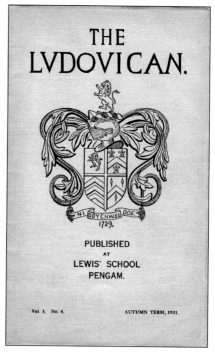

The next question was - What should go in it? Rather pertinently, because there was no such advice available in school, the editors decided on a series of articles about careers - Journalism, Accountancy, Medicine, Law, Civil Service, Banking. If possible these articles should be written by an expert i.e. someone out of school. The editorial should be gossipy and written by boy editors. Details/reports should be given for Urdd, School Societies, athletic achievements, Art society, Music society, poetry, prose, Old Boys, University news and an Oxford letter - the hope was that there would always be at least one boy in Oxford or, failing that in Cambridge. Dr Pate was elected General Editor. The boy editors to be Morris Levine VI2 and T J Howells VII. Tenders to print were received from Priory Press, William Lewis (Cardiff) and the Western Mail. The Priory Press quote (the cheapest) was accepted for a 40 page book. Cost: £18 for 500 copies, which was 9d per copy. Eight pages to be given to adverts at £1 a page or 10/6 per half-page. Form representatives on Magazine Committee Form VI: G T Hodge and W J Rees, Form V: I T Minhinnick, Form IV: G Williams, Forms II and III: K Lambert. Music: J F Templeman, Philatelic Society: T J Howells, Games: G J Evans.

By October, 1930, it was agreed that the frontpiece of the First issue should be 'Old School in 1910'. The magazine included an article on *Urdd delegation to Geneva* by Delfun Lewis, and a cartoon by L G Thomas 5B. One nice quote from Cobbett was *'Perseverance is a prime quality in every pursuit'.* When the first *Ludovican* was published it sold out within two days.

The Second Issue included an article on *Accountancy as a Career* by T D Evans BA, ACA, Clerk to the Governors and an Old Boy. Taxation, he wrote, which has been 6/- in the £ but is now 4/- in the £, has caused an increase in the number of accountants. Accountancy is a science that calls for accuracy. An accountant would ask an articled clerk for a Premium of £100 to £250: this was the amount paid to the accountant by the new clerk to be taken on. This magazine had a most interesting article predicting what life would be like at Lewis' School in the year 2000. Written in Welsh, it is reproduced in the Appendix 2 together with an English translation.

In the Third issue the chosen career was *Dentistry*. M L Symonds LDS, RCS Eng. wrote that until the 1921 Dentistry Act anyone could set up as a dentist. *An average profitable practice is worth c £600-£800 p.a.* In another article Stanley Knight, complains about the state of music in the schools of Wales. *When the floodgates of the Dissolution (16th century) were opened, her Song Schools were swept away and this loss has had a marked effect on Welsh music which is apparent even today. Throughout the whole of Wales only one candidate this year took Higher School Certificate in Music, and that was at L S P. Education is the leading or drawing out of the good gifts of a pupil.*

For the Fourth issue R G Jones' woodcut of the school (see below) appeared for the first time. This time the Careers article was *Railways as a Career* by Mr Pursall. *No premiums are necessary to enter the Railway Industry. Five grades range from £200 p.a. up to £350 p.a.* Also in the magazine a report indicated that old boy J H Griffiths BA (history) Jesus College, Oxford, had been appointed Assistant Librarian in the Manuscript Division of the Library of Congress, Washington, USA.

Copies of the first nine *Ludovicans* can be found leather-bound in one book at the Glamorgan Record Office. There are several excellent cartoons by L G Thomas in this volume including those with such captions as *On the War Path against the Canker Worm of Ignorance', On, Stanley, On* - a reference to L Stanley Knight as a knight on a horse. Also included is an article on *Journalism as a Career. Minimum salary on a Weekly £4.10s. up to £10.10s. You need to start as a reporter. Get into a Provincial paper - weeklies are probably best.*

Eighty-three pupils left during the year 1929-30. The destinations of those going on to university were Jesus College Oxford 1, University College Cardiff 7, Technical College Cardiff 3 and Medical School Cardiff 3. No one went to an English university other than the one boy to Oxford.

The Public Health Services as a Career was recommended by Mr F G Meek, Sanitary Inspector with Bedwellty UDC. *Salaries range from £200-£300 with the possibility of earning £450 a year at the top end. After qualifying you could progress to become a Medical Officer of Health or a Sanitary Inspector, but you do need good qualifications.* Another Old Boy, S C Dymond MPS, FSMC recommended *Pharmacy as a Career*, while E B Fry MA wrote on *The Church as a Calling. All Truth is God's Truth! Scientific Truth, Truth discovered by Psychology, Truth realised through Art or Literature, all are to be welcomed by, and are of value to any individual who may be in the ranks of the clergy at a future day.* Because E B Fry had written about entry into the Established Church the balance was struck by Rev. H Gwyn Lewis writing on *The Free Church ministry as a Calling.* His one very apposite comment was *Accept that you will always be a student.*

The Autumn issue of *The Ludovican* in 1932 records that the School colours had been changed that year from light blue and dark blue to black and white. This, the article said, *is more in keeping with the coat of arms of the Lewis Family, which is a silver lion on a black background. Boys will have new caps and play in new rugby jerseys.* The next issue of the school magazine was the first one with the Lion Rampant of the Lewis Arms in its correct colours of argent on sable. Another first was a 1934 photograph of the whole school taken by Panora Ltd, London. It shows about 450 boys. The cost of the magazine was now 6d which was added to the games fee of 1/4. Both were collected in the Spring term. P J Davies, who was away from school due to illness from May until September wrote a very interesting article on Capetown in the 1934 Autumn issue. He had spent a holiday there.

The School Psalter

The school psalter, which was published in March 1936, contains 137 psalms set in tonic solfa, 43 of which are in Welsh. All but six of the tunes are the compositions of staff and pupils. When selecting the tunes great care was taken by the editorial panel to see that they were not unconscious copies of the tunes of other composers. With a few exceptions the tunes by the boys were written under the supervision of Dr David Wynne Thomas, the music master from 1928 to 1961. Every one of the fourteen forms in the school, except one, contributed at least one psalm. Nine staff, including L Stanley Knight, the Headmaster, composed a total of 25 psalms, the lion's share (15) being the work of Dr Thomas. The psalter concludes with ten prayers, *The Lord's Prayer* with separate settings in English and Welsh, *Benedictus, Magnificat, Nunc Dimittis* and details for an *In Memoriam* service. The design for the front cover, which incorporates the school lion rampant, was the work of R G Jones a master at the school for thirty-nine years. R G completed his service as Senior Master. The dedication at the front of the book reads:

> *To John Herbert James, Esq., of Vaynor,*
> *A generous friend, to whom the school owes much for his*
> *munificent gift and lifelong interest this book is dedicated.*

One-off events

A lump of coal exhibited at the Welsh Industries Fair, Cardiff, in May 1936 weighed 6lb short of 2 tons 5 cwt. Brian Rice-Jones of Cwmgelli, Blackwood, made the best guess (within 8lb). He was a pupil. When the fair was over the coal was delivered to his home. At interview he said that he estimated its length, breadth and width and, knowing the specific gravity of coal, came up with his estimate.

In January 1936 King George V died. In November King Edward VIII visited the area and in December abdicated. This brought King George VI to the throne. To celebrate his Coronation the Glamorgan Education Committee agreed to pay 6d a pupil towards a tea to be held on 11 May 1937, the day prior to the Coronation. The Governors could also spend 1/- on a gift for each pupil. After the event their records show that there was no tea for Pengam pupils but there was for the girls at Hengoed. A service to mark the Coronation was held in the school chapel the day before the event. All present wished George and Elizabeth a long, happy and prosperous reign. For this service the new school psalter was used for the first time. After the service boys of Lower School went to the Palace Picture House, Bargoed, by courtesy of Mrs D Hann and Mr

& Mrs Withers. They saw programmes of Empire pictures lasting three hours.

In January 1938, with Old Boy T Glyn Jenkins as chief engineer, the Cardiff steamship *Kellwyn*, formerly the *Marie Llewelyn*, made her first attempt to run the blockade off Bilbao during the Spanish Civil War. In an air-raid on the Spanish government harbour at Valencia by a dozen planes, a bomb was dropped and exploded just twenty feet away from the ship. She was a sister ship of the *Dellwyn* which sank on 25 July at Gandia near Valencia.

Towards the end of November 1939 thieves broke into Lower School and stole chocolates valued at £1. They must have had a good Christmas.

Entrants and Leavers
Throughout the '30s roughly ninety boys a year entered the school, often almost twice as many from Glamorganshire as from Monmouthshire. Passing for Pengam depended wholly on how you did on the day. In 1934 many pupils in the Junior Schools were laid low with a fever. Surprisingly, no provision was made for those who could not attend at Pengam to sit the entry examination. The age limit for examinees varied considerably. In 1935 it was *'under 13 years 4 months on 30 July 1935'*; a year later, but on the same date, the age was *'under 12 years 9 months'*. Who determined these dates is not known. The numbers who passed the entrance examination from the nineteen different Monmouthshire feeder schools also varied considerably. For example in 1937 not a single boy from Blackwood was in the first fifty compared with the consistently high numbers who passed from the Tredegar and Oakdale schools. One can only conclude that the numbers who were successful were positively correlated with the quality of the teaching.

At the upper end of the school many left as soon as they could get a job. Between September 1932 and the following July approximately 100 boys left. The destinations of 75 of them who left between Sept '32 and July '33 were: mining 10, engineering 3, elementary teaching 2, church 3, pharmacy 3, technical college 2, medical school 1, university colleges 9, deceased 1, shop assistants 16, army and navy 7, clerks 6, and to remain at home 12. For the leavers between September 1935 and July 1936 the numbers were: university 12, medical 1, technical college 1, mining school 1, civil service 6, clerks 12, chemists 3, electricians 5, engineers 5, fitters 6, colliery workers 5, shop assistants 10, RAF 9, police 2, other education 3, miscellaneous 10, left area 5, to other schools 8, deceased 1, at home 13 - some of these being forced to leave to look after a parent or grandparent. Whatever the destination of each leaver the belief was that their education at Pengam would eventually lead to a more prosperous and satisfying life.

Hengoed

Christmas parties for Fifth and Sixth Form boys with the girls from Hengoed were held most years in the '30s, one year at Pengam the next at Hengoed. In the early days tea was provided before the main proceedings; later the practice was to take your partner to supper halfway through the evening. In 1937 it was proposed to send the Hengoed girls who wished to study Higher School Certificate physics and mathematics to Pengam, but this never materialised. Would the number of boys studying these subjects have increased?

Staff

Three new staff arrived in 1930: Ensor Jones (history), Handel Morgan (physics) and T Bryn Price (chemistry). Ensor Jones was a very dedicated teacher but found teaching challenging. Sadly he died a month before the outbreak of WWII. Soon after the war Handel Morgan (the physics teacher with the lovely resonant voice), following a period of secondment at Wrexham Training College, took up a post at University College Cardiff, and Bryn Price (Dulip) moved to Penarth Grammar school in 1950. He will always be remembered for his *Did You Ever*

T Bryn Price BSc.

See limericks at the Sixth Form parties. Harold Hoof, a former Cross Country runner, joined in 1934 to teach biology, botany and zoology and remained until he was called to war service, returning briefly in 1945.

In 1932 the staff were paid once a term, a time gap between payments that most teachers found too long. After much discussion at a staff meeting it was proposed that they seek monthly salary payments. Although the motion was passed by a substantial majority, six years later the only progress they had made was that they were paid four times a year instead of three. However, they were permitted an extra benefit - they could use the gym to play badminton every Monday evening in a recreational activity organised by Neville Richards and P J Davies. If we think that problems with teachers' pensions and pay belong only to the present the record shows that things were very serious for teachers in the 1930s. During the school year 1931-32 there was an iniquitous cut in teachers' pay, and in 1933 teachers were informed that there was a serious deficit in the pension fund. To eradicate this deficit the government stated that they were prepared to pay half of the superannuation contribution but teachers would need to pay the other half.

A shortage of male teachers necessitated three temporary female teachers being employed in 1936, but there was no question that any one of them could be made permanent - it was against Government policy. Dr Pate retired in 1937. He was School Almoner (a job he passed on to T A James), taught Greek, was very involved with the production of *The Ludovican*, and had worked in the school for 22 years. He was described as having a gentle bearing, genial pleasant manners and a keen sense of humour that had made him popular with both Staff and boys. His qualities of patience, exactness and determination, had contributed largely to the success of the magazine which he managed. Although he had taught in several schools before he arrived in Pengam, it was here that he found everything he needed in a life as a teacher. Dr Pate's post in the English department and as editor of the school magazine was taken over by D A Davies - a teacher who built up the junior library before being called to the colours. He never returned, becoming Director of Education for Merthyr when he was demobbed.

On 31 March 1939 the staff listened to Chamberlain's speech of 'appeasement' with Germany with much satisfaction. Few wanted to recognise that war was fast approaching. Two Old Boys of significance died during the year. One was Morgan Jones MP who was described as *a genial and amiable personality, an Old Boy who blazed with a passionate sympathy for the class from which he sprang*; the other John Herbert James who had given so much to the school: details of which are given elsewhere. Stanley Knight wrote that he was *a cultured gentleman whose taste for the beautiful was developed to a high degree, and this cultured discernment is reflected in the choice of gifts he made to the school: paintings, pews, library books and exhibition cases*.

Old Boys' Association

Annual Dinners for the Old Boys' Association were normally held after International rugby matches at the Park Hotel, Cardiff. About sixty Old Boys would attend. There was usually a guest speaker - in 1931 it was Old Boy James Evans, General Inspector for Wales under the Ministry of Health. In 1932, after the Wales v Ireland match, Dr George Howells was the guest. An Old Boy and formerly Principal of Serampore College, India, he had spent about forty years there. At this meeting several members commented that the younger Old Boys didn't support the association. Many expressed a wish to have a dance as well? Later in the year a Pengam and Hengoed Reunion Dance was held at Bargoed. This was also the time when rugby matches between School and Old Boys became an annual fixture as did Reunion Dances with Pengam boys and Hengoed girls. At Sports' Day, in an attempt to cement the old with the new Old boys were invited to take part once again in what was called The Old Boys' Race but the distance was reduced from 300 yards to 150 yards. Was this because they were short of breath from smoking? The first prize was a silver lighter!

No group can expect to please all its members all the time. In 1939 a letter from D C Rees (an old boy) said that during his day at Pengam it was all soccer. He was now a director of Swansea Town AFC and obviously disapproved of the change to rugby.

Maesycwmmer/Bedwellty School
Throughout the whole of the 1920s and 1930s the minds of the School Governors were much exercised by the plans for Secondary Education germinating in the offices of Monmouthshire Education Committee. In 1920-21 they had spent £3000 to convert Maesycwmmer Infants' School into a Secondary School. Monmouthshire's intention was that it should become a Grammar School for up to 130 pupils. Entry to the school would be by examination, the first entrance examination to take place in December 1920. The school opened on 8 February 1921 when 54 pupils were enrolled. The name was swiftly changed from Maesycwmmer Secondary School to the Rhymney Valley Secondary School. It was the first such secondary school in Monmouthshire. Nonetheless a search was soon on for a more suitable site and in June 1930 such a site was approved at Britannia, less than a mile away from Lewis' School on the opposite side of the Rhymney river. The new school was to be a mixed school for 360 pupils and would cost about £31,000. Cash was sanctioned for the site clearance in February 1931 and planned for the September but the depression held things back for several years. Eventually it was built between 1935 and 1937. Maesycwmmer was closed on 23 July 1937 and Bedwellty Grammar School opened in the September. By 1939 there were 245 pupils. Would Monmouthshire boys still be allowed to attend the old grammar school at Pengam or would they go to Bedwellty School instead?

CHAPTER 5

World War II and its Aftermath
The 1940s

By 1940 little had changed in Welsh Secondary Education since 1900. The Central Welsh Board offered a Junior Certificate which could be taken after two years but was phased out after World War I, and a Senior Certificate renamed School Certificate in 1923, which was attempted after four years tuition. The School Certificate examinations were very important for, to matriculate, a pupil needed to pass with a credit in at least one subject from each of five specific subject groups, a qualification that was essential for university entrance. After a further two years a pupil could sit the Higher School Certificate and for a few, the Honours Certificate, the latter disappearing during WWI. In the 1920s a pupil could legally leave at the age of 12 but by 1930 education was compulsory from 5 to 14. In 1938 the Spens Report recommended increasing technical education in High Schools so that they were equal in esteem with Grammar Schools. It proposed a leaving examination equivalent to School Certificate. However, the report spoke against bilateral schools - schools where some of the pupils are chosen according to ability while the remainder are not - and multilateral schools i.e. the equivalent of modern comprehensive schools, which was what the Labour Party in Wales wanted. An advantage of the existing system from the standpoint of the Grammar Schools was that they could return undesirable pupils to the Elementary School from which they had come. Towards the end of the Christmas term in 1940 this happened to one Pengam boy on the grounds of poor attendance. He had attended on only 15 out of a possible 115 occasions, and it was thought that he should be replaced by a boy who wanted Lewis' School tuition. In 1942 a boy was expelled for insubordination.

World War II

When the school term began in September 1939 it was under war conditions. All pupils had gas masks. The time-table was altered so that there were smaller numbers of pupils together at any one time. It was also decreed that lessons should be avoided during black-outs. The school-day was shortened. There was no assembly: school commenced at 9.00 and concluded at 2.30, with a thirty-minute break for lunch. These changes did not last very long. The following February (1940) Summer Time was introduced as was the old Time-table. School started at 9.05, ended at 4 p.m. with the lunch-break from 12.45 to 1.50. There was no Morning Assembly whenever there was a possibility of air attack, two lessons were scheduled before break, two after break and three in the afternoon. Assemblies re-commenced in October 1942 as did the former lesson times. The same month, as a wartime requirement, all Glamorgan pupils were inoculated against diphtheria.

Throughout the war the school received much distressing news about former students - deaths, injuries, men missing or being taken prisoner. France surrendered on 17th June 1940. German bombers could now be based in northern France within easy reach of south Wales. Two days later Cardiff docks were attacked. Locally the air-raid sirens sounded frequently. Most masters were on duty as Special Constables, Local Defence Volunteers (later named the Home Guard), First Aid or Air Raid Precaution wardens. R G Jones is referred to as Cadet Captain of the Rhymney Valley Battalion, Glamorgan Army Cadets. Education was forced to take a lower priority. At one stage only three staff were said to be available for fire-watching. Of these one was physically unfit; the other two were already in the Civil Defence. How could teaching be anywhere near normal in such circumstances? During the Summer vacation it was arranged for sixty students and a few staff to go to the Vale of Glamorgan to assist with farm work. They were paid 6d (2½p) an hour and charged for their keep. One consequence of the war was that the government agreed to release boys for land work provided they had passed their School Leaving Certificate.

On 3rd July a Higher examination was interrupted for a-quarter-of-an-hour by the sirens and on the 15th the boys spent 40 minutes under their desks during a CWB chemistry exam. Two days later they sheltered in shallow ditches or trenches which had been cut in the school grounds even though these provided little real protection. His Majesty's Inspector Jenkins called at the school to inspect the trenches, but his comments are not recorded. How the duties of an HMI have varied over the years! When P J Davies, H D Jones and Jerry Williams were put forward as members of the local Home Guard the Governors agreed provided that they only served locally. Their duties were not without danger. On one occasion E M Lewis of Fochriw was shot through the leg by another Local Defence Volunteer. He required first aid treatment at Merthyr Hospital.

Sirens sounded most days and there were consequences from enemy action elsewhere. For example, an order of apparatus and chemicals from Philip Harris, Birmingham, was lost en-route through bombing that burnt out the lorry delivering it. Re-ordering was necessary. The war position became more critical. Should the school form an Air Training Corps? The Governors were not too keen for they thought it would reduce school performance still further. A meeting was called by the Head to discuss the matter but in the end it was decided to go ahead. Alfred Withers, a local businessman became President and L Stanley Knight the Commanding Officer with Neville Richards as his adjutant. Boys outside the school who were not pupils were welcome to join what would become known as the Gelligaer Squadron. By April sixty boys were in training, meeting at Bargoed every Wednesday evening.

Death came to Old Boys relatively early in the war. Brian David of Fleur-de-lis died in a flying accident in January 1941. Pilot Officer WVA Evans of Ynysddu was killed in a train crash - he was a BA (Wales) and had represented Wales and Monmouthshire at athletics and Monmouthshire at rugby. In 1942 Lieut. Bernard P G Harris was killed in the Middle East and Thomas Albert Gabe died while serving in the RAF. Charles Davies a leading radio mechanic with the Fleet Air Arm and Flight Sergeant Thomas Idris Owen, who had flown more than 3000 hours, were both reported missing believed dead, and W A Box was missing over France. On the brighter side D A Lloyd won the Distinguished Flying Cross. His was the first war decoration for an Old Boy, though three had previously been mentioned in dispatches. As the years passed there was more heartbreak. In April 1943 Geraint Williams, a ship's deck officer and son of the Rector of Gelligaer, was lost at sea. Later Flying Officer M H Oddie was killed in action, Lieut. Ewart Henry Morgan RE, was killed in Italy, Rhys William Evans, son of Alderman Tom Evans and a former Head Boy and Chaired Bard, aged 22, died in action, Captain K Scudamore of the Ivor Arms, Fleur-de-lis, was killed in action in Belgium, and so the list went on. In all sixty-six Old Boys lost their lives in the service of their country. Towards the end of the war Flight Lieutenant J T James, in the Pathfinder force, was awarded a DFC, and Sgt. John Charles Hughes the Military Medal in North Africa. Reports also reached school about Old Boys detained as POWs : Gomer Lewis, RA, in Java and H L Packer, place unspecified. Even when the war was over fatalities were still being reported. Flight Sergeant Rowland J Dash (RAF) was lost over Germany and William Austin Harvey was killed in a Sunderland flying boat crash. In January 1943 M L Sweet paid a visit to school. He had been machine-gunned from a German aeroplane while on duty at St Leonards and left for dead in the service mortuary. An alert attendant noticed that he had a pulse. Careful nursing after he was removed to hospital eventually saw him recover to qualify as a teacher.

Our Armed Forces cannot fight without equipment and this must be paid for. In War Weapons Week in 1941 Arthur Wright organised a collection of £1113 in school; for Warship Week the amount was £1760, the Tank Appeal raised £1344, Salute the Soldier Week £1811 and Wings For Victory £2404. The equivalent of £2404 today (2013) is approximately £285000. What energy this member of staff possessed.

World War II revealed massive shortcomings in technical education and the 1944 Education Act aimed to do something about this. A Tripartite Secondary School System was proposed - there would be Grammar, Technical and Secondary Modern schools. The school-leaving age would rise to 15 (although this did not happen until 1947). The Secondary Modern Schools were encouraged to transfer their better pupils to the Grammar School at the age of 13 and many pupils who were either late-developers or who had had a bad day when they sat their 11+, profited immensely by this move. In 1948 the Central Welsh Board was abolished and its duties taken over by the Welsh Joint Education Committee (WJEC). Three years later General Certificate of Education (GCE) exams at O, A and S level were introduced. The former 'pass, credit' and 'very good' of the Central Welsh Board were replaced by a simple 'pass'. There were now serious doubts about the validity of intelligence tests for entry to Grammar Schools, research showing that about 10% of pupils were mis-allocated.

At the beginning of the decade the school Assembly Hall, formerly the parish church, had been referred to as 'the Hall' for some 30 years. Now it was converted once again into a chapel. The lectern was the gift of Mr D G Hall; the organ and pews were given by friends and admirers. In February of 1940 a picture damaged by water from a burst pipe was found to be uninsured, as were other pictures, the organ, lectern and pews. Appropriate action followed - insurance was swiftly arranged. Before the end of the year 'blast walls' had been erected at Lower School, behind Upper School, in front of the windows belonging to the cloakroom, lavatory, science labs and front door. In the following June all the windows were pasted with gauze and doped with cellulose to reduce the danger from possible flying glass: a procedure which the chemistry master thought somewhat questionable.

It was Wartime. What else could be done to help the War effort? Should there be a school garden and if so how should it be used? Three years later ground was prepared to grow vegetables but no record has come to light as to whether or not it functioned and, if it did, what happened to the produce.

As the war ended every boy who entered Pengam still had to surmount an academic hurdle, the later much-maligned 11+ examination. He had not only passed it but had scored enough marks in basic numeracy and literacy to be able to select the school of his first choice. These boys were drawn from the three parishes of Gelligaer, Bedwellty and Mynyddislwyn and from a broad range of social backgrounds. Many were first generation grammar school boys of working-class families, others the sons of professional families. These would include a whole range of abilities and aptitudes: Oxbridge aspirants, under-achievers, steady plodders, those who were 'games mad' and those who didn't want to be there at all - but it was what their parents wanted.

Borden Boys

The outbreak of the Second World War in September 1939 caused plans that had been made some years previously to be put into practice. One such plan was to evacuate schoolchildren from vulnerable areas of the country to areas of greater safety. Pengam therefore expected a request to have evacuees at the school. A meeting of the Governors that month agreed to admit as many boys as the surplus accommodation would allow. By May 1940 accommodation at Pengam had been found for sixty-one boys and three male staff, Messrs Highton, Snelling and Higson, from Borden Grammar School, Sittingbourne, Kent. From the same school fifty girls and three staff would join our sister school at Hengoed. These boys used the chemistry and physics laboratories where they were taught by Mr Higson, from 3.20 to 4.40 Monday to Thursday. By July 1942 twelve Borden boys were thought to be sufficiently advanced to be entered for the First School Leaving Certificate of the Central Welsh Board. Ten had very good results, one gaining seven distinctions and another six; much of the tutoring being given by Lewis' masters. By the end of July that year most of the German aircraft had been moved from France to the Russian Front. In fact conditions in Kent had improved so much that all the evacuees except two returned home. They were remembered as being well-mannered and hard-working pupils. The following month a letter appeared in the local press thanking the people of the area for all their help. In particular the generosity, kindliness and patience of all the foster parents and all our other friends. In October 1964 the Headmaster received a letter from one of the evacuees.

'I came late in 1940, was put in Form VA, and did CWB in 1941. At the time we dug trenches in the grounds and had gas mask drills. I played once in a school rugby match, took part in impromptu speeches and was disqualified because I spoke with my hands in my pockets. I was in the Air Training Corps, and took away a lasting memory of maths and history. I always felt at home.'

Entry examinations

For the 1940 entry any potential entrant whose age lay between 10 years and 12 years 9 months on the 31st of September was allowed to sit. That September the entry comprised 54 from Glamorgan and 36 from Monmouthshire. On other occasions the division between counties might be 60 to 30. Did the variation in these numbers depend on the range of marks attained by examinees in the two counties? Somewhat strangely the sister school at Hengoed invariably took 45 from each county. Again this prompts the question Why? Another surprising fact is the number of scholars who passed but turned down the offer of a place at one of the Lewis' schools. For instance of the 1942 entry 16 Tredegar boys and 11 girls declined. Why was this? Was it related to the long journeys and extra costs involved? The numbers who sat the entrance exam varied considerably from year to year. In 1948 about 280 Monmouthshire boys sat for 35 places. Of these two boys scored 167 marks out of 300. One became a university professor, the other ran his father's businesses - a café and betting shops. I wonder which one had the more satisfying life?

Until the 1945 entry the parents of boys who came to Pengam were liable to pay fees. Of the 1944 entry 11 Monmouthshire boys out of 37 paid full fees of £7.10s. a year (equivalent to roughly £1100 today), and 11 paid nothing. For Glamorgan boys 17 out of 54 paid full fees and 23 nothing. The others paid £2, £3, £4 or £5 a year, the exact amount being determined by Return of Income forms, which were due to be handed in three days before the start of term. These fees were for the first child in Pengam. For every additional boy in the school a further 10s (50p) was charged. Fee-paying boys could apply for a Maintenance Allowance. Whether the allowance was granted depended on the family income per head. For a family with a weekly income of £2.12s.6d (£2.67½) and 5 children there was a cash grant of £1.3s.4d (£1.17) but a family with 2 children and an income of £2.12s.6d did not qualify. The maximum grant was £1.6s.8d (£1.33) to be paid to a family where there were 7 children and the weekly income was £2 - roughly £240 today. Records show that the school did not always find it easy to collect the fees due.

First Impressions

For any new boy the most impressive memory of the first day would probably be the school chapel. This was the place where many key events in school life would take place - morning assembly, the annual Eisteddfod, Speech Day and Founder's Day. Originally it was built as a parish church with a tower and spire, and equipped with a pipe organ, lectern and pews - a pulpit would be added in 1945 in memory of the Old Boys who had died in WWII. It was in the chapel that boys would find that their teachers wore gowns, some even sporting mortarboards, and sat on the platform facing them during morning service - in Welsh on Tuesdays and Thursdays, in English on the other days. It was from this platform that academic and sporting successes were announced to the whole school. Everyone took pride in the successes of the few. It was here that scoldings for lack of courtesy, laziness and unpunctuality took place and here where the names of those who would spend an hour in detention after school on a Thursday would be read out.

Red-Letter Days

The intention of Speech Day, always with a celebrity as guest speaker, was to recognise, praise and reward academic success, but the school was poor and had very little reward to offer other than praise. In 1943 Lord Davies of Llandinam exhorted us *'to use the Press, wireless and cinema more, to delve into and try to understand our history, and to gain a good understanding of civics. All these should help us to develop the sense of responsibility we need in a free democracy.'* Other guest speakers included two Old Boys who had become MPs. Hayden Davies MP for the South-West Division of St Pancras and Harold Davies MP for Leek who was elevated to the House of Lords when he lost his parliamentary seat. On another occasion Sir Ben Bowen Thomas MA, Permanent Secretary Welsh Department of the Ministry of Education was guest speaker. Dr William Thomas, Chief Inspector at the Ministry of Education spoke in 1949. He said he'd like to see *every secondary school in Wales with its own chapel. He thought man was in danger of becoming 'drunk' on material wealth and prosperity and, as we gained power there was the danger that we were losing in direction, in aims and values. Peace, he said, was the greatest gift to humanity, not wealth, power or authority. There was need to emphasise the priceless value of true goodness and beauty which would bring better understanding of our neighbouring countries and give support to the body which had been set up to bring about a clearer and sympathetic understanding of other countries - UNESCO - the United Nations Educational, Scientific and Cultural Organisation.*

Another day of equal importance was Founder's Day always held during the last week of May, sometimes in Gelligaer Church, otherwise in the school chapel. As guest speaker a local dignitary would preach. In 1942 Rev. Canon Dr Lawrence Thomas DD took as his text *'A man shall be as a shadow of a great rock in a weary land'* (Isaiah 32.2). The reference was to our founder Edward Lewis. From 1946 on, Founder's Day was renamed Commemoration Day. During this service a pulpit, which was bought with money collected from boys and friends of the school, was dedicated to the more than 70 Old Boys who had lost their lives during WWII. Particularly sad was the death, at the age of 26, of Welsh poet and storyteller Alun Lewis MA. Alun, a former pupil at Cowbridge Grammar School and son of the Director of Education for Aberdare, had taught at L S P for eighteen months from 1937 to 1939 when he left to join the forces. He became a leading writer during WWII. When his book *Raiders Dawn* was published in 1941, it sold 10 000 copies and he was described as '*the most assured and direct poet of his generation and the natural successor to Wilfred Owen and Edward Thomas*'. In the same year his short story *The Last Inspection* won the E J O'Brien Memorial Prize as the best short story written in 1941. He was sent to India in 1942 where he wrote *Ha! Ha! Among the Trumpets* but died in mysterious circumstances while with his regiment in Burma in March 1944. To the older generation his work appeared over-preoccupied with the crudity of material living. It was the sense of frustration and anger of men from the mines, who had nothing to do in the early days of the war except observe events from a distance while their homes were being smashed by the German bombers, that gave him his material for his first stories *Raiders Dawn*. Alun's writings were successful here and in the US. Had he lived he would surely have become one of the greats.

The Eisteddfod is a national institution and in school our very own Eisteddfod, chaired by a local Reverend, was always one of the highlights of the year. Extra cash was needed in 1941 to stage the event. One solution was to arrange a soccer match School v Borden Boys. Perhaps the Borden evacuees didn't have enough boys to choose from for they lost 9-0 and this was their national game: a good thing it wasn't rugby! In 1942, D M Canning played his violin solo so well that he was asked to play it again. In the early 1940s highlights included 'whistling' parties, mouth-organ solos, and penillion singing, events that had ceased by 1945. One wonders why, since they were so popular. The Chaired Bard was H Geraint M Jones, son of H D Jones, the Welsh master. Geraint was described as School Captain; the earlier equivalent of the Head Boy? There were no prefects then.

School meals
More than two years into the war there was still no provision for school dinners. The best the school could do was to supply a hot drink: tea or cocoa. The Board of Education had turned down plans for a new Dining Hall some years earlier so a frustrated Governing body looked for

another venue. Was it possible to convert part of a near-by hotel or use the Labour Hall in Pengam? Before an alternative could be set up at one of these venues Glamorgan Education Committee who were now responsible for the school buildings informed the governors that they were drawing up plans for a building that would seat 370. The big problem was getting the materials, but they did appreciate that Pengam was the only school of its kind in the county where dinners were unavailable. In July 1942 the site was cleared but it was September 1943 before there was provision for 74 pupils to have school dinners. Priority was given to Juniors. During the second week of the Autumn Term they were serving 94 meals a day, a figure which rose to 226 per day by the end of the month. December 1943 saw the number rise to 260 which could be increased to 360 'if we had an extra cooker'. By May 1944 ninety-six per cent of the school's 385 boys were sitting down to a cooked school meal.

In July 1944 an unfortunate event took place. M V R West, a first-year boy, upset the dinner wagon thereby breaking eleven dozen fruit plates. Who should pay for the damage? The boy certainly couldn't afford to. A collection was made amongst the Sixth Form boys to cover the cost of their replacement, £3.6s (£3.30) being collected by the following Friday. When term started in the September the numbers were too many for a single sitting. Two sittings became the norm but an unfortunate consequence was that pupils on second sitting had no break after eating before they returned to lessons. Most pupils had to pay for their meal but there were exceptions. Where the gross weekly income of a family of three was more than £3 parents paid for the meal. Likewise if there were four children and the income was more than £3. 10s. (£3.50). The cost of a meal by the end of the decade was 5d (c.2p).

Meals at lunchtime were formal. Pupils stood and said grace before sitting eight to a table arranged with one fourth former and one fifth form boy at the head of the table. These two probably served the food in the belief that they needed more sustenance than the six hungry first-years arranged below them. It was good wholesome food, similar to that served to the staff in the same dining room. After clearing the tables, if all was satisfactory, everyone was dismissed. Pupils learned something of the social art of shared dining. Today many pupils turn their noses up at roast meat, boiled potatoes and two veg followed by rice pudding or sponge pudding and custard, but in those days it was the only type of meal available. It was much preferred to the alternative - a cold packed lunch carried from home.

Accommodation

At a staff meeting in October 1942 it was suggested that boys should not be expected to carry their books around all day. The most obvious solution was that each boy be allocated a desk, fitted if possible with a hasp and staple. Each boy was accordingly allocated a desk in his form room with a lift-up lid. In this he kept his books and other belongings. Most desks remained unlocked but this rarely presented a problem. Everything was quite safe. In the corridors everyone walked on the left in single file - woe betide you if you were found doing otherwise. Graffiti inside the building was virtually unknown, vandalism exceedingly rare. Any damage tended to be accidental rather than deliberate. Even in the boys' loos, outside of course, there was little evidence of abuse. Very occasionally two boys would fight but prefects seemed to appear out of thin air to break a fight up. There would be consequences and consequences are always a good deterrent. Bullying, in the writer's experience, did not exist, though I am assured that it did occur on the corridorless trains that came up the valley from Hengoed.

By the end of the decade the ever-present shortage of accommodation reared its head again. This time it was serious for in 1950 the length of the School Certificate course, which for many grammar school forms had been four years, was due to become five years for everyone. In July 1948 the Governors investigated the possibility of basing two forms in rooms belonging to the Welsh Congregational Church in Gilfach but it was decided that it was too far away. Their solution was to have two temporary huts erected in the school grounds which could be used until the extensions (planned in 1938, and delayed because of the war) were provided. October 1949 saw the number of boys on roll pass the 500 mark. This increase was due chiefly to the numbers in the sixth form having increased to between 70 and 80. A few years previously they had been between 10 and 12.

The Demise of the old School Building

On the last day of the decade the Governors received a Compulsory Purchase Order for land to widen the road between Gelligaer Church and the Cross Inn. On this land stood the 200-year-old house that was the original school. They decided that they would like the old school moved into the grounds of the existing school and used as a museum. The estimated cost was £3000. Application was made to The Pilgrim Trust (Dr Thomas Jones CH was a former secretary and an Old Boy) but the Trust was unable to help. In view of this and although Glamorgan C C had secured £500 from the Welsh Church Acts Committee,

Monmouthshire C C declined to help. The idea was dropped. In the event a small cairn with accompanying plaque was erected near the west door of the chapel.

Curriculum

For their first year at school, it was traditional for new pupils to be allocated at random into one of three classes but for the second year they were placed in one of three streams. Those in the A and B streams would sit CWB exams after four years while those in the C stream took an extra year, except for the few who were moved into one of the other forms. All girls in our sister school took five years. Examinees took at least one subject from each of the following groups:

I   Scripture knowledge, English, Welsh, History, Geography
II   A foreign language
III Mathematics, Physics, Chemistry, Biology, Geology, General Science, Botany
IV A practical subject.

By way of example of the numbers, involved in 1943 sixty-three sat the CWB First School Leaving certificate, of whom fifty-one passed. These included Rex Acton who was awarded six distinctions, became Head Boy and won a Welsh Foundation scholarship in Mathematics to Oxford, subsequently to become a distinguished statistician. At Higher level there were just 8 candidates, 6 passed in a maths subject, 6 in physics and 5 in chemistry, showing that science subjects predominated. In 1948 the Head complained that while there were 14 studying science in Upper Sixth there were just 2 studying Arts. An Inspection report in 1943 showed that the number on roll was 404, of whom 95 were new entrants with an average age of 11 yr 2 m. Other than English 107 pupils in the school took Welsh, 61 Latin and 268 French. Music was a particularly strong subject, instruction being given for the organ, piano, violin, 'cello and woodwind. About 280 took the mid-day meal. Subsidiary inspections were made by the County Inspectors, Archie Lush for Monmouthshire and Miss Dilys Rees for Glamorgan. H M I Owen Jones carried out the inspection for the Central Welsh Board.

A 1940s Form IV essay

How does an English master select suitable topics for his pupils so that they can show their creative writing skills to best effect? Probably by choosing those that are up to the minute and within the boy's own experience. In the spring of 1940 the only conversation in many a home would have been the possible impending disaster. This essay was written by a 12-year-old who was taking a great interest in current affairs. After completing his sixth form studies and graduating he served in the Royal Air Force prior to returning to civilian life. The topic he had been given was *A News Bulletin*.

Hamburg Bombed; German Freighter Scuttled; Greeks Push On; 16 enemy planes down.

Hamburg, Germany's second largest city felt the weight of attacks from our bombers on Saturday. In spite of bad weather the R A F attacks were long and intensive. The objects were shipyards, oil refineries, electricity works and railway yards. The Air Ministry announces:- For several hours last (Saturday) night, a concentrated attack was made on Hamburg's great and various industries.

The German freighter Phryiga (4,137 tons), one of the four German steamers which secretly left Tampico on Friday night, was scuttled by her crew, after she had been shelled by British cruisers. The other three ships are now back at Tampico. Most of the crew of the Phrygia are also safe in Tampico.

An official communiqué at noon stated that the Greek attack was continuing on the Kalamas sector, where they had crossed the frontier into Albania with the Italians fleeing before them. Greek artillery has been intensively bombarding Koritza and in the Pindus range fighting is still going on. British and Greek planes were reported to have bombed Valoria and Durazzo on the Albanian coast and an Italian ship is said to have been hit.

Sixteen enemy aircraft were destroyed during raids on Britain yesterday. One of our fighters was lost but the pilot is safe. In addition, two German planes were destroyed during Thursday night after fighters and ground defences had smashed two daylight attempts to reach London the night alert was sounded in the capital at a very early hour. Enemy planes were also reported over an East Anglian town early in the night. Three planes were shot down off Folkstone and two more in the Thames estuary area.

Staff
By late 1940 Glamorgan and Monmouthshire Councils had agreed that staff in the forces should have their salaries made up to what they would have received had they remained teaching. Some of the Pengam Governors did not agree. At the next Governors' meeting they voted on the motion that '*they agree not to make up the salaries of teachers now in*

the forces because it was not done in other industries'. The motion was defeated by 12 votes to 2, the only two in support being Alderman Evan Thomas and Blackwood County Councillor Lewis Lewis. During 1940 five staff left for the forces. Late in 1941 former teacher and poet Alun Lewis visited school; it being noted that his portrait had appeared in the December copy of *Lilliput* magazine. Several of the replacements for those staff who had left for the forces were temporary; T I Jeffreys-Jones MA was appointed to teach Senior History and Junior Welsh 'for the duration of the war', and Mrs Simmonds to teach Biology in place of H G Hoof who returned for a short time in 1947. In May 1943 the government agreed that it would accept married female teachers and in the November, in spite of the acute shortage of satisfactory replacements, for some inexplicable government reason, teachers were forced to retire at 60 or when they had completed 40 years service. In September 1944 the school received a letter from County Hall to the effect that regulations annulling the appointment of female married teachers on marriage be rescinded as from the November.

In October 1942, after 23 years of service to the school, Thomas Addison Hughes BA retired as Senior English master to be replaced by W Cecil Morgan. Tom Hughes had been appointed while Vaughan Johnson was Head and had previously taught in France, Canada and elsewhere in the UK, but once recalled that Pengam was the most talented place he had ever experienced. He had played rugby with Percy Bush, then at University College, Cardiff, and at Grenoble. After teaching English in Lyon he became Vice-principal at Old's School, Alberta. Tom was said to have had a cultured personality and a gentlemanly disposition. In the school hierarchy R G Jones became Senior master on the retirement of Arthur Wright in 1944 and held the position until H D Jones (Harri-Dai) took it over in July 1946, ably assisted by Neville Richards.

It was good to see new, younger teachers join the staff in the middle to late 40s. Len George, a former pupil, replaced Jack Perrett the one-armed PE/games teacher who could climb a rope and play a good round of golf (Jack's name appeared in the Guinness Book of Records for downing a seagull with his drive at a coastal links). W S 'Weepy' Williams replaced Arthur Wright on a temporary basis until B A Haynes (Chalkie) arrived in 1946 while J E Gibbs replaced W Handel 'Custard' Morgan. Other appointments were D T Jones to teach French, B I Evans (Mighty Atom) Chemistry, W H John History and Elwyn Jones, for one year in place of H D Jones (Welsh), before he was replaced by W G Jones. Other important arrivals were Peter C Evans and Vernon J Davies. Peter Evans introduced 'A' level Art, O level Art classes in the Sixth Form, and also started a most fascinating weekly Art Appreciation lesson. Vernon Davies was able to teach Woodwork and Metalwork in a fully equipped work-shop but he was often seen working outside the room, one example being painting names on the various Honours Boards.

One new member of staff with a particular talent for making history interesting was Major E N Edwards MA as Senior History. History badly needed a teacher who could provide stability. Since Ensor Lewis died in 1939 the subject had seen nearly ten different individuals have responsibility for it. The 'Major', after six years in the army, could paint a picture that transported you far and wide to the scene of a battle or the rough sea of a voyage. His talents were recognised afar for he was the only Welsh representative - there were five in total from the UK - at a conference on Education for International Understanding in Paris in 1947. Under the auspices of the United Nations Educational, Scientific and Cultural Organisation (UNESCO), it lasted six weeks.

Since the time of Vaughan Johnston mathematics had been the strongest subject in the curriculum. W H Hughes (Taffy) arrived from Caerphilly in 1946 to teach up to 'O' level. He had worked in industry so his experience gave the department yet another dimension. In 1948 D T Davies, a former pupil, joined the staff. D T lived in Tredegar and commuted daily in his somewhat dilapidated Austin 7. A rather teasing article in the school magazine referred to his car as The Apple Cart. The result was that he became known as Dai Apple. He was a first class maths teacher though I do have a story that shows he could also be sarcastic. Asked if I understood the solution of a mechanics problem he had just gone through in class I replied *'I'd done it already, Sir.'* to which he responded *'Sorry. If I hadn't seen your solution I wouldn't have known how to do it.'*

Teachers' salaries are often a bone of contention. In the ten years from 1939 teachers' salaries went up, on average, by 30% whereas the cost of living went up by 90%. Their salaries, compared with other professions, were poor, so they were urged by their unions to bring the matter up with their MP and with the PM. Burnham was not getting them a fair deal. Is any group ever satisfied? There's always another group doing better.

Non-teaching Staff
To pupils the most obvious member of the non-teaching staff during the 1940s was Mr W T Jenkins, the school secretary, who served three

heads: Vaughan Johnston, Stanley Knight and Neville Richards. He was a modest and kind man who had been forced to look for a new occupation because of a colliery accident which had left him with a leg injury. His charm and sincerity endeared him to all he came into contact with. His desk was in the Head's office, resulting in his often having to stand in the corridor outside whilst the Head had a confidential conversation with a visitor. He was always helpful and friendly. Usually he referred to boys by their initials: H G, D M, R T. Mr Jenkins died suddenly, at the age of 57, in November 1955. He had served the school for 34 years. A set of four chairs was subsequently given to the school by his sister in his memory.

Another long-serving member of the staff was William T Hester. He and his wife were caretakers from 1934 until they retired in 1956. When he was appointed 260 men had applied for the job illustrating the depth of the depression in the mid '30s. This number of applicants also reflects the fact that a house, coal, and electricity was included free with the job. At their first meeting the Governors produced a short-list of six and voted on them. Taking the top three they voted again. In each case Mr and Mrs Hester headed the vote. Both had to pass a medical before they were finally accepted. When they were appointed their housemaid was already in post but, as they were about to begin their new employment, whether coincidental or not, the maid resigned. The new caretakers were immediately given permission to replace her as they saw fit. Details of the duties of the 17-year-old maid are startling by the standards of today. She should start at 6.40 a.m., have several periods off (unpaid) during the day and finally be on duty from 4.15 to 6 p.m. She was paid for 9^1/2 hours work a day but spread over a period of eleven and a half hours from 6.30 a.m. to 6 p.m. She served tea or coffee to pupils at lunchtime and also worked on a Saturday from 6.30 to 1 or 2 p.m. All 19,000 square feet of floorspace in the school was cleaned by the caretaker, his wife and two cleaners. In 1946 the net pay for the caretakers, including a war bonus, was £23.18s.2d (£23.91) a month.

Scholarships
Pengam has always claimed its fair share of scholarships. During the decade more than fifty scholarships of various types, State, County, Music, Engineering and others, were awarded to boys at the school. Some, including the more important ones, are referred to below. In 1940 Head Boy David Laurence Sims and John K Brown were awarded State Scholarships. Both proceeded to Oxford. Other awards that year were a County Major Scholarship in music for Robert Smith, a Monmouthshire Medical Scholarship to Ronald Medlicott, a Glamorgan

County Scholarship to John Elfed Jones and an Engineering Scholarship to Ronald George Bailey.

The star pupil of the following year was Ronald Hammond. He achieved the grade of 'distinction' in every paper of every subject he sat at School Certificate - something that had never been achieved before at Pengam. After being awarded a State Scholarship and a Miner's Welfare Scholarship Ronald went up to Jesus College, Oxford. Before he could go he discovered that he needed French at School Certificate level, a subject he had never studied. He put his mind to it and secured a credit after five weeks study. Some brain! His experience illustrated yet again that there wasn't the guidance available that there should have been. Most pupils could expect little advice at home - their parents just didn't have the knowledge or know where to get it. In school there was no careers service or teacher with the required information. His remarkable success was marked by the people of his home town, New Tredegar. They collected for a gold watch and a wallet of notes which the Headmaster presented to him in school. Ronald Hammond gained a First at Oxford after twelve months in college on a course that normally took two years, and became an honorary Fellow. He left to take a commission in the RAF and returned to continue his studies some four years later.

Another very successful pupil was Laurence D Rosebaum. He was awarded a State Scholarship and was interviewed for a Meyricke Scholarship but was unsuccessful because he did not have School Certificate Latin. Is this another example of a lack of advice? In the latter half of the decade Rex A Acton went up to Jesus College, Oxford, while F Peter Woodford was awarded a State Scholarship and the Domus Exhibition at Balliol College, Oxford. Peter also secured the United Nations essay prize for the whole of Wales. Stanley Knight was suitably impressed and keen to point out the value of a broad grammar school education.

Not exactly a scholarship but worth recording here is the success accorded Head Boy Colin Vaughan Williams in 1949-50. Colin represented Wales at the *Hands Across the Sea* rally in Tennessee, USA, where he spent more than a month. Not only that but he was elected party spokesman for the tour.

School Trips
During the war school trips were few and far between. There was a visit to the Workmen's Hall in Fleur-de-lis for a performance of *Macbeth*

staged by the Old Vic Repertory Company starring Sybil Thorndike and Lewis Casson. Sybil Thorndike returned the following year to appear in *Medea*. In 1944 members of the Sixth Form attended the Assize Court at Cardiff to sit in on the trial of a British subject, accused of murdering a US soldier. He was acquitted. After the war it took a while before school trips ventured very far. First it was to a cinema in Bargoed to see *Anthony and Cleopatra*, then to see *Great Expectations*. As the decade came to its conclusion Len George took 36 members of the History and Geography Society to Van, Castell Coch and Caerphilly Castle. The first trip abroad was to France in 1949.

Weather Problems

As if there weren't enough problems due to the war the weather decided to give a helping hand. Glacial rain and heavy snow fell in January 1940, telegraph wires came down, traffic stopped and the electricity went off. Twenty-four degrees of frost was recorded and attendance fell to 25%. On some days it seemed to be nothing but sirens and snow. Heavy snow fell again in 1942 and once again attendance was so poor that little worthwhile could be achieved. By 1947 the war was over but the snow falls were worse than ever. At times the canteen was even without food.

A Cry from the Library

A theme that has come through repeatedly while researching material for this book is the lack of money at the Governors' disposal. In 1948, W J Morris, the classics master who also looked after the library, felt so strongly about this lack of funding that he penned the following article in the school magazine.

Extra Curriculum

Within the cramping specialising confines of the curriculum, teachers have been charged with trying to cram in more and more about less and less: there are, with apologies to a contemporary dictum in the field of economics, 'too many pupils chasing too few subjects,' either willy nilly, or, as a second former once put it, 'because it's in the time-table.'

Outside the classroom, however, we are unshackled and free to roam, to find out for ourselves, if we will, more and more about more and more; the fateful letters 'C W B' Controlling Welsh Boys, take on illimitable meaning and a boundless vista when interpreted as: 'Come Willingly, Boys' into the 'Closed World of Books' waiting to be opened in the Library. By Act of Parliament, every school is, in the future, to have its library; this will, one day be stocked, by somebody unspecified, with books, and there may even be arrangements for a librarian; but when? Of the two authorities served by this School one contributes nothing to the Library, the other has made no additional annual provision for forty years.

Nevertheless, as there is a present as well as a future need, and as Acts of Parliament are not enough, there are two libraries in Lewis' School to supplement the Official School Library, which, in memory of the benefactions of the late John Herbert James, of Merthyr, is known as the 'James Library.'

The two subsidiaries are the Boys' Library and the Sixth Form Library. These are maintained by the voluntary subscriptions of the boys, by donations from Old Boys and by gifts from past and present pupils, the Staff and friends of the School.

Further subscriptions, donations and gifts, always welcome, would enable the Library Services to be extended to a degree worthy of this School.

The Librarian has lists of books which would make desirable additions to the stock, and he would like to call attention to the practice in many schools by which every boy on leaving presents a book to the library. This has much to commend it.

Who will be the first to start this tradition in Pengam?

The House System
The House System was re-introduced in the spring term 1948 in an attempt to bring the pupils together by means of a spirit of healthy rivalry and competition. It was arranged so that loyalty to one's House embodied loyalty to one's home town or village. The numbers in each House were almost identical but it was stressed that should it arise at a later date that any House had a preponderance of Seniors the allocation of pupils to Houses should be adjusted by moving one town or village from one House to another. Two House competitions took place before the end of the school year: the eisteddfod and rugby competitions. Lewis House won both.

Clubs and Societies
A salient feature of the education provided by the public schools and older universities was a thriving debating society. Many grammar schools attempted to emulate this feature. To this end a Scientific, Literary and Debating Society, always known as SLADS, held its inaugural meeting on 9 January 1948. The Chairman, Neville Richards, spoke about the aims of the society. Following the election of officers members divided into two teams to answer questions on English literature. The society's name occasionally prompted the question 'Are you going to SLADS tonight?' to which the retort came 'No, thiS LAD'S going home.' Open to all Fifth and Sixth formers the society met weekly after school on Fridays. The

canteen provided a light tea and each meeting, which began at 4.30, was held either in the Art Room or in the chapel, depending on the anticipated attendance. From the first meeting in February 1948 Mr Neville Richards continued as Chairman; several other members of staff often attending. The activities at most meetings fell into one of the following categories: a debate, lecture, After-dinner speeches, Members' Papers, Mock Parliament, an Election, Inter-school debate or Sharp Practice.

Sharp Practice got things going for the first meeting of term. This mysterious title was linked to a 'a series of short debates' in which members wrote down motions for debate which other members proposed or opposed. Topics written on a piece of paper, were put into a hat, then drawn by members at random. Those due to speak did so for not more than five minutes on the topic drawn out. Thereby pearls of wisdom resulted from the most unexpected sources. Typical topics were:
    'That cheese should be eaten with a knife and fork.'
    'That the first requisite of a woman is beauty.'
    'That a petition be taken to the Head-Master proposing that
    Stanley (the Head) be removed from the country.'
    'That tiddley-winks and blow-football should be adopted as
    international games.'
    'That you can tell a historian by looking at his face.'

Lectures were given by a member or by an outside speaker. Further debate was encouraged afterwards. Examples of lecture topics are:
    The advantages of Dictatorship.
    The United Nations Organisation.
    Town Planning.
    The Discovery of the Nature of Air.

For an After-dinner speech a member of the society was presented with a situation and given a week to compose a suitable speech. For example on one occasion the boys were asked to imagine that they were sitting in the Royal Albert Hall listening to Professor Earnest Sutherley speaking to the Royal Society about his recent trip to the moon - Did he ever think it would happen? Another speech was to welcome home Capt. Scott-Williams, the famous Arctic explorer.

For the debates there was a proposer and an opposer, each with a seconder. After these four had had their say contributions were welcome from the floor. Four motions were:

'That further progress in science at the present rate would be a disaster'. Defeated.
'That the disadvantages of co-education outweigh the advantages'. Defeated.
'That the best school has the fewest rules.' Carried.
'That this house has complete faith in the present government.' Draw.

Inter-school debates took place with Bargoed Grammar School and with our sister school at Hengoed. One motion for a debate with Bargoed was *'That the theatre is a more valuable institution than the cinema.'* Carried. And with Hengoed *'That the modern girl is inferior to her counterpart of the Victorian era.'* Carried by 3 votes.

There was also a Mock Trial when one pupil was charged with the murder of another pupil - the prisoner was discharged - and a Mock Parliament to discuss a bill 'For the abolition of homework.' Defeated. Yet another activity was to hold play-reading sessions - with a Pengam-Hengoed Dramatic Society in mind. The only other society of note was The Geographical and Historical Association which had been thriving before the war but took a while to get off the ground after it. The association arranged lectures on events of local and national history, rambles, and visits to such places as Caerphilly Castle and Cardiff Castle.

Finally reference should be made to the Urdd which had been operating in school since it had been founded by H D Jones in 1927. The annual Urdd camp at Llangrannog was always popular. From 1949 Gwyn Jones was the master in charge. His other contributions involved playing in the school orchestra and checking-in school stores. The Bargoed, Hengoed and Pengam Music Club arranged concerts in all three local Glamorgan grammar schools and also made a significant contribution to extra-curricular activities at school.

Sport
There was little competitive sport during the war years though Old Boy D Gilmour Isaac played in an Oxford/Cambridge Inter-varsity rugby match and had a college blue for association football in 1942. He was the only Welshman on the field. No school Sports' Day was held in 1940 because of Mr Perrett's absence. He was confined to a sanatorium as he had contracted tuberculosis but was well enough to return to school in the September where he remained until his retirement in 1945 after 23 years service. In 1941 Sports' Day was a very low-key affair but it did include evacuees from Kent - the Borden boys. Tom Edwards, later to

become Head of Mathematics at the school in 1965, was second in the High Jump in 1943 when North Glam House were winners. It is often difficult for pupils at a school to accept that some of their teachers achieved sporting success when they were younger. In the 1944 School Sports Hugh Bevan Griffith (5A), Nye Bevan's nephew, was Victor Ludorum (he was again in 1945) with Alun Williams (6) and Keith Jones (4A) runners-up. All three were Monmouthshire boys. Brian Sexton followed Hugh as Victor Ludorum the following year and ten years later broke the Welsh National javelin record with a throw of 193 feet which he improved to 206 feet 4 inches in 1958.

In June 1944, at the Glamorgan Championship meeting at Whitchurch, Pengam won two cups: Gordon Robinson won the St Illtyd's Cup as Junior Hurdles winner and the school was awarded the Western Mail Cup as the Junior Champions. At the first Glamorgan Secondary School Amateur Athletic Association meeting at Mountain Ash in 1946 the Middle team carried off the Sir D R Llewellyn Cup and in the first Annual Inter-County Championships of the Welsh Secondary Schools AAA involving nine counties John F Rees was first in the Hop, Step and Jump, Discuss, Shot put and Throwing the Cricket Ball. At the 1947 Meeting Pengam were placed second behind Gowerton Grammar School.

The House system during the decade was tri-partite, North Glam, South Glam and Monmouthshire. In 1943 South Glam were victorious by a slender three points, thereby being awarded the Caldwell Cup which they had to relinquish the following year to Mon. After a further year Mon passed the cup to North Glam in 1946 so each house had won the cup at least once over the four-year period. The best athletes of the time as indicated by the Annual Glamorgan Secondary School AAA sports were Gordon Robinson (Middle 100 yds 1st, 440 yds 4th), Alan Baxendale (Senior Javelin 3rd with 134 feet 4 inches), Viv Sweet (Middle 220 yds, 1st in 25.3 sec, Shot 1st 38' 7") and Gywn Harris (Middle Long Jump, 1st 18' 0", Hop, Step and Jump, later called the Triple Jump, 1st 42' 1"). At this meeting Pengam won the Middle Section and were fifth overall out of forty-four schools.

Towards the end of the decade the star athletes were John Frowen, Viv Sweet and Brian Hardwick. John was Victor Ludorum in '48 and again in '49 when he won the 100 yds hurdles, long jump and hop, step and jump, was second in the high jump and third in the javelin. That day his high jump of 5' 2" set a new school record but it was beaten the same day by Brian Hardwick with a jump of 5' 6½". At 18 John went on to set records of 23' 1" in the long jump and 46' 1 1/2" in the triple jump at the 1950 Glamorgan S S Championships. Brian attended a special athletics course at Motspur Park, London, and in 1950 gained his sixth championship win at Bangor with a high jump of 5' 3". Three other prominent athletes were sprinters: Viv Sweet and Basil Ashford, and school outside-half John F Rees.

Away from athletics the school did well in sport but there were also dark moments. The First XV went to Pontywaun unaccompanied in February 1944. Word got back to the Head that some of those present had been smoking on the field and elsewhere. The next match, against Tredegar was, not unexpectedly, cancelled. In 1946 John Langford Roberts at the tender age of 13 and weighing 9 stone, was the youngest player on the field in the Wales v England Junior rugby international at Cardiff Arms Park. He was described as 'a wonderful loose forward, very fast with safe hands'. The next year he captained Wales against England at Leicester. Other names of note on the rugby field were Colin Bosley, Gwyn Harris, Viv Sweet, Ken Robinson and Billy Thomas. Billy went on to play for Wales at Senior level. In the '48-49 season school won 10 of their 15 matches.

Cricket was always a poor relation, one of the main reasons being that there was no satisfactory pitch after the new main road was driven through the school grounds in the 1920s. Attempts were made to play home games elsewhere, for instance in 1942 Fleur-de-lis offered the hire of their ground at 7/6 (37 1/2p) a time. Results were often below par: in 1949 three of the four matches were lost and the other match drawn. Other sporting events were Cross Country Meetings (80 entries in 1944) and School v Old Boys rugby matches.

Arthur Wright MBE, BSc, AKC

I cannot leave the 1940s without an appreciation of Arthur Wright, who probably gave more of his life to the school than any other teacher in the history of the school. In addition I include details of some of the correspondence that passed between him and Old Boys during World War II.

Born in Diss, Norfolk, the son of a farmer, Arthur Wright came to teach Chemistry at Pengam in April 1904. Prior to his arrival he had spent three years at Snettisham Grammar School in his home county. When he arrived there were still boarders at the school. 'Cocky' Wright as he affectionately became known, graduated with a BSc. in Chemistry from

King's College, London. At the college he was awarded the City of London Cloth Workers Exhibition worth £60, the Barey prize for Divinity, a gold medal for Mathematics, and the Jelf medal for Chemistry and Physics. While at King's he also earned an AKC. This qualification - an Associate of King's College - was awarded to students who attended lectures in the teachings of the Church of England and passed the appropriate examination at the end of each of their undergraduate years. Apart from his enthusiasm for science he brought his many other interests to the attention of his pupils: he was a philatelist, numismatist and campanologist. This latter interest led him to tour the highways and byways of Monmouthshire on his bicycle, often accompanied by enthusiastic pupils including Morgan Price, the author's father-in-law. They took rubbings of inscriptions and details of all the bells in the county they could access. Arthur Wright's *Church Bells of Monmouthshire* was published in 1942 and one hundred and twenty copies were printed. Always aiming to educate anyone who would listen to him he gave Lantern Lectures to numerous groups both in and out of school. One such lecture of particular interest on the *Rhymney Valley* was to the evacuee boys from Borden Grammar School, Kent.

In 1924 Arthur Wright, always a man with strong convictions, became Senior Master, a position he was to hold for the next twenty years. Five years later he applied, unsuccessfully, for the Headship of the school, although he did make the short-list. That honour went to L Stanley Knight. The defeat was accepted gracefully. Though the two men had different views on many subjects, Stanley Knight was subsequently to say of him *I could not wish for a more loyal and zealous colleague. We have not always seen eye to eye, but when a decision was reached that conflicted with his personal views, the latter were forgotten and its prosecution became his first concern.*

Arthur Wright completed 40 years as a teacher at the end of April 1941 when he was told that he should retire under the 40-years service rule, but was allowed to stay on because of the problems of wartime and the difficulty in finding a suitably qualified replacement. He learned that he could stay on until the end of the war or until he was 65, whichever came first. In January 1944 his post was advertised but there was only one applicant who the Governors did not feel able to appoint. Consequently he remained in post until the end of the Summer term. When he had been appointed there were boarders at the school and just four staff apart from the Headmaster; by the time of his retirement the number of staff had grown to more than twenty. More than 3500 boys had passed through his hands. Apart from his teaching duties he had been Hon. Sec. of the School Branch of the Assistant Masters Association for 33 years. At one of the AMA meetings complaints were made that *too many people were appointed to government posts who were the product of public schools*. Furthermore any candidate with a Welsh accent would be unlikely to succeed. The four secondary school associations also thought that all secondary school teachers, about 25,000, should be graduates. Arthur Wright eventually retired at the end of the Summer Term in 1944. At his retirement he was presented with a cheque for £75.

During and leading up to World War II, as well as being president of the male side of St John Ambulance, Bargoed, Arthur Wright was one of the joint secretaries of the Gelligaer and Pontlottyn Local Savings Committee. From 1939 to 1953 he was responsible for the Local Savings Branch collecting more than £4 million. This was one of the premier districts of the Welsh Region of the Savings Movement. His involvement with this and with the School Savings movement, which he ran from 1924 to 1944, led to his name appearing in the 1946 New Year's Honours list when he was awarded the MBE for services to War Savings. Outside his schoolwork he was chair of Gelligaer and District Mining Association, belonged to the Cambrian Archeological Society, contributed to *Archaeologia Cambrensis* and to the *Llandaff Diocesan Magazine*. Without doubt Arthur Wright's greatest extra-curricula contribution to the school was his researching and writing *The History of Lewis' School, Pengam*, which was published by the author in 1929. How many copies were printed and how well they sold is difficult to judge for they were still being sold to pupils as WWII ended. One novel way of distributing them was that all sixteen students who passed their Higher School Certificate in 1936 were given a copy by the author, illustrating yet again what a generous and well-meaning man he was.

For many former students the only contact they had with the school while they were abroad serving their country was through Arthur Wright. He was always pleased to correspond with them, many thanking him by sending interesting items for the school museum. Finally I include information that Arthur Wright had first learned on 2 June 1941 concerning Cecil Davies of the Welsh Regiment who went 'missing' in the Middle East. He had not necessarily been killed but could well be a POW. In a few months it was confirmed that he was a POW (12495) in Stalag IVD 404 Germany. Details are given of Red Cross parcels. Maximum weight 10 lb. No food except solid chocolate, 2 lb maximum, a long, long list of articles that could not be sent. His mother was Mrs J Spillar of 18

Thomas Street, Nelson. He had been 3^1/$_2$ months without a smoke. She sent 4/- (20p) to the British American Tobacco Co. for 200 Woodbines to be sent. Players No 3 cost 7/- (35p) for 200 or 32/- (£1.60) for 1000, St Bruno tobacco 2/6 (12^1/$_2$p) for 4 oz, Three Nuns and Gold Block 4/- (20p) for 4 oz. He was still a POW on 3.4.44. In one parcel Mrs Spillar sent 1 towel, 2 prs socks, 2 prs leather laces, 1 pr cotton laces, 1 pr canvas shoes, 2 boot brushes, 1 tin boot polish, 1 tin solid Dentifrice, 14 ration pieces of chocolate, 8 pieces Bournville chocolate, 1 piece Nestle's plain, 2 pieces of Fry's plain chocolate.

Arthur Wright, who was always ably supported by his wife Grace, died in May 1953 at the age of 77. He was survived by his son, former Sergeant Pilot J Lyn Wright, and his daughters Molly and Phyllis.

CHAPTER 6

A Decade of High Achievement
The 1950s

With hindsight the achievements of the 1950s were greater than at any other time in the life of the school, before or since. This was probably because it took several years after 1945 for the young men to return to the universities and graduate, or to the schools to teach, and to give time for the numerous extra-curricular activities to be re-born or stimulated anew. In 1952 and again in 1953 seven boys were awarded State Scholarships; between 1951 and 1954 ten boys went up either to Oxford or Cambridge, eight to King's College, London, and thirty-seven to the Welsh University Colleges. In sport the school produced soccer and rugby internationals, even a British Lions' captain, while in athletics there were also significant achievements.

Change of Headmaster

Towards the end of 1949 L Stanley Knight informed the Governors that he intended to retire at the end of the school year. The following January applications were invited for the headship. There would be no forms but applicants should furnish three testimonials. Fifty-five applied for the Headship including Neville Richards (L S P), A G Lloyd (Caerphilly G S), H G Davies (Head, Pontycymmer G S), E E Evans (Thornton G S, Bradford), R A Davies (Friar's School, Bangor) and Dr G Highmore (Principal of Burderop Emergency Training College, Swindon). Six were shortlisted. At the interview, held in May the applicants were given a single question: *'What do you consider to be the responsibilities of the headmaster of a county grammar school and how would you discharge them?'* An interesting voting system was used whereby one person was eliminated in each round. When it came down to the last two candidates Neville Richards BSc. secured 14 of the 16 possible votes. The appointment would take effect from 1st September 1950. Neville Richards, a recent president of the Cardiff Branch of the Mathematics Association, was at the time Senior Mathematics Master and Deputy Head at Pengam.

At the end of summer term Stanley Knight stood at the west door and bade goodbye to every pupil; in his room he spoke to the prefects. One comment from a pupil at the time was *'He sought to make us into Christian gentlemen; he was an example of it.'* My experience of him was that although his appearance and manner was formidable, at times even fierce, underneath he was gentle and fair.

L Stanley Knight - an Appreciation

What follows is the appreciation written by Huw Ballard Thomas, a former pupil, as it appeared in *The Ludovican*, Summer 1950.

The Headmaster

To be Headmaster of a school with the history and tradition of L S P is a most difficult task. The greatness of the school is something quite firmly established before ever he arrives; and his success or failure depends entirely on the degree to which he allows himself to be formed in his office by the spirit of the School; whilst directing and furthering it with his own particular contribution.

When L S Knight came to Pengam, he realised this. His humility taught him that he could not make this school great: it was that already. He could not make himself great at the expense of the School, for he came as its servant. He knew its long history (which he was so particularly well qualified to appreciate) and its fine tradition (for which he had an almost unerring intuition); and so he has found his greatness, unknown to himself, in becoming in turn the prophet of a new tradition and the priest of an old. His has been the vision of a Pengam that might arise under the perplexing changes of new education acts and schemes. His, too, has been the task of bringing home to each generation of boys the fact of their heritage, and of kindling in them a sense of pride and affection towards their old School. This he could only do by forming himself within the discipline of obedience to all that Pengam has meant for 200 years; he has made it into one of the few Public Schools that are not private.

He always set before us the fact that the end of our education was to make us into Christian gentlemen; and if we were not sure what that meant, he was there as a living example of it. Hatred of hypocrisy, delight in the good and the beautiful, joy in living, and confidence in a Faith that permeated the whole of life - these were the things that we found in him and strove to imitate. Those who were privileged to spend time in the Sixth Form were able to know him much more intimately than those who, lower down the School, were still all too conscious of his office and his powers. A member of the Sixth Form was a young gentleman to him, an individual treated with the respect due to him, and expected to show the appropriate responsibilities. The writer speaks from experience when he says that all Pengam boys have become part of a vast family for Stanley Knight; and the secret of his success has been the genuine and often deep personal affection which he felt for each and all of them. It was a disciplined affection. That is why so many were never aware of it; and why, whilst all benefited from it, only those who sought it of their own free will were able to see it for themselves, and to realise the immense bonds which bound (and will still continue to bind) Mr Knight to all those who once formed his responsibility and who now claim his interest.

The qualities which have made him a great Headmaster are those which make him a great man: discipline of thought, conduct and emotion; culture of mind and body; nobility of word and action; obedience to the Spirit of Truth and the constant waiting on the Word of God. If he made the Chapel the centre of the School, it was only because Prayer was the centre of his life; and those who criticised the former were those who never understood the latter. The writer remembers asking him once, why he came to the main building so early in the morning and spent time walking on the terrace. 'To pray where I work,' was the simple answer.

There have been mistakes and failures, disappointments and regrets; but these are part of his essential humanity. Let it be said that he has been a proud man, but proud with the legitimate pride in that which was not of his own making, but which he accepted with the deep humility of his own self. For he has taken pride in the greatness of this School; and now she sends him to his retirement, honoured with her pride in him, and immortalised in the greatness of his contribution to her old tradition, which he has kept for ever new.

Neville Richards, Headmaster

At the beginning of the Autumn Term Neville Richards gave a dinner for L S Knight and the whole staff. In his first public speech he said 'I have not promised to make L S P the best school in Wales, it is that already. I will do all I can to maintain it as such.' Other interesting comments the new Headmaster made soon after he was appointed were:

'One hears of an apparent slackness of standards of courtesy, politeness, honesty and work, and too often all the blame is placed on the school where, after all, the pupil spends far less time than at home.'

'grammar school education is essentially non-vocational.'

'it is all right for a boy to go to a Youth Club once a week but not two or three times. There is not enough control from the home.'

'boys should not watch too much television.'

'Monmouthshire interests will be protected as the set-up changes under the 1944 Education Act.'

Entry

Each annual entry was for 90 boys, roughly 55 from Glamorgan and 35 from Monmouthshire. In 1950 around 280 Monmouthshire boys sat the Entrance examination for the 35 places. Serious doubt was now being expressed about the value of intelligence tests for it was believed that about 10% of grammar school places were mis-allocated.

From time to time pupils left because their parents moved away from the area. Examinations were held in June 1952 to fill a small number of vacancies in the second and fourth years. Boys sitting these examinations had to be at least 12 years 6 months on 31 July 1952 and from one of the three parishes of Gelligaer, Bedwellty and Mynyddislwyn.

School name

The Headteachers at Pengam and Hengoed wanted to change the names of the schools, one reason being that in 1952 an examiner went to the wrong school, due to what was claimed to be an ambiguous address. The Heads and Governors proposed that the names should be changed from Gelligaer County School for Boys and Gelligaer County School for Girls to The Lewis' School Pengam and The Lewis Girls' School, Hengoed. In due time they were to have their way.

Governors

Gelligaer Governors met for the last time in October 1951. Henceforth there would be 18 governors, 8 from Glamorgan, 6 from Monmouthshire, 2 representing the Glamorgan Divisional Executive Committee and 2 co-opted members - one from Glamorgan and one from Monmouthshire. The names of the two schools would now change. The name *Lewis* should be in both names but would the Ministry of Education allow the name of Lewis in the titles of the new schools? From 1st November both schools came under the administration of the Divisional Office of the Glamorgan Education Committee. The first meeting of the new Grammar School Governors took place in December 1951 with Alderman Evan Thomas JP in the Chair. He had been Chair of Glamorgan County Council for seventeen years, was in business as a dairyman, and had recently been awarded the CBE.

T D Evans BA, JP (ex L S P) a Chartered Accountant in Bargoed had been Clerk to the Governors (part-time) for 25 years. He would remain in post for the new governing body. The most important item on the first agenda concerned a new site for Hengoed Girls' School as the proposed site at Penpedairheol had been turned down.

June 1952 saw Glamorgan C C, under provision of the 1944 Education Act, agree to make a grant of £600 a year out of income of the Lewis Endowment to the Governors of the two schools. They were allowed to award this money, as they saw fit, to past pupils to help them to further their education. Over the next few years twenty-five out of sixty applicants, drawn from Monmouthshire and Glamorgan received grants, the maximum amount awarded to any one boy being £80. Each year income tended to exceed payments so by the end of the decade there was £2550 in the Lewis Trust Fund awaiting distribution.

The governing body had clear objectives and worked long and hard to realise them. They wanted the Lewis schools to be the best of their type in Wales expending much effort in the selection of Headteachers and staff, and in improving facilities. Unfortunately there were always severe financial constraints. Their efforts resulted in much work for the Clerk to the Governors. In December 1955 D W Davies BA replaced T D Evans as clerk at the time when there was a serious problem with teachers' pay. The Teachers' Burnham salary scheme with such widespread differentiated scales was claimed to be unworkable and unjust. Teachers wanted and eventually secured a national scale based on academic qualifications and service.

School Buildings

Early in the decade the Headmaster reported that two new classrooms were being constructed within the grounds at Lower School. At the same time there were several problems due to subsidence. Bulges had appeared in the chapel floor and some pews had broken from their moorings.

By mid-decade accommodation problems had become critical. Space was required for the twenty-six staff to carry out their duties but only twenty-three teaching spaces were available. This shortage forced some classes to be taught in the chapel and in the dining hall. The problem would ease a little if the building of the new gym and geography room could go ahead.

In February 1956 Glamorgan County Council gave their consent to the erection of a new science laboratory. The new building would be sited at Upper School. On the ground floor there would be rooms for metalwork and geography, above them two chemistry laboratories. The existing chemistry laboratory would then become the second physics laboratory. Due to financial stringency the erection of a new gymnasium and changing rooms was delayed. Again the Head complained about the appalling provision in the changing rooms and shower baths. *On a Wednesday afternoon 120 boys change in a room measuring 24 feet by 16 feet.* For good measure he added that the boiler was inadequate and tree roots were causing problems with the asphalt on the new tennis courts. At Speech Day that year the Headmaster pleaded for a new Science

Wing. A few months later the building of a new biology laboratory began. It was used for the first time for WJEC Practical in June 1957.

The Head would not give up in his quest for more accommodation. In March 1957 he stressed his priorities and hopes that over the following five years he would see built:
    1958-59 a new gymnasium and accommodation for the Head's clerk.
    1959-60 a chemistry laboratory and a sixth form room.
    1960-61 a physics demonstration room.
    1961-62 rooms for woodwork and metalwork.
    1962-63 rooms for geography and music.

In more general terms he referred to the inadequacy of the dining arrangements (the local authority were experimenting with combined dining areas/classrooms) and pointed out that the school needed a main hall big enough for everybody to assemble together at the same time. The chapel seated about 250, which left about 300 standing in the aisles or around the classroom doors. One possibility, he suggested, was to extend the chapel and erect a gallery.

Glamorgan Education Committee announced in June 1957 that they had approved spending £25,000 at Pengam as part of their school building programme for 1958-59. Plans were now submitted to the Ministry of Education to build, at Upper School, a chemistry laboratory, a physics demonstration room, metalwork and engineering drawing rooms, together with rooms for the sixth form.

At a Governors' meeting Councillor J King commented that he had seen cars in better accommodation than the school library. The school he said *'could have some desks from the girls' school since they were about to move from Hengoed to Ystrad Mynach and everything there would be new'*. Though the move was due in March 1959 it did not take place until the September.

In November 1957 the Ministry of Education approved the new science block. It would be in the major building plan for the next year. By January the plans showed that the new two-storey building would be at Upper School and provide accommodation for metalwork and geography on the ground floor with two chemistry laboratories above. Under the new set-up there would be five science laboratories, twice as many as previously. Until then sixth form boys would use the new chemistry laboratory at the girls' school in Ystrad Mynach. The new block should have opened in May 1959 but it was not ready until the November. The former chemistry room would become a physics laboratory and the small room, once used for biology, an administrative office. There was still a problem with the gym which was the oldest in the county.

Almost every report made by the Headmaster complained about the terrible state of the school fields. In 1954 the school fields were declared unplayable: teams had to play elsewhere. In spite of all the problems staff commitment showed that academic excellence was achieveable with minimal resources.

Numbers on roll
The number of pupils on roll continued to increase gradually from 516 in 1950 to 555 in 1958. For the year 1950-51 there were 17 in VIA2, and 28 in VISc2. The staff allocation was one member of staff for every complete unit of twenty pupils resulting in a staff complement of 26 plus the Headmaster. The result of a survey in February 1953 to determine the number of pupils being taught Welsh yielded the following figures:

	No. of pupils	No. taking Welsh
Glamorganshire	283	156
Monmouthshire	210	88

Site for new school
For years the proposed site for a new girls' school had been Penpedairheol. Turned down in December 1951, the eventual site at Ystrad Mynach was approved by the government in January 1956. The early thoughts had been for a girls' school at Penpedairheol and a college at Ystrad. Tenders were invited for the new school in March 1956 with the hope that the building would be ready for March 1959.

Eisteddfod
The annual school Eisteddfod which was held on or around St David's Day was always a high point of the school year. Boys unmasked their all-round talents often surprising their fellow pupils and teachers. The event was usually conducted either by a local minister (Rev. Rhys Bowen, Rhymney, being a popular choice) or by the Headmaster. The house system stimulated competition but during this period Jones House, composed of all Monmouthshire boys, dominated. They won by just 18 points in 1950 but the margin increased inexorably until it reached 148 in 1956. The other three houses took it in turns to be last. Those who came top in the proceedings tended to be at this acme for more than one year: in 1950 Haydn Jones was the Chaired Bard (awarded for a poem in

Welsh) for the third successive year, Islwyn Roberts of Bedlinog won it in 1951 and 1952, K F Price of Deri in 1953 and 1954, John F Hopkins of Tredegar in 1955 and 1956, while in 1958 and 1959 L C Davies, a science student, was Bard. Alwyn James of Tredegar won the Crown in 1956 and 1957 for writing a poem in English.

Two names stand out towards the end of the decade. In 1957 Head boy, P J S Williams, scored 46 of his house's total of 99 points. This was more than any other pupil in the school and was the fourth eisteddfod for him to do this. The following year Headboy J D F Jones of Blackwood had the distinction of scoring the most points. That year the morning activities were conducted by Rev. Fred Secombe of Machen, Sir Harry's brother. *(For more details of the successes of these two Headboys see Appendix 7)*

The House System
In 1957 the House system was declared 'Not fit for purpose' epitomised by the results of the eisteddfod. That year Jones House won the eisteddfod for the eighth successive year. They also won more than half of other House competitions during the same period. The question was 'How should it be reorganised?' First thoughts were to allocate boys on entry in accordance with the alphabetical list, a thought that was swiftly dismissed; after all loyalty to a locality is important - it would be quite ridiculous for brothers living in the same home to be in different houses. A committee of ten (half from Jones House) was formed to conduct a survey. Every boy was given a form on which he was asked to record his name, home town, position in form in the last three terminal examinations and the way he travelled to school, how many points he had scored in the last two eisteddfodau, whether or not he intended staying in school into the sixth form, and finally would he list the school teams he belonged to.

Analysis of the results revealed that pupils from Monmouthshire were generally of a higher overall standard than those from Glamorganshire. After careful analysis of the forms that were returned together with comments from other sources (including the staff) it was decided that houses should be defined by the following geographical areas:
Lewis: Bargoed, Aberbargoed, Gilfach, Glanynant and Pengam.
Johnston: Tredegar, Rhymney Valley, north of Bargoed, Deri and Fochriw.
James: the rest of Glamorganshire.
Jones: the rest of Monmouthshire.
These redrawn boundaries were an attempt to equalise the abilities of

the four houses so that pupils travelling on the same bus or train belonged to the same house. The new arrangements were very successful. In their first year Johnston won the eisteddfod, James the rugby and Lewis the cross country. Jones House, who had won all three the previous year were runner-up each time.

Speech Day

For his last Speech Day Stanley Knight invited the leading BBC commentator Wynford Vaughan Thomas CBE who had previously travelled around the globe in eight days and will always be remembered for his commentary from a RAF Lancaster bomber over Nazi Berlin during World War 2. He had been a pupil at Swansea Grammar School, LS Knight's former school. Other inspiring guest speakers who followed after Neville Richards became Headmaster included Dr Alan Trevor Jones, Senior Administrative Officer for the Welsh Regional Hospital Board, and the son of former Headmaster Roger W Jones; Gerard Hodge, who died so tragically in a Japanese air disaster, an old boy and brother of Sir Julian Hodge; T J Morgan MA DLitt, Registrar for the University of Wales (said by some to be the best uncapped rugby player in Wales), who emphasised that we need more technologists; Alan Oldfield Davies BBC Controller for Wales and Dr Wyn Griffith OBE, author, lecturer and broadcaster. Dr Wyn was a member of the Welsh Round Britain Quiz team. In his address he passed on these thoughts:
'The test of a good education is that it should give us an intense, insatiable and enduring mental curiosity, an unquenchable and untiring desire to learn more, to open wider the windows of the mind. No education is worthy of the name if it leaves a man satisfied. The world has so much to offer to those who seek, so little to give away to those who have not the curiosity to search.'

Speech Day also provided a platform for the Headmaster to share his thoughts with governors, pupils and parents. Here are a few:
It is amazing how many colds, headaches and stomach upsets there are on Friday afternoons.
Very many boys want to study science but most have no desire to be teachers. This is sad.
We should begin to teach Russian, for Oxford will now accept Russian or German in place of Latin as an entry qualification.

Neville Richards' address to the Headmasters' Association

We are always trying to improve the education of our children, always trying to provide them with the skills that will lead to a satisfying, profitable and fulfilling life. In November 1956, when the change to comprehensive schools was uppermost in many teachers' minds, Pengam's Headmaster, Neville Richards, gave the following address to a branch of the Headmasters' Association.

The Curriculum of the Grammar School

This afternoon the President of the IAHM spoke on the topic 'Are Grammar Schools in danger?' to the Headmasters' Association. If they are and if we whose work is concerned with grammar schools think that they are worth defending then we must give due thought to the curriculum and ask ourselves if it is suited to the needs of the present generation of pupils. Great changes have taken place over the years in what is taught and in the manner of the teaching in our schools and I believe that in general the schools have been alive to the needs of the times and have made the adjustments naturally.

The aim of any school is to give the pupils equipment to live in the society in a very complex world. Not only must he earn his living but he must be able to come to terms with his fellow men and also, this of course is most important, come to terms with himself. The school's task is therefore to provide the facilities by curricular and extra-curricular activities to enable the pupil to develop physically, academically, spiritually, aesthetically and socially. The grammar school, in common with all other schools, attempts to do this. But in our grammar schools we have the nation's ablest children: we have to assume that their intelligence enables them to understand logical processes and to follow a line of argument: they must be able to think in abstract terms. We must also realise that we are concerned with two classes of pupils, those who remain at school until the age of 18 or 19 and go to the universities and professions and those that leave at 16 or 17. Admittedly we should try to increase the number in the first class and diminish those in the second.

The main criticism of the grammar school education has been that it is too academic and that in the VIth form it is too specialised. We all know that practical subjects do feature in the present day curriculum and that crafts, engineering drawing etc., are widely taught. However in the main academic study in science and the humanities is, we consider, educationally sound for our pupils and I believe that we can meet the challenge of our times, which is to provide the scientists and technologists that the age requires and at the same time preserve in our pupils the love of the spiritual and humanistic studies without which life would not be worth living. From our VIth form must come the technologists and the backroom boys in ever-increasing numbers - at the same time the other professions will continue to make their recruitment. Our pupils will still be required for medicine, dentistry, pharmacy, agriculture, the teaching profession, the preaching profession, law, civil service and local government, banking, etc., and let us hope that we shall still produce writers, poets, painters and musicians. A grammar school curriculum must be non-vocational and yet when one considers the wide variety of callings followed by our pupils, it surely must be vocational in its widest sense.

We should have therefore a very comprehensive course for the major portion of the pupil's life at the grammar school followed by a course with some special study in depth. This will be accompanied by general studies which represent a widening of the comprehensive course previously followed.

My attempts to follow this are as follows:
1st Year: English Language, English Literature, mathematics, two other languages (Welsh and French), history, geography, general science, religious instruction, physical education, music, art and woodwork.
2nd Year: still two languages other than English, only in this year the two are chosen from 3 (French, Welsh, Latin). General science is replaced by the full subjects physics, chemistry and biology.
3rd Year: another language, German, is added for a limited number of pupils in place of music or art, so that in this year some pupils are taking 3 languages, some 2 and some only 1. Otherwise the subjects taken are all as in the 2nd year.
4th and 5th Years: A basic course for all consisting of English Language, English literature, mathematics, general history, a language, religious instruction and physical education, to which a pupil adds four subjects chosen from a large group consisting of 3 languages, 3 science subjects, history, geography, music, art, woodwork and technical drawing. There are no direct alternatives. The subjects are offered on the time-table in such a way that the pupil is usually able to make his own choice.
In the VIth form 3 subjects are studied as main subjects by the majority of the pupils together with a course taken from the following: English, German, history of science, appreciation of music, appreciation of art, social science, religious instruction and physical education.

Coronation
The Coronation of Queen Elizabeth II took place at Westminster Abbey, London, on 2 June 1953. As souvenirs pupils were presented with a copy of the Authorised Version of the New Testament. Those belonging to Roman Catholic families received copies of the Douay version of the New Testament.

The Ludovican

The school magazine, *The Ludovican*, which had been published, apart from the war, since 1930, and in 1950 costing 2/- (10p) a term, always contained interesting articles on varying topics. In the Lent 1950 edition the case was made for cricket compared with rugby as enunciated in 1888. The summer magazine in 1953 gave details of the oldest former pupil of Lewis' School still alive: Mrs Elizabeth Parfitt (née Thomas). She entered school in 1859 when Rev. D Mosley, a very quiet man, was Headmaster. The Rev. Alfred Pullen followed him. The character of the school, she said, changed with the 1870 Education Act. She left in 1872, trained to become a teacher and began teaching at Hollybush, near Blackwood. In 1879 a new Girls' School was opened in Pontllanfraith and she became the Headmistress. She strongly denounced the government of the day for incorporating the school endowments into the Glamorgan County Scheme. She believed that this meant the Governors were losing control of their school. (This was finally implemented in 1896.)

A few of the many amusing contributions to the school magazine are included below.

A committee is composed of the unfit, chosen by the unwilling, to do the unnecessary.

A committee is composed of people who individually can do nothing, and who collectively decide that nothing can be done.

If Moses had been a committee, the Israelites would never have moved out of Egypt.

Teacher to father: Your son spells atrociously.
Father: Splendid! I couldn't spell it myself.

A synonym is a word you can use when you don't know how to spell the one you first thought of.

Quotation by a pupil who found difficulty in reading Gordon Jones's comments in his exercise book *'I can tell Killer's 'i's from his 'r's now'.*

Debating Society

'SLADS is the senior, the most ambitious, and the most exclusive of all the various school societies; it is also the most successful and most famous.' So claims the Summer *Ludovican* in 1958. During the year, as in other years during the decade, outside speakers, often old boys, drew the largest gatherings, sometimes more than a hundred. After Friday school and

after tea, meetings were held either in the Art Room or in the chapel, depending on numbers. Apart from discourses the meetings included a Musical Evening, a Brains' Trust, Members' Papers and Sharp Practice. The latter was always entertaining. Pupils drew, in turn, a piece of paper from a hat. This was either blank or gave a topic. Should you draw a topic you were expected to speak about it for not more than five minutes. So successful was SLADS that a junior version was suggested to train younger boys and hence improve the senior society.

The society obviously generated a great esprit de corps, for trips were arranged to Plymouth in 1951 and to Oxford in 1953. The girls' school at Hengoed sometimes joined the boys for an Inter-school debate or the two schools combined to debate with another school such as Quakers Yard. On one occasion the motion before them was *The best system of education is coeducational*. In October 1959 a school election was organised by Bill John over several days. Pupils stood as candidates for the various political parties. The result, which was hardly surprising for the area, was: D J Jones (Labour) 276, Huw Thomas (Conservative) 111, Des Hughes (Welsh Nationalist) 105, Barrie Wilcox (Liberal) 32, John Miles (Communist) 17, Ian Puzey (Independent) 14.

Dramatics
Performances by the Pengam and Hengoed Dramatic Society became annual events. In 1951 it was G B Shaw's *Dark Lady of the Sonnets*, a short play performed by the sixth formers from the two schools. *She Stoops To Conquer* was chosen for 1952 with performances at Ystrad Mynach during the day for Forms 3 to 6 and public performances on the Wednesday and Thursday evenings of the week. All the reports were very good.

Other plays performed in the decade were Jane Austin's *Pride and Prejudice*, Charlotte Bront's *Jane Eyre*, Shakespeare's *Twelfth Night* and *The Admirable Crichton* by J M Barrie. This was produced by Mrs Haynes, Miss Young and Mr Griffiths. Three performances were staged at the Workman's Hall, Ystrad Mynach. Many claimed it was the best performance to date. For the production of Shaw's *Arms and the Man* at Ystrad Mynach Church Hall, 350 pupils went by train from Pengam for an afternoon performance.

Other societies
The Film Society, formed in 1950, thrived. By showing several films each term in school and having discussions about them its aim was to promote the cinema. Other societies were formed to further interest in Jazz, the

Scouts (during 1957-58 there were fifteen regular members) and Christianity but none of them kindled any appreciable enthusiasm. The Urdd continued its lunchtime meetings which took the form of members' papers, quizzes, and singing, including a Noson Lawen with girls from the sister school at Hengoed. In 1954 John Hopkins represented Monmouthshire at the St David's Day Festival of the London Welsh Society at the Albert Hall. Later, others went to a camp at Llangranog, some sold books on Wales while others collected funds for the Welsh League of Youth.

Almost every member of staff was involved with one society or another. Mr H W Jones, supported by Gordon Jones, formed a branch of Christian Union, but the new society did not attract large numbers. The union met every Tuesday at lunchtime and once a month after school to listen to outside speakers. Their subjects included *Communism and Christianity* and *Science and Religion*.

Commemoration Day in Bi-centenary Year
The most important Commemoration Day of the decade was 1953 when one thousand pupils from both the Lewis' schools travelled by special train to attend a service at St Martin's Church, Caerphilly, (not Llandaff Cathedral as had originally been planned because the cathedral was still undergoing repairs) to celebrate the bi-centenary of the decision to establish a school near St Catwg's church at Gelligaer. The service was conducted by Canon J O Williams, Rector of Caerphilly and presided over by the Lord Archbishop of Wales, the Most Reverend Dr John Morgan. This was the only church in the Rhymney Valley large enough for the occasion.

Other Commemoration Day speakers during the decade included Prof D W T Jenkins MA, Vice-Principal of University College Bangor, Rev. J Ithel Jones MA, BD, Canon T M Hughes MA, vicar of St John's, Cardiff, whose memorable advice was *'Tradition in itself is not enough; it needs to be enriched continuously'* and the Venerable J G James, Archdeacon of Llandaff, whose message to the assembled congregation was *'It is better for a thinking boy to have no religion at all than to be a half-hearted Christian.'* At all of these services the tradition was that the Head Boy and Deputy Head Boy read the lessons.

Trips
One hundred years after the Great Exhibition of 1851 the Festival of Britain was held in London to sell the country to the world. Early in the

Autumn Term ten staff took more than 200 boys to the London South Bank. Two highpoints and lasting memories of the day were viewing the Skylon and visiting the Dome of Discovery. A general observation was that the exhibition divided into two categories: what Britain is and what Britain does. It was a long but satisfying day.

Visits were made to the New Theatre, Cardiff, to attend performances by Welsh National Opera: Six staff and fifty boys went to see *Nabucco* while other large parties attended performances of *Die Fledermaus* and *Il Trovatore*. A visit to a cinema is always popular. In 1950 the whole school saw *Hamlet* at the Hanbury cinema, Bargoed, while another group saw *Treasure Island* there. Forms 4, 5 & 6 went further afield. They visited the Queen's cinema, Cardiff, to see *Martin Luther*.

Fifteen sixth form boys went to the Temple of Peace, Cardiff, in October 1955 to listen to Madame Pandit, the London High Commissioner for India. This was to celebrate the tenth Anniversary of the founding of the United Nations. Madame Pandit was the first woman president of the UN Assembly. A few years later a sixth form group attended a two-day conference at Cardiff High School for Girls; two of the subjects were *Feeding the World* and *Pakistan*. In 1959 eight boys and ten girls from the Lewis' schools attended a conference organised by the Welsh Association for Education in World Citizenship. They listened to lectures on *Economic aid to under-developed countries*, *Britain and the United Nations*, *Disarmament*, *Colonialism*, and *Public Opinion*.

Pupils always enjoy playing matches against other schools but combining the occasion with an over-night stay is an even more exciting prospect. Interchanges were established with Friar's School, Bangor, another long-standing grammar school. In 1953 a party of forty-two pupils and two staff visited them. The schools engaged in tennis, cricket and athletics matches, the whole thing being repeated five years later.

Other trips worthy of mention are: a sixth form visit to the National Museum in Cardiff, a visit to the Caerphilly Local History Exhibition at Caerphilly G S, a sixth-form visit to Penylan observatory, Cardiff (made more interesting by the fact that it was Rag Week in the city), a three-day trip for four staff and forty boys to London, and a tour around Ebbw Vale steel works by a group of sixth formers. Would this trip have encouraged them to seek employment there or work harder to get as far away as possible?

Stratford Trips

In May 1952 four masters, W H John, W J Jones, W J Morris and P C Evans, took 60 boys to Stratford to see *The Tempest*. It was a most enjoyable spring day with boat trips on the river but a problem evolved out of nothing as a result of a stop at Monmouth on the way home. Seeking liquid refreshment, and unable to be served in one public house, a group of sixth formers (all over age but wearing school blazers) walked to another where they were served. The clock ticked too quickly and they were late returning to the coach. Back in school rumour spread that these same boys were *under the influence of drink*. This news reached the Headmaster. What should he do? He gathered them together to investigate, the outcome of which was the order *Give me your prefect's badge; now get off the premises and don't return until you bring a parent.* The boys temporarily excluded included the Head boy, Deputy Headboys and several prefects. On the Monday each boy returned with a parent and all was quickly forgiven. One parent, a Baptist minister, is reported to have commented to the Headmaster: *Mr Richards, you administered punishment while you were in a temper. You should never administer punishment when you are in a temper.* Neville Richards could be excused for his reaction. He was relatively new at the helm and felt that he had high standards to follow. With hindsight his reaction was perhaps understandable. The event was not mentioned by the Head again, excellent references and testimonials being given for the boys involved.

Perhaps it was because of this event that trips to Stratford did not recommence until 1956 when 89 boys accompanied by 10 staff (what a pupil/teacher ratio) went to see *The Merchant of Venice*. The following year the Headmaster and 7 staff took 99 boys to to see *As You Like It*.

Duffryn House

For more than a decade sixth form boys, a few at a time, were able to join a residential course at Duffryn House near Cardiff. The visits were extremely popular. Study groups discussed art, music and drama, and listened to lectures on modern poetry, archaeology, history, music and radioactivity. Boys who went to Duffryn always enjoyed the experience - after all there were girls there: it was so different from school. At the first meal only the most forward of young men would sit at a table where young ladies had already taken their seats. Returning to school, when the group photograph of the sixty or more boys and girls on the course was shown around, it was not uncommon for the owner of the photograph to be asked 'Which one?' How many, who were later to marry, met while on a course at Duffryn? What follows is the report written by sixth form student R Meadows as it appeared in *The Ludovican* in the summer of 1956. It sums up so well the thoughts of many who attended over the years.

Dyffryn House

It is easy to be facetious about Dyffryn House, the subject of multitudinous jokes and tall stories about the exploits (amorous and otherwise) of its old inmates.

Its not my intention, however, to write in such a vein. In their more serious moments, all who have been to Dyffryn will admit that the courses provided are extremely beneficial and do much to create an interest in culture and education. Many of the courses, such as those dealing with French or Welsh or History, are highly specialised and have proved to be invaluable as aids to Advanced studies. The General Course (the most popular!) is important, not so much as an intensive course of instruction, as in furthering an understanding of society and culture.

This year, as in other years, the Glamorgan Education Committee has provided several courses which have been attended by boys of this School. The French Courses, two in number, have become a virtual monopoly of 'some few vipers' in Second Year Six but it must be admitted that now they have no fear of the Oral Examination, normally the bane of all language students. The Welsh course, unfortunately, was held at the same time as our terminals. so, naturally, no boy from Pengam attended. The General Courses (one in November and another in February) are great favourites and it is with great delight that one greets the news that one has been picked (probably out of a hat!) for this course. The History Course was also popular since it provided an opportunity for certain members of Third Year Six to receive personal tuition from Mr W H John who brought great honour on the School by being chosen as one of the Lecturers for this course. At the time of writing, no other courses (which we can legally attend!) have been held, although rumour has it that the authorities have had compassion on the First Year French class and have laid on a French Course for them in the summer, since they were cruelly deceived by 6a(ii) who will stop at nothing to enter once more the 'academic' atmosphere of Dyffryn!

Although it is difficult to speak seriously about the Courses which have been held so far this year, it is not difficult to write or speak seriously about the purpose and obvious benefit of these courses. Although there are many lectures, much time is allowed for the boy or girl to get to know those who are also attending the Course. Needless to say, many new friendships which will, perhaps, prove life-long, are made. It is this prevalent and instantaneous spirit of friendship which is one of the most important factors of a Dyffryn Educational Course. The necessity of providing your own entertainment brings out much latent talent and also serves to illustrate the fact that T.V. and radio are not necessities of life. Thus, working together to entertain others in a spirit of friendliness, gives everyone who has the good fortune to be chosen to go to Dyffryn a sense of responsibility and importance which does much to make the burden of work appear much less than it actually is. A spirit of renewed enthusiasm is the most important thing that the student brings back with him from this wonderful and, so I understand, unique establishment.

On behalf of all who have been to Dyffryn, I can do no better, in thanking the Glamorganshire Education Committee for this invaluable Educational Centre, than to repeat those famous words of Gladstone when leaving Windsor after a Dinner Party. With great sincerity and humbleness he said two words - 'Thank you.'

Trips Abroad

Germany and Austria proved to be the popular countries for school visits, influenced no doubt by a strong German department and an enthusiastic teacher who had been an intelligence officer in Germany after the war. In the summer of 1952 M I Morgan accompanied by the Headmaster took a party to Königswinter on the Rhine, a town that another school party visited a few years later. It was an excellent centre with good communications for visits to the National Parliament at Bonn and the city of Cologne with its beautiful cathedral. Although seven years after the end of the war, a half-an-hour walk from a Rhine steamer into Koblenz did not find a single inhabitable building standing. The Headmaster must have enjoyed the experience, for two years later he accompanied another party to Niederlandstein near Koblenz. Up to this time the cost of insurance for medical treatment abroad had been the responsibility of the county, but henceforth a directive from County Hall made the school responsible.

A coach load travelled to Spain via Paris in 1957. The visit left two vivid memories - the revulsion of viewing a bull-fight, and the antics of a reckless coach-driver. A 10-day trip was made to Austria (Innsbruck) and Holland in 1958 and an 8-day trip to Cologne the following Easter. The only visits to France were to Bertincourt in 1950 and to Paris at Easter in 1957.

School Inspection

On the whole the school received satisfactory inspection reports. If there was any general criticism it was the total inadequacy of the buildings and the fact that there were too few staff for the amount of work undertaken.

Music

The new Bechstein Grand piano which Dr Thomas so much yearned for was delivered on 13 December 1950. It was placed, adjacent to the organ, on the stage in the chapel. It could hardly be kept in the timber framed building covered by corrugated sheeting known as the music room which had been erected as temporary accommodation in 1902.

For Dr Thomas (as a composer he was known as David Wynne: his Christian names) these were exhilarating times. In September his violin concerto was performed at the Festival Hall in London. Given by the The London Philharmonic Orchestra the soloist was Ian Sevidka. Better known perhaps was his piano sonata which had received six London performances as well as performances at Cologne, Aachen and Paris. However, Dr Thomas's visit to the National Eisteddfod grounds in August 1956 was a visit he would probably not wish to remember. He was asked to leave because he wanted to speak in English about his new Symphony No. 2. Speaking in English flouted the all-Welsh rule which had been introduced in 1950. He was 55, one of the top Welsh composers of the day, and had been commissioned to write a symphony for the Guild for the Promotion of Welsh Music. It was to be played in the Eisteddfod Pavilion and Dr Thomas was to speak about it in the overflow pavilion on the Eisteddfod field. However, he went off-site to a chapel half-a-mile away to speak, in English, to those who wanted to hear about it before it was played by the London Symphony Orchestra, a performance that cost £700. Dr Thomas was a Welsh speaker but felt that he could only do justice to his composition in English.

The following year Dr Thomas was commissioned to compose a work for the National Youth Orchestra. When it was played the orchestra included five boys currently at the school and two former pupils. Such was local appreciation of his numerous successes that Maesycwmmer Choral Society presented him with a clock and an illuminated address.

The success of a teacher in a particular field often stimulates pupils into that area of learning. In 1957 Mansel Bebb was intending to go to Aberystwyth to read agricultural science. He had already studied the school subjects he needed to do this but changed his mind and went instead to the Royal College of Music. Mansel, even though he had had no private tuition, played his violin in the school orchestra and became leader of the National Youth Orchestra. He acknowledged the vast amount of help he had received from former pupil, German teacher and instrumentalist, M I Morgan, and from Dr Thomas. Being a member of the National Youth Orchestra of Wales, which had been founded by Irwyn Walters HMI in 1946, enabled him to go to Holland for a ten-day tour, performing with the orchestra in Amsterdam and Rotterdam. Other instrumental scholarships were awarded to Neil Cadogan and to Paul Griffiths. These successes in music were even more remarkable as there was no suitable teaching space for Mr Brinley Lewis, the part-time wind and brass teacher or other peripatetic music teachers. They had to use the dining room.

Annual Carol Concerts began in the late 1950s. They took the traditional form: the nine lessons, interspersed with contributions from various school choirs and soloists. For the last concert of the decade four soloists contributed including Neil Kinnock, a future European Commissioner.

Lunchtime
Pupils bought their dinner tickets for the week on a Monday morning but, for varying reasons, did not always use all their tickets. This caused problems and there were times when much food was wasted. To try to reduce this, from May 1951 pupils had to pay for the first untaken meal each week. To enable a reader to compare the cost of a school meal then with the cost today it increased from 7d (c.3p) in 1951 to 9d (c.4p) in 1953, a consequence of which was that 113 fewer meals were served per day with a further knock-on effect that a member of the kitchen staff was made redundant. A staff lunch cost 1/4 (c.6p).

Crossing the Main Road
The most important decision concerning the school grounds at this time was how to provide a safe way of crossing the busy main road. In June 1957 the Governors decided to suggest to Glamorgan Education Committee that a bridge or subway be built between Upper and Lower School. The Ministry of Transport had raised the speed limit on the road so it was decided to carry out a survey of the number of vehicles travelling along the road where the crossing would be sited. On the first day between 8.45 a.m. and 4 p.m. 2163 passed. The next day it was 2003. A traffic census a year later recorded 250 vehicles an hour so there was obviously a need.

The Headmaster, Neville Richards, wanted a subway, but the council opted for a bridge. Its construction was included in the minor building programme for 1959-60 and by November the building of the bridge was proceeding at an estimated cost of £5000.

Examinations

For the summer examinations in the years up to 1950 subjects were placed in the following groups: I scripture knowledge, literature, Welsh, history, geography, II Foreign languages III mathematics and science subjects, IV all other subjects. In all subjects each pupil's work was graded Pass, Credit or Very Good.

In 1951 new examinations at three levels were introduced under the over-all title of General Certificate of Education (GCE). 'O' level would replace the former School Leaving Certificate, 'A' level Higher School Certificate, and a new Scholarship or 'S' level was introduced. To sit 'O' level papers examinees must be at least 16 in the September of the year in which they sat. Teachers deplored the new age-conditions for external examinations: for it meant that some boys could have been in the school five years and still not qualify to sit. In previous years hundreds of pupils had passed their School Certificate examinations at the age of fourteen. What were they supposed to do with this extra time? Some opted to begin their 'A' level work before they sat 'O' level, but this was hardly a satisfactory position. After a re-think and after much pressure the age restriction was removed. Another radical change was that instead of being graded Pass, Credit or Very good, there would be a single grade: Pass. The brighter stars in the firmanent would in future be more difficult to detect. The scholarship papers were used to award State Scholarships which continued to be offered every summer until they were abolished in 1963.

Other changes soon followed. In 1953 Additional Ordinary level exams were introduced which pupils could sit after one year in the sixth form, and two years later an Autumn 'O' level was introduced for Summer failures to resit, rather than have to wait until the next summer. The pass mark at 'O' level was set at 50%. For 'A' level the grades would be A to F. 'A' was equivalent to a VG or distinction; D a bare pass.

For the new 1953 General Certificate of Education examinations the school entered 116 candidates. At 'A' level 32 secured 1, 2 or 3 'A' levels. At the next Speech Day the Guest speaker was all for the new 'O' levels but Neville Richards was quite cool on the matter. He claimed that it was holding good students back. Belonging to the golden period 25 students passed A levels in 1953, seven being awarded State Scholarships including Howard Prothero (Trinity College, Cambridge) and Michael J Bird (King's College, London), both of whom had two distinctions.

In 1954 the school was once again proud of its results. At 'A' level 32 had passed generating two State Scholarships. By comparison the numbers passing at 'A' level in other local schools were: Bedwellty 3, Caerphilly 21, Nantyglo 14, Pontllanfraith 11, Rhymney 12, Tredegar 21, Hengoed 15 and Ebbw Vale 32. In 1955 forty-six sat 'A' level yielding three State Scholarships. One hundred and thirty sat GCE in 1954 of whom 128 passed in 1 or more subjects, while 146 sat in 1955 of whom 134 were successful in 1 or more subjects.

Library

Most boys in every secondary school are more interested in sport than in reading. In an attempt to get greater readership a new library rule was introduced in 1951. *Every boy whether he reads it or not, must take out a book every Friday. He is responsible for the book and must return it the following Friday; failure to do so will result in a fine of two-pence per week.*

One-off Events

Head boy Colin Vaughan Williams was chosen in July 1950 to represent Wales in New York for an International Friendship tour of six weeks organised by Youth Incorporated, Nashville, Tennessee. In New York he was put up at the Waldorf Astoria, and given a camera, clothes and spending money. In the following September he spoke to Cardiff Rotary Club about his trip. The USA, he said, are ready for war with Russia. He was pessimistic with regards to the future, thought that a degree in the southern states was equivalent to Higher School Certificate here, saw many slums and thought that race relations in the country were poor. *'Electricity is so cheap that they let street lamps burn throughout the day. It is cheaper than employing a man to turn them off.'* The tour, which took in nine states, covered about 10,000 miles. At the White House Colin met President Truman where he was the group spokesman. He broadcast twelve times on three stations in Tennessee and on Voice of America, a programme beamed to Europe.

Early in 1951 Colin flew to Oslo to support the nomination of Allen Dobson, of Nashville, Tennessee, for a Nobel Peace Prize. Mr Dobson was President of the body that had sponsored the international friendship tour (there were 21 in the party) that Colin had been on the previous summer.

An important event for the combined Lewis' schools took place in October 1954. With John Ellison and Robert MacDermot in charge, the Lewis' team of P J S Williams and Gareth Williams from Pengam, and

D R Davies and J Prosser from Hengoed, competed in BBC's *Top of the Form* against Cardiff High School for Girls. They lost by a single point: 40-39. The recording took place in early October and the programme went out on 25 October.

For the first time in 200 years the father of a pupil at LSP was summoned to appear at Bargoed Magistrates' Court on 1 April 1955 because his son was not attending school. The boy, aged 14, had attended *'no times'* out of a possible 103 occasions. The father did not appear to answer the summons; he was fined £1.

Much effort was put into training cyclists in 1957. There were many Safe Cycling successes. Pupils from Lewis' School won the individual and area team awards at Junior and Senior levels. School teams also took second place in the team competitions. Many boys received Road Safety certificates.

The bravery of Kenneth Humphries helped to save an 8-year-old and a 12-year-old boy trapped on the edge of a quarry pond 25 feet deep in the summer of 1957. He stripped off, swam across and held both by their legs until they were hauled to safety using ropes and ladders.

When World Youth League Day came around messages were read in school in English, Welsh, French and German.

Unforeseen events and illness
Peter Gillingham of Blackwood was knocked down in October 1950 while crossing the road between the two schools. He was the very first pupil to be involved in such an accident. Though taken home by ambulance as a precautionary measure Peter was able to return to school almost immediately. Of a more serious nature fifth form pupil Gwyn Thomas was killed in an accident in a quarry in May 1951. The Headmaster accompanied by fifty boys attended his funeral.

Occasionally a most unusual death occurs. In July 1952 the body of 16-year-old Brian Morgan of Gilfach Street was found in the pool at Bargoed Swimming Baths. Brian went bathing on a full stomach and died of shock due to a condition known as *status lymphaticus*. The attendant, Miss Doris Rogers noticed that a basket of clothes had not been claimed when the baths closed. On checking the pool she found the body in ten feet of water. No one had realised he was missing. The medical report stated that there was a large amount of undigested food in his stomach. Brian did not drown; he had a lesser hold on life than the average child and was always likely to die suddenly. It could have happened anywhere. He was the eldest of four; his mother had died the previous February. The funeral took place at Gwaelod y Brithdir cemetery. The Head boy and two Deputy Head boys were three of the bearers; the other three belonged to the local YMCA club where Brian had been an enthusiastic member.

In December 1956 the funeral of 17-year-old Brian Lucas took place at St Catwg's Church, Gelligaer, Rector John Ivor Jones officiating. Brian had died from stomach wounds sustained when a friend's single barrel 410 shotgun went off by accident in the friend's home. Brian died within 10 minutes. The gun had been bought two days earlier. Neville Richards, the Headmaster, together with several staff and sixty-two pupils attended the funeral service.

Senior mathematics master D T Davies died, in 1955, while a patient in St James's Hospital, Tredegar. He had been admitted suffering from bronchitis. Affectionately known as Dai Apple he was appointed in September 1948 to the school where he had earlier been a pupil. D T had been in school up to the previous Thursday. Always associated with his Austin 7 car in which he used to travel between Upper and Lower School, he had won a six-year scholarship to the school in 1921. D T won scholarships from Monmouthshire and Glamorgan Education Committees, a Reserve State Scholarship and the Caldwell Cup for the best boy in his year. He got a First in Pure Mathematics at University College, Aberystwyth, in 1930 (once again he was the best student in his year) and shortly afterwards won a travelling scholarship to Germany but was taken ill and could not go. D T Davies was awarded an MSc., interested in sport, a competent pianist and read widely, but he was not averse to the occasional sarcastic remark. When Paul Shreder announced that he had been accepted by an Oxford college D T's comment was '*I suppose they want big men to row the boats in Oxford Paul.*' An oak bookcase given in his memory was presented to the school by his parents. His widow gifted all his mathematics books to the school.

The passing of a member of staff while in post is comparatively rare but it occurred again in April 1959 when W J Cecil Morgan MA collapsed and died. Cecil was Senior English teacher, aged 54, and had been at Pengam for more than 20 years. He was an excellent Upper School teacher who loved to read the part of leading Shakespearean characters when studying a set book - a good example being Shylock in *The Merchant of Venice*.

142

Sad news also reached school about Old Boys. On a Saturday in February 1956 nineteen-year-old Cpl Desmond Thomas Jones (RAF) was shot dead by a terrorist in Nicosia. His parents were expected to pay £300 to bring his body home. In January 1954 another Old Boy, David John Goldstein, a junior official at Britannia Colliery, died in a motorcycle accident near the Barn Hill.

Overheard in the Corridor

All girls who go out with me should pass an intelligence test.

I only know her vaguely, I went out with her for eighteen months.

I wasn't looking at her as a girl, but as a beautiful building.

Then she asked me if I'd like to try on her sweater.

I often feel sorry for people with only one living room.

You know the headmaster doesn't like seeing boys running around the grounds naked.

Foreign Assistants

Monsieur Jacques Detain, the French Assistant, gave a talk at Bargoed Literary and Debating Society entitled 'Some aspects of France, Britain and Spain.' A later French Assistant, Mlle Simone Picot, commented that 'every Sunday, the friendly homely Welsh put on their best clothes and go to chapel whereas the French play football'.

Interesting Extras

As a new development, Report Books were introduced for First Year pupils in the summer of 1955.

When W E Park retired in 1955 the keeping of the school log-book passed to W H John. At the last assembly of the year ties were presented to the top boys in Forms 1, 2 and 3.

For the year 1951-52 the sports fees were 2/6 (12¹/₂ p) a term; by 1958-59 they had doubled.

A full school roll-photograph was taken in November 1952.

Due to severe weather, attendance in the two weeks 29.11.52 to 10.12.52 fell to 50%.

A request to close the school on Bedwellty Show Day, the first Monday in September, was turned down in 1952.

Parents of three pupils who applied for the release of their sons before they had completed the agreed five years were ordered to pay £10 each to secure their release.

The programme for Parents' Concerts held in March each year, and chaired by the Head Boy, comprised the best items from that year's school eisteddfod.

In 1956 the school bell, in use every school day, was more than 100 years old.

Urdd camps at Llangrannog and Bala were still popular.

The Crowther Report (1959) reaffirmed raising the school leaving age to 16.

Miss Doreen Green became Headmistress of Hengoed Girls' School on 1 September 1959 on the retirement of Miss Ethel Moore. This change was in preparation for the move to the new school at Ystrad Mynach on 7 September.

Non-teaching staff
Mr William Thomas Hester, the caretaker, retired in 1956 after 22 years service. From a shortlist of three William M Dwyer was appointed caretaker in February 1958.

Towards the end of the decade a canteen cook was paid £9.11s.8.d (£9.58) a week and a part-time maid £4.10s.3s. (£4.51) for 20 hours.

Staff
Several new staff were appointed to start in the Autumn term 1950:
Miss R Kathleen Thomas BSc, biology (so at last Mrs Simmonds, who was still temporary, had a female colleague), Bryn Jones BSc. (PE, games and economics), S I Jones BA (Welsh), P C Evans ATD (art), B I Evans BSc (chemistry) and J Gordon Jones BSc (mathematics - coming from Newbridge G S with a nickname of 'Killer' he had no discipline problems). The following January the mathematics department was strengthened still further by the arrival of Harold Jepson BSc but he was to move to Southampton five years later.

Every pupil up to School-leaving Certificate level studied mathematics. This required a large number of well-trained staff. H W Jones MA (Cantab) joined the department in 1954 and Thomas J Edwards BSc. in 1955. Other appointments during the second half of the decade were M J B Cook BA, Junior English, history and games; Gerald Bowditch BA, French; Raymond Hurley BSc., senior chemistry; Geoffrey Dolby BSc., mathematics and David B Davies BSc., physics (the latter two were the only applicants); Keith Marshall Horner BA, English; Ian Lloyd Davies PE and L E G Paul, metalwork. In November 1959 Myfyr Islwyn Morgan (known to the boys as MI), who had been on the staff from 1949 to 1958 before he left for Canada, was offered a history post which he declined.

In 1950 David Morris BSc, mathematics and Thomas A James MA retired after 29 years and 26 years respectively. In 1955 W E Park BA, geography, retired after 35 years: he had been a pupil in 1905. J M Williams BA, French, who had been Senior master, retired in July 1959 after forty years service. He had

David Morris BSc   Thos James BA

been president of Rhymney Valley and Bargoed Literary and Debating Society, a society he had helped to form 14 years previously which met at The Settlement, Bargoed. The following year Clifford Murray Harris retired after 40 years and two terms. No one had served the school longer. In 1959, H D Jones MA who retired as Senior Master in 1948 was given an Honorary degree for his work on a Welsh dictionary. The oldest living ex-master in 1954 was H B Pittway MA who was 83.

Sport
Two athletes stood out in the early 1950s: John Frowen and Brian Hardwick. In the 1950 Glamorgan Secondary School Championships John Frowen, aged 18, won the long jump with a distance of 23 ft 11 in and the hop, step and jump (or triple jump), with 46ft 1½in. Both were Championship records. He also played for Wales in a Boys' Club Soccer International and went on to play for Cardiff City. Brian Hardwick was primarily a high jumper. He gained his sixth championship at Bangor when he won the Welsh Secondary Schools AAA High Jump rising to 5ft 3in. In

June 1952 he showed his versatility by being Victor Ludorum in the school sports and coming first in the Long Jump at Port Talbot in the match between Glamorgan and the North West Midlands with a leap of 20 ft 9¹/₂ inches. Brian was one of eight Welsh boys to be selected to go on a special athletics course at Motspur Park, London.

The Annual School Sports produced intense competition between the houses. Around twenty-seven events were staged in three categories: Junior under 13, Middle 13-15, Senior over 15, the winning House each year (usually Jones!) being awarded the Caldwell Cup. The Victor Ludorum was the boy scoring the most points in the Senior section. Winners included Basil Ashford, D Paske, E Gummer and V Paget (joint), Richard Davies and John Dawes (joint).

The programme for the school sports in 1959 listed the existing school records. Up to that date the oldest was O C Beckett: 10.0 seconds for the 100 yards in 1923. John Watkins held the pole vault with 8ft 6 in using the old bamboo pole, a record which was raised to 11ft after the introduction of fibreglass poles some years later. The end of the decade saw John Clive Jones become a member of the Welsh Team at the Empire Games.

We cannot leave athletics without reference to cross-country running which became so popular around this time. It was introduced in 1952 and was described by one teacher, who shall remain nameless, as *fine exercise for undergrown, underdone little boys who found playing rugby a little too tough,* but progressed into a super team sport with matches against other schools. A year after its introduction the school team beat Howardian High School (twice), Newport H S, Barry G S and Bargoed G S losing only to Pontypridd G S. In 1956 the school team won both the Junior and Senior events in the Glamorgan Secondary Schools' Championship at Mountain Ash. The star runner was Don Edwards, the captain. In the 1959-60 season the school team raced fifteen times losing just twice. In the Glamorgan Championships they were second to Cardiff High School by a single point. Captain David Morgan was the best runner the school had produced to date, becoming Indoor Champion for the second time. In various competitions representing the school he ran seven times, breaking the course record on five occasions.

Rugby continued to be the most popular sporting activity. During the 1953-54 season J Byron Jones played for the Welsh Secondary Schools against Yorkshire at St Helens, against England at Leicester and France at

146

Cardiff, while W G Derek Morgan played against France and against Yorkshire in the December. Byron, who could play at centre or prop forward, was captain in the Welsh Secondary Schools match against South Africa. Derek Morgan would go on to play for England at Senior level and become President of the Rugby Football Union 2002-03. Other boys who secured schoolboy international honours were J P O'Shea and C J Padfield in 1957-58, and Dennis Hughes and John Prince in 1959.

First team rugby was exceptionally strong. At the end of the '54-'55 season the record read: played 18, lost none, points for 295, against 29. At one period they were undefeated at home for five seasons. A successful First XV depends heavily on younger boys being enthused and trained by members of staff. Apart from the First XV the school ran four other sides: Seconds, Colts, Under 14s and Insects. Soccer was never encouraged. Even so, Teifion Harris, aged 16, played for Wales YMCA against Ireland at Swansea in 1950. By the school-year 1957-58 the school had two fields, one each side of the main road. The question some asked was *Shall we re-introduce soccer?* The immediate answer appeared to have been *No*. Rugby would remain king. For House competitions the winner of the rugby competition received the Rocyn Jones Memorial Shield which had been given by the Old Boys in memory of the great man. The annual match against the Old Boys did not always produce a win for the school.

Summer sports were never particularly successful. For cricket there was no facility at school but the Headmaster was able to arrange for home matches to be played at Trelyn. Up to the end of the 1951 season the best stand by two school cricketers was by Alan Moore and Gethin Evans. For the second wicket in a match against the staff they scored 74 out of a total of 108 for 4. In reply the staff scored 19 for 8 wickets to draw the match; they were saved by the clock.

Similar difficulties existed in trying to run a tennis team. Apart from a lack of facilities the weather was often a problem. In the mid '50s Peter James was the best player. Of the 14 matches arranged for 1959 half were lost because of the weather. Of the 7 played victory was secured in four. Again the Headmaster helped by arranging for home matches to be played at Gilfach. 1954 was the most successful season. The team won all seven matches.

Table tennis, for sixth form pupils only, was introduced in 1959-60 after the purchase of one table. Ever mindful of expanding the options and the wisdom of every boy being able to swim, Bargoed Baths from 1952 on, was reserved for the school from 11.45 to 12.45 on Mondays and Wednesdays.

John Sidney Dawes

Without question the most important sportsman to have been produced by the school is John Dawes. Neville Richards described him as *the complete allrounder with a pleasing personality*. A Monmouthshire boy, who rose to become captain of the First XV for the 1958-59 season, John went up to University College, Aberystwyth, where he graduated with a degree in chemistry, before proceeding to Loughborough College for further studies. He played rugby for Newbridge and London Welsh and won his first international cap in 1964. In total he played for his country on twenty-two occasions, six as captain, including the all-conquering Grand Slam side of 1971. Success followed success. John was captain of the only British Lions' team to win a series in New Zealand and captain of the Barbarians side that beat the All Blacks in that memorable game at Cardiff in 1973. He never lost as a player or coach to an England side. During the period 1974-79 John Dawes was coach to the national side winning the Five Nations Championship four times in five seasons including two Grand Slams. Pengam has produced many fine international rugby players but John Dawes stands head and shoulders above them all.

Old Boys

The First Annual Dinner of a revived Old Boys' Association was held at the Royal Hotel, Cardiff, in September 1950. Sir Rocyn Jones, who had been a pupil at the school for three years from 1886, was the speaker. Two years later (1952) the Association bought £120 of War Loan 3¹/2% to provide the R W Jones Memorial Prize. Sir David died shortly after this, at the age of 80, and in July 1953 the Old Boys Association presented a shield to the school to be awarded annually to the house that won the Rugby House Competition.

Paul George Smith Shreder was a pupil at Pengam going up to Jesus College, Oxford, in 1951 to read mathematics. Paul was familiar with six languages including Russian and Chinese. Paul's father, Peter, was the electrical engineer at Bargoed Power Station. An Honorary Graduate and Gold Medal winner at St Petersburg University he was responsible for installing much of the original plant at Bargoed colliery. A talented artist, Paul found that at Oxford he was able to draw portraits of the great and the good, resulting in an exhibition at St Giles, Oxford which received more than a thousand visitors. His portraits included the Duchess of Marlborough, The Maharajah of Dhrangadhra, The House of Commons Speaker, Mr Herbert Morrison, The Archbishop of Wales, Prince Obolensky and Lord Pakenham. Following an Oxford degree he completed a further degree course in Civil Engineering at University College, Cardiff. In January 1957 Paul was a member of the South Wales team for *What do You Know* on BBC Light Programme. For a while the author understands that Paul was attached to Eton College to tutor boys in the solving of *The Times* crossword.

Ugo Neil Phillips (of Tredegar) became President of athletics at Sheffield University in 1954. A fifth year medical student, he was reserve wicket keeper for British Universities v South Australia. Neil was associated with Middlesborough Football Club and Alf Ramsey, the England Manager, was so impressed with him as a medic that he asked him to become team doctor to the England squad. Neil accepted, was team doctor for the 1966 World Cup and remained with them until Ramsey was replaced in 1974.

Dr Thomas Jones CH, one of our most famous former pupils died in October 1955. He had been adviser to four prime ministers: Bonar Law, Earl Lloyd George, Ramsey McDonald and Earl Baldwin. At the time he had written more cabinet speeches than any other civil servant and in 1951 his biography of Lloyd George had been published. Starting work at 13 for 9/- (45p) a week, he was a timekeeper in the local steelworks, but left the Rhymney Valley to enter University College, Aberystwyth and then Glasgow university. He was the first secretary of the Welsh National Health Insurance Commission and member of the Unemployment Assistance board 1934-40 becoming a Companion of Honour in 1929. Dr Jones founded Coleg Harlech in 1927. He was Secretary of the Pilgrim Trust, 1930-45, which used American-based funds to improve social and educational services in Britain, and was awarded the Gold Medal of the Honourable Society of Cymmrodorian.

Victor Erle Nash-Williams, a pupil at L S P 1909-15 died in December 1955 following a hernia operation. He had been Head Boy in 1914 but his studies were interrupted by WWI when he served in the Infantry Regiment. He returned in 1918 and was Sir Mortimer Wheeler's first student in archaeology at

An Old Boys' Society blazer badge from the 1950s.

University College, Cardiff. He gained a First in Latin and an MA in archaeology and was appointed Keeper at the National Museum of Wales.

Lewis Boddington was awarded the CBE in 1956. He did work on angled flight decks for aircraft carriers and was the leading authority in naval aeronautics, eventually becoming Director General of Aircraft Research and Development for the RAF.

Scholarships

During the 1950s an abundance of State Scholarships were awarded to Lewis' boys; twenty between 1951 and 1954, seven in the summers of 1952 and 1954, another five in 1957. Science subjects provided the most popular 'A' levels; dominated by pure maths, applied maths and physics for which the school had an enviable name.

Many of the state scholars secured even higher honours before leaving school: Alwyn James an Exhibition in History at Gonville and Caius, Cambridge, Philip J S Williams an Open Scholarship in Science to the same college; J T W Morgan an Exhibition in Science to Pembroke College, Cambridge; Robert Laurence Thomas a Sambrooke Science Scholarship to King's College, London. Other awards were: Aeron G Evans, a Glamorgan County Scholarship to University College Aberystwyth; J Cleaton, a Royal Scholarship in Engineering at Imperial College, London; David James Matthews, a Cooper Open Scholarship in Physics to Nottingham University and John I Howells, The Evan Morgan scholarship at University College, Aberystwyth. In the field of music Glamorgan Music Scholarships went to Brian L Crowley and D N Cadogan.

To give an example of the number of examinees involved; in 1958 forty-eight pupils secured one or more 'A' Levels, eighty-six one or more 'O' levels, and three pupils State Scholarships.

Bilateral schools

J Stanley Jones, Principal of New Tredegar Technical School and a former old boy complained bitterly in January 1956 about the structure of secondary education. There were he said *too many grammar schools and not enough technical schools. There are too many teachers, preachers and black-coated workers and not enough skilled technicians and technologists. In the Rhymney Valley there are seven grammar schools and two technical schools. This proportion should be reversed. There is no secondary school for* technical/commercial subjects for girls. The Welsh Council of Education is to establish bilateral schools - this is no solution. Some grammar schools should convert to independent technical schools. He was not listened to by those in power. The grammar schools at Pontllanfraith and Caerphilly became grammar-technical schools.

Bargoed Rotary

J D F Jones and Mary Thompson (Head Boy/Girl) were invited to speak to members of Bargoed Rotary Club in May 1958. Their speeches dealt with the country's need for scientists and technologists. J D F, an Arts student, thought that, in general, students studying arts subjects were more interested in general matters than science students whose aim was usually to solve specific problems. Scientists he declared have little sympathy with religion or politics. One most pertinent point the two speakers made was that few sixth formers anticipated returning to the area after completing their university/professional training - there just weren't the career opportunities. Studying any prefects' photograph brings home the truth of this statement.

First Rugby XV 1933-34.
Back row: D H J Jones, I D Thomas, W L Sweet.
Second row: L Stanley Knight (Headmaster), A R Lewis, L Meredith,
J W Davies, H Thomas, E Richards, R M Williams, R Pearce, J W Perrett
(Gamesmaster).
Front row: A P Thomas, H G Williams, P Jones, B Davies (Captain),
A D Evans (Vice-captain), G T Roberts, R J Richards.

The First XI in 1934.
Standing: L Stanley Knight MA (Headmaster), S J Gouldstone, G Roberts,
A P Thomas, I Foulkes, T Hughes, T G Thomas, J W Perrett
(Gamesmaster).
Seated: E B Walters, J R E Saunders, E Richards, P Jones (Captain), R Pearce
(Vice-captain), J W Davies, H E Bailey.

152

A young David Morgan soon after he was first employed in 1888.

David Morgan when he was about to retire in 1934 after 46 years service to the school.

A cartoon by Sixth form student Daniel Cusack from the *Ludovican* in 1933 with the title *The Lion's Share Again*. It illustrates how Lewis' School was devouring Meyricke scholarships, given each year to the top students in Wales. The school had been awarded three of these scholarships in the previous five years.

Another cartoon *A Midsummer Night's Dream* by the same artist impressing on the students that playing cricket in the summer will not lead to success in the Central Welsh Board examinations in the summer.

School Prefects (seated) and Sub-Prefects (standing) 1934-35.
Standing: F Evans, J H Brown, D S Pember, J Browning, J Jacobs, K R Lambert, S J Goulestone, I R Matthews, A Evans.
Seated: B P G Harris, A A Edwards, G Williams, J E Saunders, L S Knight MA (Headmaster), H Jones, G T Roberts, R Pearce.

E M Lewis setting a Long Jump record of 20ft 1½ins in the School Sports, 1938.

Lower school in the early 1930s. The former upstairs dormitory has been turned into a classroom.

The school floodlit for the Coronation of King George VI in 1937.

The school in the summer of 1939 just as World War II was about to begin. Many former pupils would lose their lives in this conflict. One important difference is the window in the south wall of the classroom on the left. Subsidence, due to coalmining, necessitating the re-building of this room.

In 1941 an Airforce Cadet Squadron was formed in school with the Headmaster, L S Knight, commanding officer and Neville Richards adjutant. Local businessman Alfred Withers was President.

Prefects (seated) and Sub-Prefects (standing) 1941-42.
Standing: T G Evans (Prefect), L Tucker, A L Davies, A Luke, D J Bowen,
D D Davies, G M Jones, M Williams, F J Davies, T L Rees, J D Phillips
(Prefect).
Seated: T D Harris, D E Jones, J H R Edwards, D B Jones (Head Prefect),
L S Knight MA (Headmaster), J S Turner (Deputy Head Prefect), E R Tudge,
B C Lougham, K G Williams.

The view of the school from the main yard in 1949. The cycle shed is
adjacent to the woodwork room. On the ground floor, from the right, are
the Physics, Biology and Chemistry laboratories. The two rooms above the
Chemistry laboratory are teaching rooms.

Roll of Honour.

1939——1945.

NI DDYCHWEL DOE.

ANDREWARTHA, S.	-	RHYMNEY
BAILEY, H. E.	-	YSTRAD MYNACH
BENNETT, R. G.	-	BLACKWOOD
BERRIMAN, C. D.	-	BARGOED
BOX, W.H.	-	YNYSDDU
CONNOLLY, T.	-	BLACKWOOD
CREW, K. B.	-	CEFN FFOREST
DASH, R. J.	-	CWMSYFIOG
DAVID, B.	-	FLEUR-DE-LIS
DAVIES, C.	-	BARGOED
DAVIES, H. D.	-	RHYMNEY
EVANS, D. K.	-	BLACKWOOD
EVANS, G. H.	-	YSTRAD MYNACH
EVANS, R. W.	-	PENGAM
EVANS, W. V. A.	-	YNYSDDU
FINCH, A. J.	-	PONTLOTTYN
FRANCIS, E. N. J.	-	NEW TREDEGAR
GABE, T. A.	-	BARGOED
GABRIEL, P. Z.	-	HENGOED
GARRETT, T.	-	BLACKWOOD
GAUNTLETT, G.	-	ABERBARGOED
GOODMAN, P. D.	-	NELSON
HAMMERSLEY, F. A.	-	PENGAM
HARRIS, B. P. G.	-	BARGOED
HARRIS, G. F. J.	-	BARGOED
HARTMANN, J.	-	HENGOED
HILLS, L. P.	-	PENGAM
HOWELLS, A.	-	RHYMNEY
ILLINGWORTH, W.	-	GILFACH
JAMES, T. S.	-	YSTRAD MYNACH
JENKINS, J.	-	BRITHDIR
JONES, B.	-	RHYMNEY
JONES, H.	-	YNYSDDU
JONES, H H.	-	RHYMNEY
JONES, K. I.	-	CWMFELINFACH
JONES, J. M.	-	GILFACH
LEWIS, D. G.	-	RHYMNEY
LEWIS, A. R.	-	BLACKWOOD
LEWIS, I.	-	YSTRAD MYNACH
LITTLEWOOD, H. G.	-	YSTRAD MYNACH
MEEK, R. T.	-	ABERBARGOED
MERRICK, W. J.	-	RHYMNEY
MORGAN, E. H.	-	BARGOED
MORGAN, I. T.	-	OAKDALE
MORGAN, R.	-	BARGOED
MORRIS, A.	-	PONTLOTTYN
MOSELEY, C.	-	RHYMNEY
OWEN, I. T.	-	RHYMNEY
PITT, W. J.	-	TRELEWIS
POWELL, A. E. E.	-	BARGOED
PRICE, C. E.	-	RHYMNEY
PROSSER, G. G.	-	ARGOED
REES, K. V.	-	BARGOED
ROBERTS, E.	-	FLEUR-DE-LIS
ROBERTS, W. G.	-	TRELEWIS
SAUNDERS, W. O. E.	-	PONTLOTTYN
SCUDAMORE, J.	-	FLEUR-DE-LIS
THOMAS, J. I.	-	TRELEWIS
THOMAS, W. G.	-	BLACKWOOD
TUDGE, E. R.	-	YSTRAD MYNACH
WILLIAMS, E.	-	YNYSDDU
WILLIAMS, G. J.	-	YNYSDDU
WILLIAMS, J. G.	-	GELLIGAER
WILLIAMS, K. R.	-	TIRPHIL
WILLIAMS, N. E.	-	CEFN FFOREST
WRIDE, I. C.	-	GILFACH

"WE WILL REMEMBER THEM."

The School Roll of Honour for the Second World War.

A W Hancock JP, Chairman of Governors, congratulates Neville Richards BSc after his appointment as Headmaster in 1950 as successor to L Stanley Knight MA.

Pupils on the front steps after receiving their certificates in 1950.

The staff who taught the successful candidates pictured on page 160.
Back row: V J Davies, W J C Morgan MA, W J Morris BA, W J Griffiths BA, B Haynes BSc., T B Price BSc., L Alden BSc..
Middle row: L C E George BA, W Hughes BSc., D T Davies MSc., E L Jones BA, E Edwards MA, T D Jones BA, M L Simmonds BSc., J Gosset, L-es-L, W Jenkins.
Front row: D W Thomas Mus Doc, P J Davies BSc., W E Park BA, N Richards BSc., L S Knight MA (Headmaster), J Williams BA, C M Harris BA, D Morris BSc., T A James BA.

The Prefects 1951-52.
Standing: B J Davies, B J Stephens, A E Jones, S D Probert, J T Griffiths, J H I Lloyd, P D Jenkins, G N H Evans, A L Jones.
Seated: D M Jones, A G Veysey, H G Morgan (D Head Prefect), E P Brooks (Head Prefect), Mr N Richards BSc (Headmaster), E B Smith (D Head Prefect), C P Lewis, T Lewis.

The school chapel with its pews c. 1950. There is now a pipe organ, lectern, pulpit (in memory of those old boys who lost their lives in WWII).

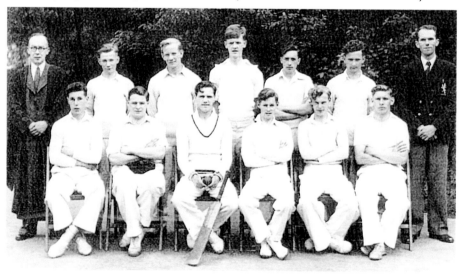

Cricket XI 1951.
Standing: The Headmaster, David Brooks, Rowland Yemm, Jeffrey Eschle, Gordon Walbeof, Peter Brooks, Peter Evans ATD.
Seated: Gethin Evans, John Phillips, John Golding, Rowland Exall, Alan Moore, Norman West.

Islwyn Roberts winner of the Chair at the School Eisteddfod 1952. Also in the photograph J M Williams BA (Senior Master), Alun L Jones (winner of the Crown), W G Jones BA, S I Jones BA, Neville Richards BSc. (Headmaster).

A year of exceptional results - 1952. Seven pupils were awarded State Scholarships. From the left: Peter Jenkins, Gethin Morgan, Bryan Stephens, David Jones, Douglas Probert, Geoffrey Veysey, Vivian Lewis. This degree of success was repeated two years later.

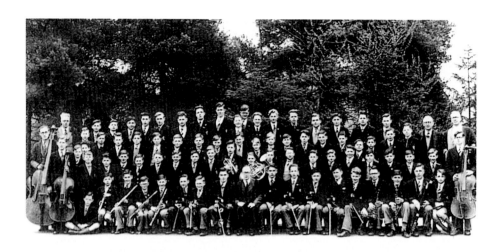

The School Choir and Orchestra 1952.
Staff: Left W G Jones, Dr Thomas, and on the right Gordon Jones, M I Morgan.

Schoolboy rugby internationals Derek Morgan and Byron Jones (Headboy) in 1954 with the Headmaster Neville Richards and Gamesmaster Bryn Jones. Derek went on to play for England at Senior Level.

The School Orchestra with Neville Richards BSc. (Headmaster) and the staff responsible for organising it c. 1954. On the left of the Headmaster: B Lewis, to the right M I Morgan MA and D W Thomas Mus.Doc.

The School Orchestra 1955. Staff: on left B Lewis, M I Morgan. On right: Gordon Jones, Dr Thomas.

The Headmaster Mr Neville Richards, with the Cross-Country team 1956-57.

The Cross-Country Team 1959-60.

CHAPTER 7

Uncertain Times
The 1960s

Transition at the Top

The 1960s were not good times for stable leadership at the school. Neville Richards' health was beginning to fail but he fought manfully on - as anyone who knew him would have expected. On 10 July 1963 he received a letter that must have made him feel a very satisfied man. It was written by the parent of Eric Alfred Bonner Cole who had been awarded a First in mathematics at Cambridge. His father expressed *deep and lasting appreciation of all that you and the Lewis' School have done for him. I am hoping that his performance at Cambridge will add something to the lustrous reputation of the Old School.* On the thirteenth of the following month the Head was taken seriously ill and rushed into hospital where he underwent an operation the next day.

When term began in September 1963 Deputy Headmaster Leslie G Alden BSc. stood in for the Head whose condition had not improved as had been hoped. Eventually the Head returned to continue at the helm but on 23 March 1965 was taken seriously ill again in school and rushed to Caerphilly Hospital. Leslie Alden stood in once more, being Acting Headmaster until the following May, when Neville Richards returned. He had made a good recovery but as the year progressed it was manifest that he would not be able work as he would have liked. Accordingly he resigned at the Governor's meeting on 17 November 1965. The year before his resignation he had become a Justice of the Peace and on St David's Day 1966 he was presented with a collection of records as gratitude for all he had done for the school. Leslie Alden remained in charge until Fred Evans took up post in May 1966 but following his election to parliament in July 1968 the Headship became vacant again. By this time Leslie Alden had retired so Len George acted as Head while Fred Evans was away electioneering. In June it was the turn of Len George to have a spell in hospital, during which time W J Griffiths (Buck) took over. Len George returned to school for the Autumn term 1968, and W J Griffiths acted as Head until Glyn Rees arrived in April 1969.

Following Neville Richards' retirement, former Headboy Hugh Griffiths (1960-61) was asked to write an appreciation of his contribution to the school. The result was a moving article which was printed in the Summer copy of the school magazine in 1966. It expresses sentiments endorsed by so many that it seems appropriate to reproduce it here.

IN GRATEFUL APPRECIATION

Nothing could have pleased me more than to have been asked to write this tribute to Mr Richards as Headmaster of the Lewis' School.

I offer no excuse that my inevitable feelings of personal involvement make it an emotional contribution; for I am certain that all Ludovicans who knew him as Head, shared that sudden sadness which the news of his ill-health and retirement brought.

There is always in all of us a little of the disbelief that our intimately - remembered pasts can alter beyond recognition. And it is difficult indeed to imagine Pengam without Mr Richards.

The loud, gruff voice along the corridor, the abrupt manner and the severe countenance in morning assembly which first frightened a small boy in short trousers, became a human being only by stages. But the sixth former was in a position to appreciate three striking qualities in his headmaster:- the passionate interest in the job and in individual people; the ever-energetic attention to detail; and an overwhelming sense of integrity.

All these qualities were directed and dedicated to the School's well-being. It was apparent in all that Mr Richards did and said, that he was proud of the School, and his sense of pride inevitably transferred itself to us, so that the studious attitudes and high standard of behaviour he demanded, were made that much easier and more natural for all.

There was little of the double standard that often makes school life so artificial. The Head expected the values taught to be carried beyond four o'clock and the School grounds, and to a large extent they were. Woe betide the pupil whose behaviour reflected badly upon the school.

Pengam, of course, has behind it a long and honourable academic tradition. But it is a headmaster who makes a school what it is, and Mr Richards was in so very many ways the good headmaster. His was no nine to four o'clock day. He was in his office well before the early morning bell, and long after the noisy corridors had emptied. More often than not his green Wolseley was also to be found outside the front porch on a Saturday.

He took the greatest delight in academic achievements, but his interest in pupils did not stop there. Whether it was in the back seat of the Chapel at SLADS on a Friday evening, or on the First XV touchline on Saturday morning, he was a frequent spectator of sporting and social events.

For such a busy man his attention to small details of administration was amazing; and whenever responsibility was delegated to others, he always kept himself informed of what was happening. Many's the time as Head Boy I ruefully experienced that reproach for something forgotten, something not done.

His memory for people - pupils and the generations beyond - was extremely retentive. Often the like of this conversation: 'Jones 1b takes after his father .... not like his brother in 4a .... the father used to write poetry for the magazine .... quite good' (and over to the bookshelf he would go to check relevant issues of The Ludovican). How hard for members of form one or two to have recognised in that mighty authoritarian figure such interest and concern in their personal welfare.

Visit Mr Richards tomorrow, and ask him in which desk you sat as a member of 1c, Room 11 in 1953. He is as likely to tell you the names and places of the majority of your classmates - many you have long since forgotten. And if a name does stick on the tongue notice that familiar snort of impatience. He is as demanding of himself as he always is and was of other people.

Mr Richards' headship saw the external face of Pengam alter almost beyond recognition. The Lower School gained two classrooms and a new gymnasium; bulldozers gouged out a new playing field; the old hard court was resurfaced and fenced for tennis; Biology, Chemistry and Physics were extended and rehoused; new and elegant surrounds were built to keep the savoury smell of school dinners from starving students till the bell rang; and a swimming pool, where the toil and sweat of classrooms would wash away was sunk in the old gym.

Many of these badly-needed improvements were due to the persistence with which the Head pressed the relevant authorities, and, in the case of the swimming pool, the initiative which he took to find means of raising money. One needs to list the changes to realise the extent of the achievement.

In much the same way Mr Richards greatly extended the curriculum. He was a genius at the vital timetable compilations which made this possible. The various A Level combinations offered to the sixth former were enormous, and, given the necessary staff ability, I am certain that Esperanto, Zoology and Metalwork would have presented little difficulty to arrange.

It was obvious during the last few years that Mr Richards' health was not very good - even though it had little effect on the amount of work he undertook, or the vigour with which he pursued it. Last Easter, by a strange quirk of fate, we found ourselves sharing the same hospital ward whilst he was recovering from a major operation. The circumstances were enough to dampen the enthusiasm of any normal person. Yet what struck one above everything was the mental vitality and impatient desire to be up and about life. It was a salutary experience for me to realise that life as he meant it, was almost wholly dedicated to his work at school.

Unfortunately, for some time now it has clearly been a case of 'overwork' rather than 'work'. His illness and premature retirement must largely be attributed to this selfless devotion to the School's welfare; and Pengam and its pupils must recognise the heavy debt of gratitude they owe him.

If anyone has deserved a quiet and enjoyable retirement it is he; and we sincerely hope that under more favourable conditions his good health will return. Yet at the same time it is difficult to think of such a man inactive; and true to nature, as Justice of the Peace, his service to the community continues.

He has always been aware of the School itself as part of this greater community. The careers and achievements of ex-pupils have been followed with avid interest. Letters, newspapers, personal meetings and second-hand accounts have all kept him constantly in touch with the School's contribution to society. If you are to visit him, you will be assured of a friendly welcome, and will likely learn what happened to many of your contemporaries.

As final comment, it is a rare privilege to encounter the kind of admiration in which Mr Richards is held. (No false eulogy this.) Head-masters are traditionally subject to irreverent treatment. But, in my experience the verdict for him is unanimous. Whenever the Old Boys gather, the subject always drifts at some stage to the past and to Pengam and at Pengam for us there is always 'Nev', who through all the wilful exaggerations and reminiscences retains nothing but our respect and affection.

There could be no greater tribute than this.

HUGH GRIFFITHS. (Headboy 1960-61)

Neville Richards did not enjoy a long and active retirement. He, who had given his life to the school, died on 9 August 1968 at the age of 64. The funeral service was held at Holy Trinity Church, Ystrad Mynach. After cremation his ashes were interred near the west door of the church. A small plaque, half covered with turf, reads

Neville Richards BSc., JP,
9.8.68.

It does not even record the fact that he was Headmaster of Lewis' School. This seems a totally inadequate memorial to a man who had given so much to so many though, as a modest man, it may have been what he had wished.

Careers

In the period immediately after WW2 there was no careers advice: in fact there was virtually no advice of any kind; you found out what you could where you could and were at a great advantage if your parents were fully tuned in. By the 1960s there was a vibrant careers service, Denzil Cole the Careers Officer for Bedwellty, even coming to Pengam because there were still Monmouthshire boys at the school. His visit was additional to the service offered in the Rhymney Valley by the Youth Employment officer.

Carol Service

The annual carol service, now organised by the Old Boys' Association, continued during the new decade. In the summer of 1961 David Wynne (Thomas) retired to become a full-time composer. Dr Thomas who had been in charge of music since 1929 was replaced by John F Williams BMus., ARCO who remained at the school until the summer of 1966. John, one of his former pupils, inaugurated several changes at the first opportunity. For his first concert two new carols were introduced: *O Come O Come Emmanuel* and *I Saw a Maiden*, together with his own arrangement of *Adam lay Abounden*. The following year there were carols in Welsh which had been translated from the English by S I Jones BA the Welsh teacher, and the next year more new carols: *Lullay my liking, Blessed be that maid Mary* and Joubert's *Torches, Torches*. Again the total inadequacy of the chapel was made evident for the choir was conducted by John Williams standing on a desk while scores of boys listened to the proceedings from the adjacent rooms. What would Health and Safety make of that?

Clubs and societies

In an attempt to improve the quality of photographs in *The Ludovican* the Headmaster held a competition. He was able to select what he wanted from about fifty photographs, but a more important consequence was the setting up of a photographic society which flourished for several years. One of the first speakers was David Blatchford a well-known local photographer. Another club that blossomed for a short while was a Chess Club under the watchful eye of new teacher D H Elias BSc. Success was slow coming; most of the matches played during the first three years of the club's life being lost.

Enthusiastic sixth form boys set up a Table Tennis Club for themselves in 1960, and an Archaelogical Society was formed in 1962-63 with L Hargest BA in the chair. They visited Cardiff museum, studied aerial photographs, and listened to talks on the Greek colony at Cyrene, N Africa, and about recent discoveries in E Africa. During 1963-64 film strips, slides and photographs were shown on prehistoric and Roman Wales. Another club that was re-formed the same year as the archeological society was the Stamp Club. In the time of Arthur Wright the Philatelic and Numismatic Society thrived so it was good to see that an attempt was made to get it going again. It met fortnightly and during its second year held an exhibition of rare and unusual stamps organised by the Stamp Collecting Promotion Council. Unfortunately the initial enthusiasm was not maintained but it did re-start again in 1969 after a two-year gap. The Angling Club which practised its art at Penallta, Roath Park, Butetown and Llangorse had about thirty members.

An attempt was made in the autumn term 1962 to re-start the Jazz Club which had operated briefly back in 1957-58. The 1962-63 attempt was no more successful. Twelve meetings were arranged during the Christmas term; the number attending declining from about 50 to 6. For a few years at the beginning of the 1960s a Modern Languages Society flourished under the guidance of two members of staff: W A Thomas and T D Jones. Often during the lunch-hour but occasionally after school, German or French films were shown or the group listened to talks, often given by one of the foreign students. One highlight was a talk in German on *Education in Germany*.

W G Jones BA of Lewis' School became secretary of the area committee of the Rhymney Valley and Monmouthshire Urdd (Youth) Eisteddfod. Following in the steps of others, several groups went to the Urdd camp at Llangranog; others to the Senior camp at Glan Llyn.

Crossing Road
The building of the bridge across the main road continued. L E G Paul, the metalwork teacher kindly agreed to the challenge of designing and making a school badge which was on completion attached to the bridge. This advertised the school to all those who passed beneath it. The badge was fixed to the bridge during the 1960 Summer vacation.

The move towards Comprehensive education
The reports in 1966-67 by Plowden and Gittins endorsed comprehensive schools. In future entry examinations into secondary schools would be abolished; primary school assessments would be used instead to give an idea of the abilities of new entrants. In this new scheme after pupils had moved from primary to secondary the first two years should be transitional; all pupils should have a common curriculum for at least six months. In May 1967 the final plan for the area was announced: *we shall all move to Ystrad Mynach and become a mixed school.*

Headmaster A T Evans reported that under the Glamorgan Education Committee plan the boys' school would be on a single site at Ystrad Mynach. This was not greeted with joy by the local residents for it could mean up to two thousand pupils plus the students from Ystrad Mynach college invading their small village every school day. They could see many problems ahead.

Shortly afterwards the structure for comprehensive education in the area was revealed as:

1. A two-tier comprehensive school for boys with the first two years at Graddfa School, Ystrad Mynach with 210 in each of years 1 and 2 (i.e. 420 in total there) and years 3, 4 and 5, with 210 in each year (i.e. 630 in total) plus a sixth form, at Lewis Boys'. This gave a combined total of 1050 + VIth form for the new school.

2. A comprehensive school for girls with 210 in each of the first two years at Ystrad Mynach girls' secondary school i.e. 420 in total, and 630 at Lewis Girls' giving a total of 1050, plus a sixth form. The intention was that all pupils would eventually be taught in a single girls' school on one site.

How the school had changed since its foundation. Under the Will of Edward Lewis it was a charity school for 15 poor boys; then, in 1849, an elementary school for 150 boys and 100 girls; next, in 1875, a privately owned endowment grammar school, evolving into a county intermediate school in 1889, and then a grammar school with a highly selective intake in 1905. It had become one of the best grammar schools in Wales. Now it was proposed to cater for one-third of all the pupils in the urban district of Gelligaer. It was to lose its Monmouthshire boys who had done so much to raise its standards.

Another organisational problem was the Raising of the School-leaving Age (ROSLA), due for implementation in 1970. In preparation for the change to comprehensive education in March 1969 a conference on school reorganisation was held when many of the foreseeable problems were addressed; few staff looked forward to the change with eager anticipation.

During the 1960s great changes were in the air for education. 'Education for all' was the cry of Labour politicians. By this they meant that all children in a local area should attend the same school. In the valleys of south Wales all the local councils were Labour controlled so it was quite natural that all our local state secondary schools would become comprehensives. Nearby Tredegar was the first to change, in 1965. Many were the arguments from both sides. In Pengam two opposite viewpoints were presented by two sixth form students in *The Ludovican* published in the summer of 1966.

For Comprehensive Education

The principles of comprehensive education have long been argued, both publicly and privately. To suggest that a large section of our younger generation is either extremely forward or extremely backward is beyond ridicule. What is certain is that those who are forward, given a reasonable amount of tuition, will advance at more or less the same rate, by dint of their innate aptitudes. The backward form a social problem which must be considered apart from the general question of secondary education. There remains, therefore, the mass, who fall under the title of 'average'.

Since the 1944 Education Act, even the most uneducated parent had come to realise that 'book-learning' is at least a way of acquiring a satisfactory income. When the outgoing Conservative government decided therefore, to raise the school leaving age to 16 in 1970, they as surely declared that 'O' levels (or some equivalent), will then form a social norm while a fair percentage of our children will somehow become capable of 'A' levels. How then, when there is an obvious shortage of both schools and teachers, can we satisfy these educational requirements?

The government, because of the economic problems it has to face, will obviously not be able to increase educational expenditure greatly. We will, more or less, have to make do with our present schools. Also, we cannot snap our fingers and have a few thousand new teachers. How can we solve our problems then? Will re-organisation of the secondary moderns alone do? The immediate question arising from this is, have they the resources for mass 'O' level work? And then 'A' level work? The answer is simply and unquestionably, no.

We must, therefore, take and remould the whole system of secondary education. It is obvious that our schools must become more efficient, but, for the economic reasons mentioned above, we are unlikely to have larger school units - the obvious answer for increased efficiency. We must next consider, therefore, the old idea of specialisation, Should graduate teachers, capable of 'A' level teaching, be overtaxed with 'O' level work? Surely many of the secondary modern teachers, who nowadays quite often work with no educational aim, are quite capable of 'O' level instruction? We cannot afford, in a society dependent on material progress, to neglect these potentialities.

The idea of specialisation on 'A' level work immediately leads us to the idea of 'sixth-form colleges.' However, to imagine grammar or comprehensive schools without their sixth-form work is as implausible as to imagine universities without their post-graduate work. What is certain is that with our present resources a break is necessary. We have a choice between a two-tier or a three-tier system, but if I may for once be subjective, I fear that the three-tier system will be too disruptive to the course of education. We have thus to decide when should this break be? The majority of education authorities, as well as the Education Minister, seem to favour 13.

The question which now arises is, should all children then transfer to the senior school, or should each individual have a choice? Unfortunately, a combination of parental pressure and headmasterly advice would tend to make this latter a form of wasteful selection. In Leicestershire, however, they only expected 40% to transfer to the senior school (at 14), whereas actually 80% decided on the transfer. The county authority, therefore, now intends to introduce automatic transfer in its whole area by 1970.

Finally, it must be remembered that comprehensive education is not a revolutionary idea. It has existed in some areas, such as Anglesey and the Isle of Man, since the 1944 Education Act. Other areas, such as Westmoreland, have had a mixture of the grammar-secondary and comprehensive systems since the Act. Bristol's educational system was over 70% comprehensive before the Conservative Party decided that a little emotion stirring would create some useful political capital- yet now the more progressive Bow Group of the Conservative Party has come out in support of comprehensive education.

In conclusion, all over the country the 'Eleven-Plus' has proved to be much more a test of social background than educational ability, and its wastages must be swept away. Neither I, nor any serious advocate of the comprehensive system, would suggest that it could replace our present system without one snag. The problems which it does raise I have set out and attempted to answer in this discussion. What is certain is that if the system is put into effect, it will have glorious benefits for our dynamically changing society, and also for everyone involved in the process of education, whether they be educationalists, teachers, students or parents.

Glyn D.G Davies

Against Comprehensive Education

Do we need reform of our educational system? This is an important question at a time when the future of the grammar schools is in the balance. At the present time children are streamed at the age of eleven into three types of schools: grammar schools, which give an academic training, technical schools which give a practical training and secondary modern schools which give a training which suits their pupils for a working life.

It is proposed to do away with these three separate types of school and to combine them into a system of comprehensive schools. The pupils of these schools will be streamed, also at the age of eleven, into an academic stream, a practical stream and a general stream. What is the difference? Practically none. Yet it is being carried out, at a cost of half a million pounds a time, in a time when this country is in the most perilous financial position in which it has ever been.

What are the advantages of comprehensive schools? Supporters of the system say they are many but on closer inspection it is seen that they are few indeed. It has been claimed, for instance, that in a comprehensive school it is easier for a child to move from one stream to another. That this theoretical ideal is not possible has been shown by the 'class war' in an Islington comprehensive school where the different streams do not speak to one another and anyone from the lower streams who works in an attempt to gain admission to a higher stream is ostracised by his or her class mates.

Compare this state of affairs with that between a modern secondary and a grammar school. A pupil in a secondary modem school is able to find his own level of academic study without the shadow of his more brilliant counterparts hanging over him. If a mistake has been made in the selection at 11 (and such mistakes occur as often in comprehensive schools as in grammar schools) then he has a much better opportunity of transferring to a grammar school at 13 than he would in reaching the 'A' stream from the 'D' stream in a comprehensive school.

On the other hand, though, the comprehensive school, on the whole, caters more for the average pupil than for the brilliant one. Intelligent pupils cannot be expected to work as well in a school where less than half the pupils care about the education they are receiving. In a grammar school, competition, especially in the 'A' streams, encourages the more intelligent pupils with a corresponding rise in the standard of academic work.

Another advantage claimed by supporters of the comprehensive system is the abolition of the class distinction between those who go to a grammar school and those who go to a modern school. This is totally untrue. Class distinction of one sort and another exists throughout the animal world and wherever there are people there are class distinctions. The intelligent pupils tend to regard the 'D' and 'E' stream pupils as riff-raff and the less intelligent pupils feel out of their depth among the brighter ones.

A very big disadvantage of comprehensive schools is their large size. Instead of schools of 500-600 pupils there is one school of 1,500-2,000 pupils. This is an unmanageable size for a school. The personal aspect is removed from teaching and each pupil becomes a name and a number instead of an individual. The headmaster only comes into personal contact with 25% of his pupils and of these nearly 15% are wrong doers. The classes become too large and it is a well known psychological fact that large classes tend to smother individual thought and creative thinking.

While the comprehensive school has a few advantages 'pseudo comprehension' as practiced by some education authorities has none. These authorities are determined to follow official party policy, irrespective of whether comprehension is good for the area or not, and so, since they are unable to build new schools, the old schools are combined in their original buildings. This is pseudo comprehension and results in the farcical situation, as is the case in a nearby town, of distances of up to two miles between classrooms. This is reform for reform's sake and is utterly wrong.

On the whole therefore, the disadvantages of a comprehensive school far outweigh its merits and therefore I think that the secondary education system is not in need of such radical reform as that contemplated by the introduction of comprehensive schools at the expense of grammar schools.

A L Ogilvie

Decades have passed since comprehensive education was introduced into the south Wales valleys. There is still no consensus of opinion as to which is the better. Some pupils would benefit more from a grammar school education than from a comprehensive school education. For others the converse is true.

Courses
South Wales Switchgear, Pontllanfraith, under the guidance of Alfred Nicholas (later Sir) engaged hundreds of young people from the valleys as apprentices, building up a business which supplied transformers and other electrical equipment to many countries throughout the world. In February 1963 local schools received notification that they intended offering apprenticeships to fifty boys and five girls (no gender equality then) in the age group 16 to 18-year-olds. Any pupils with four or more 'O' levels were welcome to apply. Links between schools and the company remained strong: during July and August 1965 SWS ran five courses so that pupils could see exactly what working with the company would be like.

Curriculum
Twenty-two 'A' level subjects were taught at the school when the Autumn term began in 1960 viz. English, Welsh, Latin, French, German, history, economics, geography, geology, pure mathematics, applied mathematics,

pure and applied mathematics, physics, chemistry, biology, botany, zoology, art, music, woodwork, metalwork, geometrical and engineering drawing. Three years later it was proposed to introduce Russian. The subjects offered at 'O' level in the mid 1960s were English Language, English Literature, history, geography, Welsh, French, German, Latin, Russian, biology, chemistry, physics, art, music, woodwork, PPSG, metalwork, geometrical and engineering drawing, calculus and geology.

In the middle of the decade the Headmaster regretted that fewer students were doing mathematics at A level. By 1969 the position had improved. That year the records show that the entries were:
For VI2 X (the scientists) pure and applied mathematics 10, pure mathematics 8, applied mathematics 8, physics 24, chemistry 20, biology 10, botany 1, zoology 0, geology 3 and use of English 27.
For VI2 Y (arts' students, some of whom take a science subject) English 4, Welsh 1, Latin 0, French 6, German 5, Russian 0, history 10, geography 16, economics 16, pure mathematics 3, zoology 1, geology 9, music 1, art 1, woodwork 1, metalwork 1, use of English 23.

Debating
During the long post-war period SLADS was one of the most important societies in the school. In particular the Autumn term 1960 was one of the most successful in the society's history. A meeting under the heading *Six Ess Three Show* attracted an audience of 260 - a record. Always well attended were the inter-school debates with our sister school. These were held annually; one year at Ystrad Mynach and the other at Pengam. Motions debated at two of these meetings were *Life is so short that Man is justified in enjoying himself as much as possible* and *That this generation has no faith, whatsoever, in the present educational system.* Interesting talks by members of staff included *Witchcraft and Demonology* (J Young BA), *In search of the Welsh Red Indian* (S I Jones BA) and *Wales and Welsh Culture* (Miss R K Thomas BSc). Outside speakers of note included Reverend Vaughan Walters BA who spoke on his experiences as a Baptist missionary in India, and Dr Gwynfor Evans MP, president of Plaid Cymru for thirty-five years. The society owed much to the support it received from members of staff, particularly to T D Jones BA.

Dramatics
The decade opened for the Pengam and Hengoed Dramatic Society with two performances of G B Shaw's *Androcles and the Lion* at Ystrad Mynach in the November. During the following season they staged three one-act plays at the same venue: *Birds of a Feather* (about bishops and poachers in mid-Wales), *Brother Wolf* (the story of a robber converted to an

honest life) and $X = 0$ (which pointed out the futility of war). *The Rose and the Ring* by W M Thackeray was the choice in 1962 but the intended production of *The Alchemist* failed to materialise due partly to a lack of enthusiasm on behalf of the pupils and partly because Mr Elias had to go into hospital. Three lean years followed, the rejuvenated society rehearsing *Henry IV (Part I)* in January 1966, and putting on films of *The Bible* for Forms 1, 2 & 3 and *Othello* for Forms 5 and 6 in the October; at the same time staging a production of *She Stoops to Conquer*.

This new enthusiasm continued with *A Man for All Seasons* at the Girls' School at Ystrad Mynach in 1967 and *Arms and the Man* at Pengam in 1968. In February 1969 Shaw's *Candida* was the choice followed by an impressive performance of *Under Milk Wood* in the September. The main force in choosing such a large-scale production was Miss Sally Davies BA who had joined the staff that term. David Nutland played Rev. Eli Jenkins and June Cocker Polly Garter.

Eisteddfod
The St David's Day eisteddfod continued to excite. In March 1960 Barry Horsman won the Chair and Robert Lewis the Crown poem. Johnston House won the Alden Cup which had been presented by Deputy Head Leslie Alden for the House scoring the most points, and Robert Lewis secured the Cup for the most points. Neil Kinnock won the Senior English Essay the following year, perhaps an earnest of his skill in communicating in English.

In March 1965 Dafydd Walters, the son of a Welsh-speaking Baptist minister, won the Bardic Chair for the third consecutive year while L C Thomas won the Crown for the second consecutive year. There were now more than sixty competitive items in the eisteddfod. Johnston House dominated the event year after year and in 1969 Teifion W Davies won both the Chair and the Crown, not unique but unusual.

To the end, and in spite of his ill-health, Neville Richards continued to think of his first love; the school. Just a short time before he died he donated a new bardic chair, valued at £55, to the school.

Entry
The number of new entrants remained just above 90 each year with fewer than 40 coming from Monmouthshire. In 1963 every boy was instructed to present a *Health Certificate and have cap, black blazer with badge, grey flannel trousers, grey or white shirt, school tie, rubber shoes for gym, gym shorts and a vest for athletics (to be bought at school), football*

knickers black, boots, jersey - red blue and green yellow. All clothing was to be clearly marked with the pupils' school number. Monmouthshire pupils living more than 2 miles from school were advised to apply to the Director of Education for Monmouthshire for a travel permit or season ticket. Also new this year was the sending from each feeder primary school the relevant record cards for the new pupils. There were no Monmouthshire pupils in the September 1965 entry and the following year, of the 99 new entrants, eleven were transfers from Secondary Modern Schools.

When Glyn Rees became Head (September 1969) the requirements for each new entrant were a little more strict. In addition to the items mentioned above, every pupil was to have a light grey pullover and descant recorder.

Number on Roll
As in the 1950s the number of pupils in the school slowly increased. At the start of the decade there were 570 on the register including 101 in the Sixth Form. Ninety-two pupils had left, 21 of whom had gone to university. In October 1963 the breakdown of the 609 pupils into year-groups was: I -91, II - 99, III - 101, IV - 103, V - 105, VI - 110. By the beginning of the Autumn term in 1968 the total had risen to 618.

Examinations
In spite of the many changes of Headship, results in external examinations continued to be excellent. In June 1961 44 boys got one or more 'A' levels while 106 got one or more 'O' levels. Mathematics remained the strongest subject: in 1962 44 sat 'A' level including 11 pure and applied maths, 7 pure maths, 7 applied maths and 15 physics. A new examination 'Use of English', was introduced in March 1963 in an attempt to improve the English skills of sixth formers. Another instruction that year was that henceforth 'A' level results were no longer to be published. It was now the norm each year for around fifty boys to secure one or more 'A' levels.

Changes continued to be introduced. Pupils sat the first examinations of the Certificate of Secondary Education (CSE). Though primarily for secondary modern schools, grammar schools entered some of their weaker pupils in some subjects. The pupil's result for each subject was graded from 1 to 5 or, in extreme cases, ungraded. Whereas GCE (General Certificate of Education) was for the top 20% only of that year's students the new CSE examination covered a very broad range. Quite soon it was appreciated that each examination (GCE or CSE) was associated almost exclusively with one particular type of school. This was considered unacceptable so moves were made to solve the problem by combining the two into a single examination. The change took a while to implement and it was in 1988 that the General Certificate of Secondary Education (GCSE) was introduced. From that date all pupils sat the same examination.

Miscellaneous
In April 1961 the Headmaster was still asking for an amplifying system which would enable boys, forced by lack of space in the chapel, to stand in the adjoining classrooms and participate in morning service and other such activities.

That year the Belgian driver who drove the party through Germany to Austria and Italy spoke five languages. This advantage was somewhat negated by the fact that he drank too much!

Dover, Printers, Abergavenny, quoted £3.13.6 (£3.67^1/$_2$) plus tax at 4/6d (22^1/$_2$p) in the £ for 1000 Christmas cards. Envelopes would be extra.

In July 1968 a pupil was suspended for setting a desk on fire.

Language teaching was changing. The language laboratory was making its appearance. In 1964 school decided to spend money on tape recorders, a gramophone and projectors.

French and German assistants continue to come to spend a year at the school.

International referee Gwyn Walters took charge of the match with Neath at L S P in 1968. School lost 6-5.

In 1968 the swimming pool was used for canoeing demonstrations. Students came from as far as Carmarthen and Cardiff to observe.

A live locust was found in school in a pack of bananas delivered by a local shop.

Miss D Madigen from Immigration House for Australia, London, came to school in December 1966 to give a lecture on her country.

Founder's Day
Guest speakers at Founder's Days during the decade included Rev. Glyn Parry-Jones MA, BD, Welsh Regional Organiser for BBC's Department of Religious Broadcasting (Welsh region); Rev. Dewi Morgan BA, editor and press secretary SPG (Society for the Propagation of the Gospel), London

(an Old Boy 1927-34); Rev. N Leslie Stokes BA BD, West Green Baptist Church, London (an Old Boy 1926-34); Rev. Canon T G King, rector of Stoke Charity, Winchester, Hants (an Old Boy 1923-29 and brother of one of the Governors); Rev. Chancellor Derek G Childs, Principal Trinity College, Carmarthen, and later Bishop of Monmouth; and Rev. Fred Mudge, vicar priest Llandaff Cathedral.

Governors

The composition of the Governing Body in the early 1960s consisted of representatives of various committees as follows: Glamorgan Education Committee (8), Caerphilly and Gelligaer Divisional Executive (2), Monmouthshire Education Committee (6), Co-opted members: Glamorgan (1) and Monmouthshire (1).

Gymnasium

With a new gymnasium being built - it was used first in November 1962 - thoughts turned as to how the old one could be used. The options eventually reduced to two - either a library or a swimming pool. Some thought that to convert it into a pool was impracticable but that is what was finally decided. During the year the Head sent out hundreds of letters to Old Boys. Very quickly he collected £220 including £5 from Harold Davies MP for Leek and a similar amount from Aneurin Davies MA who had just become Registrar at Kings' College, London. By the time the fund closed the necessary £4200 had been raised.

Head boy

The Headboy was gifted a fair amount of authority. He could:
Remove a Sub-Prefect's badge for refusal to do a duty.
Give a C (conduct mark) for failure to wear a school cap at the designated times and in the prescribed places.
Take detention after school on a Thursday on his own. This could mean looking after more than fifty boys for an hour.
Arrange car parking and programme sellers for the school play.
Even teach. When Bryn Jones was absent through illness in January 1968 the Head Boy took six of his eight lessons.
Enter the names of 'sinners' in the detention book.
Be off school premises at any time between the hours of 9 a.m. and 4 p.m. if he chose to be.

Alfred T Evans BA

Alfred Evans took up the appointment of Headmaster on Monday 2 May 1966. Born in 1914 and the father of three children he won a major and an exhibition scholarship for the best candidate in Arts when he entered University College, Cardiff. For his BA finals he took French, German,

English and History (gaining Honours in English), obtained a Diploma in Education and a First Grade in Advanced PE. A keen sportsman Fred Evans was Captain of the university boxing team, and represented the university at rugby, swimming and cross country. His stay as Headmaster would be short for his main interest was politics. He was parliamentary candidate for Leominster in 1955, Stroud in 1959 and, when Aneurin Bevan died, he was short listed for the Ebbw Vale constituency. For the 1964 election he was asked to contest many seats but refused because of the serious illness of his wife. He was an Executive member of Glamorgan Federation of Constituency Labour Parties and on many other committees. In education he had held the posts of Head of English, Bargoed Grammar/Technical School 1937-49, Headmaster of Bedlinog County Secondary School 1949-66, before becoming Headmaster at Pengam. Fred Evans remained in post until 18 July 1968 when he won the seat for the parliamentary constituency of Caerphilly in a by-election called because of the death of Ness Edwards MP. In Parliament he was offered a seat on one of the Boards for Wales. He was now doing exactly what he had always wanted to do with the wish to serve on the Welsh Hospital Board, or something to do with education, but with the plea *not electricity or gas please*.

In May 1967 Mrs Shirley Williams, Minister of State at the Department of Education and Science had been guest speaker at the school Speech Day. In his report for that day Fred Evans stated that *The number of scientists, technologists is dropping. More are doing economics and geology. Are mathematics and science subjects too rigorous?* (The writer's answer to this is No. The curriculum in mathematics offered in the 2010s is not as rigorous as it was when Neville Richards was getting scores of boys through 'O' and 'A' level. It should also be remembered that many of the boys in earlier years sat the equivalent of 'O' level at the age 14+ and not 16+ as became the case for 'O' levels.) One month before Fred Evans was successful in his parliamentary quest he wrote to Mrs Shirley Williams asking if he could continue to pay his teachers' pension contribution (*I've done thirty years*) so that he could get a full teachers' pension at 60. I find this a strange request. Do not MPs receive a pension?

Head Boy's diary
The 1960s saw the innovation of the Head Boy's diary. John Fletcher Davies was Headboy and David G Griffiths his Deputy for the year 1967-68. One of his first duties was to compile a list of possible prefects and sub-prefects which the Headmaster would scrutinise and approve. After distributing the tassels for caps (black and white for prefects, black for sub-prefects and white for himself) the prefects were presented to the

whole school at the next assembly. At first only the Headboy was allowed out of school between 9 a.m. and 4 p.m., but this rule was later relaxed allowing prefects and sub-prefects off school premises during the lunch hour to visit the Tuck Shop. However, they were not allowed out during mid-morning break.

As time passed the duties of the Head Boy expanded. He seemed to become an unpaid additional member of staff for he was asked to enter on their record cards, the 'A' Level results of boys who had left to assist in arrangements for the WJEC examinations and to send out invitations to guests for Speech Day.

One of his notes refers to Dancing Classes at Hengoed which he writes were taken by Mrs Buck. It is assumed that since W J Griffiths's nickname was 'Buck' the classes were taken by his wife. One of the biggest problems with the combined Lewis' schools dancing classes was getting boys to dance.

Hengoed
The official opening of the new Lewis Girls' School at Ystrad Mynach was on Thursday 17 May 1960 at 2 p.m. The building they were leaving had been opened on 1 November 1900 to accommodate 80 girls but it was never large enough. By 1905 the number on roll had reached 138.

Leavers
At the end of July 1968 (a typical year) there were 81 leavers, 30 of whom went to a university and 14 to a technical college. One summer, after the examination season, a parent sought permission for his son to finish school before the end of term to enable him to take up a job to earn money to go to university. The Head replied that he could not stop him as he was over age. On the odd occasion a pupil was asked to leave because of his poor work.

Lewis Trust
Each year the Lewis Trust Fund continued to receive £600, plus a small amount of interest, from the original Lewis Foundation. The Trustees looked after this money carefully and in April 1960 had an accumulated balance of £2562. Very many former students benefited with grants of amounts up to £80.

Lunchtime
It is estimated that each year in the 1960s 68400 meals (averaging c.350 per day) were prepared requiring 36 tons of potatoes, 2500 gallons of gravy and 2300 gallons of custard. To service these meals 241,920 pieces

of cutlery were washed. In April 1962 there was a shortage of vegetables which caused them to be rationed for school dinners. The suggested substitutes were scones, pastry fingers, bread, rice, spaghetti or dumplings. Later that year the average number of meals served per day had increased to 409. The unit cost of providing a meal was 11.2d (4.7p). A few years later a new kitchen was opened, but the most impressive advance was that the new dinner plates bore the school name.

Magazine
The standard of *The Ludovican* was fairly consistent throughout its life from 1930 but by the mid-1960s there were significant problems, not least with the printers. When the 1967 magazine was published it was using the third different printer in four years. The loss of the Monmouthshire boys (now Gwent boys) also had an influence, as did the fact that the magazine published in the Summer of 1965 was the last magazine while the school was nominally an endowed school. Ultimately the professional printer was sidelined; the school resorting to its own photolithography, a process that would never produce anything of a quality equal to that of previous publications. Advertisements from local businesses had always helped to keep down the cost at which the magazine could be sold. In 1968 they were £8.8s.0d. (£8.40 for a full page and £5 for a half page.)

Former pupil Gerard Hodge (brother of financier Sir Julian Hodge) who had left in 1932 and had been an instigator in converting the old gymnasium building into a swimming pool, made an interesting contribution to the 1962 magazine:
I had no right to receive the grant from public funds which took us to university. Forget your rights, think only of your responsibilities. Be neither a rejector nor an acceptor of new things but a discriminator. (i.e. don't be prejudiced, think things through.)

Monmouthshire boys
New entrants to Pengam from Monmouthshire ceased in 1964 but those already in the school were allowed to complete their education there. The two counties were often at loggerheads over their costs. In November 1969 a list of Monmouthshire boys was sent to the Director of Education for Glamorgan seeking financial readjustment from Monmouthshire County Council.

Neil Gordon Kinnock (Baron Kinnock of Bedwellty)
Without doubt Neil Kinnock is the best known name, both nationally and internationally, of any former pupil of Lewis' School. Tredegar born, Neil

made the long journey to school from 1953 until 1961, when he left to become a student at the University College of South Wales and Monmouthshire, Cardiff. There he graduated with a degree in Industrial Relations and History. After a few years as a tutor with the Workers' Education Association he replaced Sir Harold Finch as MP for Bedwellty in 1970 and subsequently became MP for the new local constituency of Islwyn. Neil rose to be leader of the Labour Party and leader of the Opposition from 1983 to 1992. He was the longest serving leader of the Opposition in British political history, and the longest never to have become Prime Minister. He resigned as leader in 1992, and from the House of Commons three years later when he became a European Commissioner. In 1999 he was appointed Vice-president of the European Commission under Romano Prodi, a position he held until 2004. Neil Kinnock entered the House of Lords in January 2005 after being created Baron Kinnock of Bedwellty. After leaving Pengam Neil was very critical of the practice of caning which he claimed was prevalent in the school while he was there. Since I was totally unaware of any pupil being so treated during the years I was a pupil I made further enquiries. I have been assured by a pupil who was in Neil's year that caning certainly went on: my informant had been caned for being cheeky to a prefect. Thinking back to Lloyd George's comments when he re-opened the school in 1905 I think he would be impressed that one pupil got almost to the very top of an extremely greasy pole.

Non-teaching staff
In November 1962 the total area of the old school involved in daily cleaning was given as 25 716 sq ft plus the laboratories, giving a total of 35 220 sq ft. Each cleaner was responsible for 6000+ sq ft. The duties of the caretaker included stoking all boilers at 6.30 a.m., 10 a.m., 1 p.m., 4.30 p.m. and 7 p.m.; and attending to cloakrooms and towels, etc., for which he was paid about £12 per week.

An advertisement for Laboratory Assistants offered wages at a weekly rate from £4.14.6 to £4.17.5 for those under 21, thereafter from £11.10.4 to £11.17.5. A Senior Laboratory Assistant's wage ranged from £10.6.9. to £10.13.1 at 18 and from £12.13.11 to £13.1.9 at 20.

One-off events
The audiovisual teaching of French using film strips and tape recorders was introduced in January 1963.

The first-year pupils in September 1963 were the first who had to stay on in secondary school for five years.

In 1964 the Ministry of Education became the Department of Education and Science under the Robbins Report.

Form Captains and Vice-captains were introduced in 1966-67.

H B Edmunds, the German master was taken ill and entered Caerphilly Hospital where he died on 17 October 1967.

Prince Charles was invested as Prince of Wales at Caernavon Castle on 1st July 1969. Pupil representatives from all the secondary schools in Wales were invited.

New Tredegar, with former Ludovican J Stanley Jones as Principal, became the first Bilateral Secondary Technical School in Wales in September 1960.

Vandalism
Serious vandalism had never been a problem at the school but that changed in 1967. One Sunday in May, during the Whitsun holidays, an intruder gained access to Lower School by smashing a window and started a fire. Smoke was observed by a passing motorist who gave the alarm. The Staff Room and form rooms in Lower School were extensively damaged but the hope was that it should be possible to get the building usable again and re-open on Monday 5th June. This did not prove to be the case for a report in July states that *clearing of fire damage at lower school is proceeding.* The approximate cost of the books lost was £192.14.6.

On 1 May 1968 the police received a telephone call to say there was a bomb in school. Six months later there was a break-in. Damage was sustained to a teacher's desk and registers in three rooms were torn to pieces, but nothing was stolen. A year later there was another break-in, this time into Head's study. No money was kept there and nothing went missing.

Parents' Concert
Each year the concert was chaired by the Head Boy. The whole point of these concerts, probably the most popular of all the official school functions, was for parents to become aware of the standard of work achieved. They could listen to a boy playing a piano, organ, trumpet, trombone, clarinet, violin or viola; they could listen to boys singing, either on their own or in small groups; or they could be impressed by the boys' language skills in Welsh, English, French or German. There were recitations and the evening usually concluded with an excerpt from a classical play.

The Parents' Concert in April 1960 included solos by John Watkins (viola), D G Jones bassoon ('Dai bassoon') and M P Beynon (keyboard). The former two were members of the National Youth Orchestra. Other items included some of the recitation-winners from the eisteddfod and an extract from the recent production of *She Stoops to Conquer*. With Head Boy Paul Reed in the Chair the parents were also made aware that there was currently a petition in circulation against the exclusion of Monmouthshire boys from the school.

At the 1963 concert the first public performance was given of a song composed by Brian Russell, a pupil at the school, and an anthem was performed composed by Mervyn Burtch (a former pupil), then in charge of music at the girls' school in Hengoed. The evening included recitations in English, Welsh, French and German, and an excerpt from the Jones House play *The Rivals*. At this event a collection was made, the proceeds of which were shared between the *Freedom from Hunger Campaign* and the school swimming pool fund.

In 1964, the school choir of 100, conducted by John Williams and with Gordon Jones at the organ, sang Vivaldi's *Gloria*. This was the first performance of a complete work at the Parents' Concert. The concert in 1969 was acclaimed by many present as the best yet. Included in the programme were renderings of *Ye Boundless Realms of Joy* by Handel and *Be Not Afraid* from Mendelssohn's Elijah.

Prizes
Many former pupils who belonged to the Old Boys' Association recognised the lack of prizes and set about doing something about it. By 1962 the list of prizes was: The R W Jones Memorial Prize, The Headmaster's Magazine Prize, The Old Boys' Association Form Prizes, The W E Park Reading Prize, The David Meurig Thomas Cup for Excellence in Modern Languages, The Moore Cup for Noteworthy all-round achievement, The Anthony Jenkins Cup for Excellence in Natural Sciences, The Hugh Griffiths Prize for the most promising student of History at 'A' and 'O' levels of G. C. E., and the Old Boys' Association Blazer Badge and Tie, presented by Trevor Rees, Esq. to the Head Boy.

The Gerard Hodge Memorial Fund
A former pupil who did much for the school was Gerard Hodge. He prospered in business becoming Managing Director of a company known as Mining & Chemical Products. Gerard Hodge felt that he owed a great deal to his old school for the start it had given him in life, and did much to initiate the conversion of the old gym into the swimming pool.

Unfortunately life dealt him a very unkind hand. After taking off to fly home from a business visit to Tokyo in 1966 his plane crashed. He was one of two survivors who escaped, shaken but unhurt. The following day he tried again but was most unfortunate. His plane crashed on take-off killing him. A Memorial Fund in his honour was set up by the Old Boys' Association. When it closed in July 1966 the balance stood at £355.2s.7d. (£355.13) This money was invested to establish The Gerard Hodge Memorial Fund. The hope was that the interest generated would be sufficient to award annually four £5 prizes for: Best School Magazine contribution; Art; Music, and Outdoor Pursuits. Gerard had been guest speaker at Speech Day in 1961.

School Buildings

While a great deal of building and rearrangement was taking place at Pengam in the 1960s; at Governors meetings, at County Hall and at Westminster, thoughts must have been expressed that one day, and soon, the outdated old buildings would be bulldozed to the ground and be replaced by a new purpose-built comprehensive school. However, that was in the future; the more pressing need was the present. To that end a new physics laboratory was built which came into use in January 1960 and a new two-storey block for geography, metalwork and two chemistry laboratories was opened a few months later. The physics laboratory now had a store room and the old chemistry laboratory had become a second physics laboratory. There was also a secretary's office and so there was now no need for the secretary to stand outside when the Head wished to hold a private conversation.

Two years later more major building work took place: a new kitchen and dining room were sited adjacent to the main dining room while the two existing dining rooms were converted, one into a music room, the other into a drawing office. An HMI report had stated that the Music Chamber was a menace. It requested that *this unsightly corrugated iron building be pulled down and replaced.* How on earth did Dr Thomas put up with it for so many years? It must have been very cold in the winter. A minor building programme then gave rise to the creation of a library on the site of the existing Music Chamber and also new playing fields on land east of Lower school.

The available accommodation in April 1963 was 16 classrooms, 5 laboratories, plus specific rooms for art, woodwork, metalwork and geography; also the library, and old and new gyms. Of these, 21 teaching rooms had been built before 1945. The Staff Room, which measured 15' 9" by 13' 3", remained totally inadequate. In 1964-65 it was the base for thirty permanent staff, two part-time musicians, a French assistant and five university students in training. Imagine what it must have been like at break-time when everyone was attempting to acquire and consume a cup of tea or coffee.

In May 1967 the new dinning hall was opened and on Friday 12 May at 3 p.m. Councillor K G Turner, Chair of Governors, officially opened the swimming pool. Former Headmaster Neville Richards and Alderman L Heycock were also present. The cost of its construction, complete with water treatment plant, was £2628.60.

Scholarships
Success followed success. From 1951 to 1963 pupils at the school were awarded thirty-seven State Scholarships, fifteen went up to Oxbridge and there were seven open scholarships. In the 1960s Gareth Hughes and Lyn Carey Thomas won Meyricke scholarships to Jesus College, Oxford, Keith Alan Shore an Exhibition Scholarship in Mathematics to Jesus College, Oxford, P T Atkinson and E H Walters Entrance Scholarships to the same college while Geoffrey John Rowlands won an Entrance Scholarship to Magdalene College, Oxford.

In 1967 three A level mathematics students entered King's College, London, where Aneurin Davies (LSP 1938-44, who had been taught by Neville Richards) was Registrar. In music Michael Beynon was awarded an Instrumental Scholarship at the Royal Academy of Music and Michael Crump won a General Music Scholarship Competition.

Pupils who won Scholarships to Welsh colleges included Ralph Coombes: the William Jones Williams Scholarship at Bangor and a Major Open College Scholarship at Swansea (he opted for Bangor); William J Morgan: a College Open Entrance Scholarship to University College, Swansea and Rhys Evans, grandson of Alderman Thomas Evans, an Open Scholarship to University College, Aberystwyth (Economics and Geography).

Other awards were: Bryan Arthur an Entrance Scholarship to the London School of Economics, Geoffrey Powell a Post Office University Scholarship for Electronic Engineering, Gerald Osborne an Industrial Scholarship to John Laing & Co Building Engineering and J Roberts an Industrial Scholarship with Rolls Royce.

Speech Day
Important people who graced the platform in the school chapel on Speech Days during the decade included Col C G Traherne TD MA, Her Majesty's Lord Lieutenant of Glamorgan; Dr J H V Parry CMG, CBE,

Principal, University College, Swansea; Gerard Hodge who sadly was to die in an air crash, Dr Emlyn Stephens MSc, PhD, Director of Education for Glamorganshire (he and his wife would die in a car accident the following week), Dr Elwyn Davies, Secretary of the Welsh Department of the Ministry of Education; Professor L J Lewis (an old pupil) University of London Institute who would speak at Neville Richard's last Speech Day; Trevor Jenkins BA, Director of Education for Glamorgan; Mrs Shirley Williams Minister of State Education & Science; Mervyn Jones CBE Chair Wales Gas Board and Professor Bowen, University College, Aberystwyth.

Sport

Pengam rugby players continued to gain international honours. John Prince and Dennis Hughes were selected for the WSS Rugby XV in 1960, as was A I Beddoe a few years later. The First XV always seemed to be strong. They won 13 of the 16 matches played in the 1965-66 season but lost 24-7 to the Old Boys in 1967. Some idea of the high consistency of rugby and soccer throughout the school is indicated by the results for the last three years of the decade.

1966-67	P	W	D	L	Pts for	Against
First XV	18	14	2	2	209	57
Second XV	16	12	1	3	267	47
Under 14, Under 13 and Colts all did very well.						
Soccer	6	2	2	2		

1967-68	P	W	D	L	Pts for	Against
First XV	20	14	4	2	209	69
Second X	13	5	2	6		
Soccer	8	2	5	1		

1968-9	Played	won	drawn	lost	pts for	pts agst.
First XV	22	10	2	10	253	199
Second XV	16	11	5	-	206	83
Under 15	16	15	-	1	403	36
Under 14	12	7	1	4	170	83
Under 13 A	10	5	3	2	105	70
Under 13 B	3	1	0	2	6	30
Under 12	3	2	-	1		

| | | | | | Goals | |
					For	Agst.
Soccer	5	2	2	1	20	21
First XI	8	4	1	3	31	28
Under 15	7	4	-	3		

In March 1968 the First and Second rugby XV went on a tour to Devon at Half-term. They won all their games.

In athletics 1962 was a good year. The junior team (under 15) won the Glamorgan South Area Championship's Shield while the middle (15-17) and senior teams (17-19) were runners-up to Caerphilly. Three area records were broken by Pengam boys: R A Williams, senior 200 yds hurdles, E W L Williams, middle 200 yards hurdles, and T I Jarrold, the middle pole vault. Jarrold continued his winning streak by clearing 11ft 6in at the Open Welsh Championships which broke the Youth (15-17) record. At the Glamorgan AAA Championships G Jones threw the javelin 175 feet - a county record - and followed this with 179 ft 10in at the Welsh Inter-county Championships in Bangor. (Former pupil Brian Sexton's Welsh Javelin record of 218 ft still stood.) In a Four-way meeting at Gloucester the school team won 21 out of the 40 events. To round off the season the school sports produced ten new records.

In 1963 the school transferred from the Glamorgan South Area to Glamorgan North. At these championships the juniors won the shield, the middle team were second to Pontypridd while the seniors missed first place to Mountain Ash G S by a single point. Three boys represented Glamorgan in the Welsh Championships at Aberystwyth and Pengam won a Five-school meeting at Gloucester against four Gloucester schools.

At the WSSA Championships at Colwyn Bay in the summer of 1967 the school secured three firsts and two seconds. J K Powell won the mile, C R Williams the 440 yds and Lee Morgan the pole vault. J Lee was second in the 220 hurdles and J M Davies second in the triple jump.

One of the strongest athletic activities was cross country running. During the 1962-63 season, with H L Williams in charge, the school ran junior, middle and senior teams. In total the teams competed in twenty-seven matches winning twenty of them. They were Glamorgan champions and defeated West Mon G S who were the reigning Monmouthshire champions. In twelve years of competing in the Glamorgan Secondary School Championships Pengam had been first on five occasions. The star senior the following year was D H Parry. He represented Glamorgan against Monmouthshire and ran in the Welsh Inter-county Championships. By the end of the decade N J Preston was the teacher in charge and Gareth Morgan the best runner. Gareth was Glamorgan Champion, Welsh Schools runner-up and Welsh Boys' Club Champion.

In the last summer of the decade an Outdoor Pursuits club was formed, with three associated staff. The first organised event was a hike from the Rhymney Valley to Crickhowell. A three-day camp followed at Crickhowell and later another at Talybont. Great enthusiasm would project the club into the next decade. In October 1966 Pengam boys helped Glamorgan smash Monmouthshire in the Cross Country competition. All three teams won.

Tennis matches were played in the 1960s with the support of two members of staff, D B Davies and Bryn Jones. Again the weather interrupted arrangements. In 1960 only 8 of the 12 fixtures could be played. This resulted in 5 wins. 1963 saw House championships in tennis, Lewis becoming the first victors.

The cricket XI still did not have a home pitch in the second half of the decade. Home matches were played on the National Coal Board pitch at Ystrad Fawr, Ystrad Mynach. During the 1969 season school won half of the eight matches played.

The School Swimming pool was officially opened in May 1966 and was an instant success. The following year five Amateur Swimming Association gold medals were won at Cardiff. In 1968 Alan Evans was chosen to swim for Wales. By that year more than 450 bronze, silver and gold medals from the Amateur Swimming Association had been awarded to Pengam boys.

Golf, another newly introduced sport, was closely linked with Bargoed G C. A Golf Foundation coaching scheme operated from September 1966. The school paid half the coaching fees at £1 per hour plus half the professional's travelling expenses at 6d per mile. Up to 16 hours coaching would be given over the year, a normal course being eight one-hour lessons for ten to twelve pupils. The strength of the school club resided in about thirty boys who were members of one of three local Golf Clubs.

T Dilwyn Jones BA the senior French master was the driving force in the formation of an angling club and was able to negotiate the use of Taff Fechan water at reduced rates. Another popular new sport associated with water was canoeing. Club members had built seven canoes in three years and by 1967 had thirteen usable canoes.

Although education was nominally 'free', fees (five shillings or 25p, a term in 1969) were still collected. They were called sports' fees but covered the cost of the school magazine and helped to pay for books for the library.

Staff

When the decade opened in January 1960 there were twenty-nine teachers on the staff but only twenty-seven separate teaching areas. Enthusiasm for the orchestra increased and by April 1963 there were two part-time wind instrument teachers each coming one day per week and a strings teacher coming two-and-a-half days a week. Most teaching posts were easy to fill but the shortage of well qualified staff in the two principal subjects of English and Mathematics was illustrated by the fact that David Elias was the only applicant when he was appointed to teach English in 1960, and Walter Case the only applicant when he was appointed to teach Mathematics in 1961.

W A Thomas, responsible for teaching German, represented Wales at Table Tennis in West Berlin in 1962. He was captain of a combined England/Wales team against Czechoslovakia and against West Germany. In 1967 Mr Thomas enjoyed a Schoolmaster Fellowship for Easter at Emmanuel College, Cambridge. Mr N J Preston BSc (1966-70) who was second in the physics department, must have been a bundle of energy. Apart from being in charge of the Cross Country team and the Canoe Club during the Autumn term 1969 he helped with rugby, athletics, swimming, and Christian Union.

Several staff who had taught in the school for long periods retired during the decade. They included:

Len C E George BA (1945-70)
Len George, who arrived at Pengam in 1945 to replace Jack Perrett and teach PE and games, retired after 25 years service in the school. A former pupil, he had played in the centre for the school XV before going to University College, Aberystwyth, where he read geography. Remaining there he acquired a Teaching Diploma and a Diploma in Physical Education. Len rose through the ranks becoming Deputy Assistant Head, acting Deputy Head and finally Deputy Head towards the end of the 1960s. He was a man of integrity with a rounded personality. Many former pupils have a picture of Len with a tie to support his gym trousers encircling his rather full midriff. He would beat time with a short stick on the wallbars saying *Promise me boys you won't let yourselves go to seed.*

Les G W Alden BSc., (1948-1967)
Les Alden came to Pengam in January 1948 replacing J E Gibbs in the Physics Department. He was a lovely man, gentle and deeply committed to the school, who carried a metal plate in his head as the result of a war injury. Always interested in his church and in local affairs he was Vice-

Chairman of the Seventh Post-War Horse Show and Gymkhana at Trelyn Park in June '51. As Second Master Les Alden had acted as Head during Neville Richards' absences and during the inter regnum until Fred Evans was appointed as Headmaster. He retired in the summer of 1967.

Clifford M Harris BA (1920-60)
After his education at Howard Gardens Secondary School, Cardiff, where his Form Master was R T Gabe, the famous rugby player, 'Cliff' as he was affectionately known to his pupils, graduated at University College, Cardiff, and joined the staff in 1920. Apart from teaching English, Latin and chemistry he gave yeoman service outside the classroom - as editor of *The Ludovican*, and as an assistant coach for both soccer and rugby. When faced with a miscreant he would be quite likely to say *You think you're clever don't you mister. Well you're not!* In later years he became somewhat dreamy, partly due to declining eyesight. Outside school his interests included the YMCA, Bargoed Horse Show, Bargoed Chrysanthemum Society, the Glan-y-nant Welfare Association and the Rhymney Valley Schools Rugby League.

David W Thomas, DMus., (1929-61)
Dr Thomas (Gandhi to his students) left school at the age of twelve, worked twelve hours a day in a warehouse, then spent eleven years underground where he developed nystagmus, the dreaded eye disease. With help from the local Congregational minister he matriculated in 1924, and shortly afterwards was awarded a Glamorgan Open Scholarship in Music which allowed him to embark on a music degree course at University College, Cardiff. In 1929 he arrived at Pengam where he was to spend the whole of his teaching life in a corrugated zinc-sheeting shed with the exalted title of the Music Chamber. 'Gandhi' was a kind and tolerant man, never selfish, ever a perfectionist both with his pupils and with his first love - musical composition. Subsequently he was awarded the degree of Doctor of Music by the University of Wales, won numerous Open competitions and composed music that was performed at the National Eisteddfod, on the BBC and by numerous chamber ensembles and orchestras. Many of his compositions are still performed today.

William J Morris, BA (1923-61)
Another master who gave a great deal more to the school than he was obliged to was W J Morris, though many would say that he could have done more inside the classroom. He never forced a pupil to learn. If you chose to study you would have all the help you could possibly expect, but if you didn't want to learn any Latin, so be it. I recall one classmate's paper in Latin. His script was blank other than a few words at the top:

Dear Willie J. Je ne sais pas. The boy was bright enough for he qualified later with a PhD in biology where a basic knowledge of Latin would have been very useful. As G E Woodberry wrote in *John Goffe's Mill: Education has really only one basic factor - one must want it.*

'Fritz' was educated at Porth County School and University College, Cardiff, where he graduated, in 1922, with first class honours in Latin. The following year he was appointed to Lewis' School. In the matriculation year he chose 'unseens' over set books believing that they were a far better training in logical thought. Fritz put a great deal of effort into establishing an excellent school library, was the school's first Careers master and collected information on local youth employment which set many a pupil on the right path. For a period in the '40s a notice appeared in the library: *Tolle, Lege, but bring it back.* For years his brilliant witty Chron.Peng. articles in *The Ludovican* were eagerly awaited. One of the best brains on the staff he was not content until that day's *Times* crossword had been completed.

The author recalls going to Llangynidyr with him and a mutual friend for a drink. On the way home we stopped on the top of the mountain to relieve ourselves. We got out and walked, in different directions, some distance from the car. As I turned and looked towards him he licked an index finger and raised it above his head. My demeanor must have expressed puzzlement. He looked at me and raised his voice *'Must know which way the wind is blowing my boy'.* Another example of learning from experience.

Another story relates to Gethin Morgan's visit to Cambridge for interview. A few days before he was due to travel Fritz gave him some papers. On inspection they were found to give all the necessary travel details - the times of the trains from Maesycwmmer to Newport, Newport to Paddington, how to cross London and the times of the trains from King's Cross to Cambridge. This thoughtfulness was very much beyond the call of duty.

Philip J Davies, BSc., 1924-1964
After his education at Tredegar County School and University College, Aberystwyth, where he obtained a first in physics, Percy was appointed to Lewis' School in 1924 and served the school for forty years with diligence and power. Many a sixth-former awaited the return of his Practical Book in trepidation hoping that the corners of its pages were not turned down with cutting comments written in thick red or blue pencil scrawled across them. In the middle years of his reign, he suffered greatly from poor eyesight. It became so poor that the author recalls

six-formers playing shove-halfpenny across the benches during some of his lessons. For all that a close look at the examination results over the years will show what a fine teacher he was and how many boys had much to thank him for as they look back.

W H John 1949-60
'Bill' John was educated at Cardiff High School from which he won a Glanely & City of Cardiff Major Scholarship to University College, Cardiff in 1941. His undergraduate time was interrupted by three years in India and Burma as a Lieutenant in the Royal Artillery from 1942 to 1946. After graduating from Cardiff where he was President of the Student's Union and a member of the First Cricket XI he came to Pengam in 1949 as Senior History Master. Apart from his excellent work in the classroom he was a powerhouse in the Pengam/Hengoed Dramatic Society and arranged numerous trips to Stratford. When the Korean war started, he breezed into a lesson one day saying *Sorry the quality of the maps in the newspapers are poor - they'll improve soon.* He was speaking from experience. Outside school he was active in church work and a BBC script writer.

Gordon Jones BSc. (1950-65)
Gordon Jones arrived at Pengam from Newbridge Grammar School with the nickname of *Killer*. What a start that must have been for him. Appointed as second in the mathematics department he followed D T Davies as Head of Department and remained in post until he retired. An excellent sixth form teacher he was not averse to the odd mistake. I can hear his voice now as he thought he had completed a solution but a pupil pointed out an error: *Now you've upset the apple cart.* An accomplished musician, he contributed much to school music. Outside school his interests included bowls and his beloved Methodist Church in Blackwood.

Tuck Shop
The death of Mrs Emily Moore, a widow aged 90, occurred in April 1963. Her first husband had died 65 years earlier and her second husband in 1917. Mrs Moore kept the Tuck Shop in the village and is remembered with affection by hundreds of old boys. You could buy cigarettes singly and smoke them in the back room safe from the prying eyes of all authorities.

Trips and visits
In July 1960, and again in 1963, boys from Friar's School, Bangor arrived for one of their Sports' Meetings with the school. They did not have a happy time in 1960 losing by 26 runs at cricket, 6-3 in tennis, and both senior and middle athletics competitions.

In the mid-60s the Council for Education in World Citizenship (CEWC) was going strong. In 1963 2500 students, including two from Pengam and twelve from Lewis' Girls attended their meeting at Central Hall Westminster where the theme was *Freedom from Hunger*. Talks were given by four people who had done Voluntary Service Overseas: two in Africa and one each in Polynesia and India. It was a superb gathering with a strong social aspect. One of those present was Rolf Harris. The following year five boys went to a similar gathering. The theme this time was *The United Nations* and the principal speaker Jan Smuts the South African who had helped to frame the Charter. It was said that the best speaker this time was Dennis Healey the Labour politician. Those attending came away with the not unsurprising impression that the meeting was anti-USSR.

It is sometimes thought that in many schools rugby has preferential treatment but events in March 1966 contradict this. The Canoeing Club which had been formed in 1964 were given permission by the Director of Education for 20 boys and 2 staff to canoe from Glasbury to Ross (but with no financial assistance), whilst he refused leave of absence for staff to take a rugby XV to Devon during term time.

Other visits were arranged to *HMS Tiger* at Cardiff Docks; the Dental Hospital, Cardiff; the Geology Department, Cardiff; Treforest College of Technology and the Royal Shakespeare Theatre, Stratford-on-Avon.

Trips Abroad
Germany and Austria were the favoured destinations for school trips abroad at this time. At Easter 1960 W A Thomas BA (Head of German) took a party to Germany. In the Summer holidays he led another party of four staff and thirty boys on a further German adventure. In July 1962 thirty-three boys and three staff (W A Thomas, Tom Edwards and M B Cook) went to Ostend, Brussels and Cologne. A significant change introduced for this trip was that the county would not henceforth provide cover for medical expenses.

In 1964 pupils had an eleven-day trip to Austria during the Easter holidays with W A Thomas, Tom Edwards and Les Alden. Things got off to a poor start for they had a rough crossing. Many of the boys were quite ill; hand basins full of vomit do not engender a feeling of well-being! The coach ride took them via Brussels, Limburg, Ulm (the Danube was brown not blue) and Oberammergau to Innsbruck which was to be their base. On the return journey they stayed at Heidelberg, enjoyed a steamer trip on the Rhine and visited Bonn. The food, said one boy, had been an endless variety of sausages.

It was Germany again in 1966 and Sölden, Austria, on skiing holidays each year from 1966 to 1969. In 1966 Vivian Rowe was awarded a Grade 1 Certificate of Merit after a skiing course and John Hughes Jones awarded a Grade 2. For the skiing holidays the height and shoe size of each boy needed to be forwarded so that suitable equipment awaited them. France was not totally out of favour: Two staff and twenty-five boys went to Paris in 1965 while Dilwyn Jones BA (Senior French teacher), R B Ellis BA and E J Williams organised an 8-day coach trip to Brussels, Paris and the Loire Valley in the summer of 1969.

Perhaps the most exciting trip of the time was that made by fifteen boys and two staff to Russia during the Easter vacation 1966. Led by E G Lea BA, the Russian master, and assisted by Dilwyn Jones BA and Mr Lea's brother, the group headed for Moscow via Ostend, Cologne and East Berlin. Unfortunately pupil Paul Darch broke his leg in Warsaw while getting off a train at a station that didn't have a platform. Paul was confined to hospital but T D Jones, who had the necessary linguistic skills, stayed with him and eventually arranged for Paul's return to the UK. T D Jones then found his way to Moscow where he linked up once more with the party. The trip entailed five days in Moscow and five in Leningrad. Maintaining the Russian contact seven boys went on a cruise to Leningrad in 1968.

Courses and Conferences
During the school year 1960-61 the First National Residential Sixth Form Conference in Britain was held in north Wales at Coleg Harlech. In total seventy pupils attended, the subject under discussion being *The Birth of New Africa*. Another group of sixth form pupils attended the following year when lectures were given on *Education in South East Asia*. From the college a visit was made to the Italianate village of Port Meirion where Clough Williams Ellis, its designer, showed them around. In 1963 the visit to Coleg Harlech was termed 'The best yet': the dominant topic was *The causes of war*.

Links with other educational establishments are important. Cross-fertilisation of ideas and practices benefits everyone. Just to observe the educational environment of pupils in other schools stimulates the mind. In June 1967 it was arranged for three boys go to Atlantic College for six weekends on a canoeing course, while another boy went to the college for a National Life-guard Examination.

An even more exciting prospect was an ocean cruise. In May 1966 a small group cruised from Swansea to Lisbon and back aboard the *M.V. Devonia*, while in July 1968 seven boys from Pengam and nine girls from Lewis' Girls, accompanied by Miss M Hughes, went on an Educational Cruise on the *S S Nevasa*. What the weather was like is not recorded but it seems that a good time was had by all.

Old Boys
Paul Shreder, who has been referred to in the previous chapter, was continuing to make a name for himself. In September 1961 news reached school that he was going to study art under Annigoni in Florence and in 1963 his reading of the news on BBC caused the Headmaster to write to him concerning his mispronouncing of the definite article before a consonant while reading the news. The Head pointed out that *'thee' should be used only before a vowel or for emphasis*. Whether or not Paul took notice of this the writer does not know but such action epitomised how closely the Head followed the careers of so many of his former pupils.

At the same time Neville Richards was hearing of the successes of several other past pupils. Colin V Williams, a former Head Boy, had become Staff Officer to the Chairman of the NCB; Mervyn Morgan (at L S P 1921-27) was Superintendent of the Communications and Navigational Research Laboratories at Marconi; Paul Griffiths had been appointed Head of Music at Canon Hill Art Centre, Birmingham.

Rugby continued to dominate the 'Success in Sport' category. Five old boys represented their country at senior level: Dennis Hughes, John O'Shea and John Dawes (Captain) at rugby; Trevor Williams and George Renton (Captain, Welsh Amateur XI) at soccer. Was it unique for the captains of two national football sides (round ball and oval ball) to have attended the same school? Other senior rugby internationals were Billy Thomas, Peter Rees and Derek Morgan.

CHAPTER 8

Changing Worlds
The early 1970s

Catchment area

The school year 1970-71 was the last time that Monmouthshire boys attended the school. For the few remaining in second year sixth one wonders how they travelled to Pengam from such disparate places as Tredegar, Newbridge and Abercarn for there would have been no school buses. At the same time the school severed connections with the Upper Glamorgan side of the Rhymney Valley i.e. from Bargoed up. Apart from the Gelligaer area Lewis' School drew its intake from Llanbradach, the new Caerphilly housing estates, and Nelson. In 2013 boys still travel to Pengam from Llanbradach while boys from the nearest junior school (Pengam) go to Pontllanfraith and many boys from nearby Gilfach attend Bargoed Comprehensive. For its current catchment area Lewis' School is very poorly sited: it lies on the periphery.

Comprehensive education

A report in September 1970 stated that comprehensive education at Pengam would progress in three stages:

First in 1973 the school would lose its pupils from Llanbradach (it didn't) and Caerphilly but the numbers would be compensated by taking sixty per cent of the 11+ intake between Gilfach and Ystrad Mynach and by catering for ROSLA (Raising of the School Leaving Age) pupils, that is, those who would then have to remain in school until they were 16.

Second, in 1975, when the new comprehensive school would become available in Bargoed, the Pengam/Ystrad Mynach area of the Rhymney Valley would go comprehensive in two tiers. Pengam would become the Upper or High School, and would take all 13-18 year-olds while the Secondary School in Ystrad Mynach would take the 11-13-year-olds.

Finally, at an unspecified date, the complete comprehensive system would be located in a purpose built school, perhaps at Ystrad Mynach, near the then existing girls' school. (It wasn't)

A Departmental conference on the Caerphilly Scheme took place in June 1971 and at a December Staff meeting in Pengam the Head reported that the school would probably go comprehensive in 1973.

Plans proceeded apace. In June 1973 the staff of both the Lewis' Schools and the Bedlinog and Graddfa schools met with County Advisers to discuss the new comprehensive schools. Finally in July Lewis' School, Pengam, and Graddfa Secondary School, Ystrad Mynach, combined.

Eisteddfod

The school Eisteddfod carried on as usual. James House were the winning house in 1970 while Teifion Davies won the Chair and the Crown for second year running. The following year Gary Lewis won the Chair and Rowan Edwards became Crowned Bard. Yet again James House were top, the result being decided by the final event. For the last Eisteddfod as a Grammar School James fell to bottom place, the winners this time being Jones.

Other Regular Annual Events

The usual annual events proceeded as in previous years. At the Commemoration/Founder's Day service in May 1970 Rev. A K James, Vicar of Marshfield spoke and in 1971 the guest speaker was Rev. Norman Williams, Rector of Checkenden, nr Reading. Formerly of New Tredegar Rev. Williams did much work with handicapped children.

The numbers for the carol service became too large for everybody to fit into the chapel so two Houses held their service in the chapel, the other two in the gymnasium.

Entrants

For the first September of the new decade there were 604 pupils on the register. The new intake included pupils from Coedybrain J S, Llanbradach, Cwm Ifor J S and Penyrheol J S. As in previous years new pupils needed a cap, blazer, etc, and finally a descant recorder. Prior to entry pupils were advised that all clothing must be clearly marked with the pupil's name and number. An interesting school rule which staff and pupils were made aware of stated that: *For no homework to be set is unacceptable. Show revision.*

Examinations

The summer results for 1970 were more than satisfactory: 56 out of 58 sixth formers got 1 or more 'A' levels, 79 out of 87 got 1 or more 'O' levels, 24 got 'O' level re-sits and 41 out of 43 got one or more CSEs. This was the first occasion that there were no Monmouthshire candidates. The following year 51 sat 'A' level, four boys obtaining grades that would probably have earned them State Scholarships had these not been discontinued some years earlier. The Head Boy, Neil Moses, went up to study at Trinity College, Cambridge, and there was much praise for Walter Paget a pupil who carried on with his school work in spite of extreme difficulties.

Clubs

Clubs that thrived in the years leading up to the change were the Choral Society, Railway Society, Writer's Club and Chemistry Club. In a talk to the Film Society in 1974 S I Jones reminisced. The Film Society had met in the old dormitory room at Lower school as it was the only room that could be blacked out. More than a hundred boys attended but their total weight was more than the floor could stand. Parts of the floor above the library began to break up. Afterwards the meetings were held in the old Dining Hall. On the other hand the CEWC (Council for Education in World Citizenship) group disbanded and the railway and modelling, after two good years, was in decline due to lack of numbers.

Fire in school

The vandalism of the 1960s continued into the 1970s. A cutting in the *South Wales Echo* in February 1970 reported that there had been another fire in Lower School, the second in four months. The fire destroyed one wing of Lower School including the library which had been established in 1875 by Herbert James and later enlarged by his son Charles. The whole Lower School building was declared unsafe. From the day after the fire Forms 3 and 4 stayed at home. The following Monday the Primary School at Gelligaer was available for Forms 1 and 2: transport was provided and staff commuted. After about a week the school was said to be *working normally* - a statement that was probably stretching the meaning of the phrase a little. The cause of the fire was stated as *unknown*.

The Headmaster's report in 1970 records that, due to the fire, school was deprived of six teaching spaces plus the library, staff room and a textbook store. Five temporary teaching spaces were provided but there was no provision for the sixth form for private study, the Youth Employment Officer, Medical Officer or any Official visitor. The damage could not be repaired, so with ROSLA and the school changing from a three to a five-form entry the authorities put in place preliminaries for a vast building programme which would shift the centre of gravity of the school from the Upper site to the Lower one. The problem was probably exacerbated by attempting to teach certain subjects in sets not forms. Prior to comprehensive education a boy took all his lessons with the other boys in his form but larger schools made setting possible. For example, if all the mathematics classes were time-tabled at the same time the top thirty, selected purely on mathematical ability, could be placed in one set or group, the next thirty in another set and so on. The argument was that each set was more homogeneous than would otherwise have been the case and thus would be better for the teacher and the taught. For English, mathematics or science, the subjects most likely to use setting because every pupil was taught them, a given pupil could well be in a group with or without his form friends.

After the fire in the library many people offered replacement books but there just wasn't the space to accept them. Donors were encouraged to hold on to their books until the following year when, hopefully, there should be a new library. As if to remind the school that they could not relax vigilance a warning was received seven months later claiming there was a plan by pupils to set fire to a wing of the school. The police were informed, the planned fire did not materialise and, as far as I am aware, no person was apprehended for any of the earlier fire problems.

Gifts

An oil painting of the original school at Gelligaer, painted by John Coslett Jones, Art master at Bargoed Secondary School and an old boy, was donated to the school by W T James OBE in October 1970. It was unveiled by Dr Alan Trevor Jones, son of Roger Jones, a former Headmaster. Later a second picture - The First Lewis' School at Pengam - was presented to the school and on 26 February 1971 a service of donation, dedication and unveiling of the two pictures took place in the school chapel.

Dr Trevor Jones gave a substantial cheque towards a new library. The old library in Lower School used to be the Headmaster's house and Trevor had been born in it. He also donated a fine pipe organ, originally standing in the Presbyterian Church, Caerleon Road, Newport. It was moved from Newport and installed in school in the February, the total cost involved being about £300. On January 17, 1973 the official presentation, dedication and inauguration of the organ in memory of R W Jones MA, Headmaster from 1888 to 1919, took place in the school chapel. It was presented by his son and dedicated by Rev. D L D Chiverton BA, Rector of Llanfabon. Its qualities were demonstrated by the guest organist, Richard Elfyn Jones BA, MMus., FRCO. Also present was the guest composer Dr David Wynne, formerly music teacher at the school.

Other gifts worthy of mention were a complete set of Dickens, presented by Richard Williams, son of T R Williams, who had been a former teacher at the school; and a piano from the daughter of Tudor Jones, another former teacher. The Chairman of Governors, Lewis Lewis, both of whose sons had attended the school, also donated books.

Hair dispute
The first day of the autumn tern in 1970 caused quite a stir both in and out of school. The Headmaster, Glyn Rees, sent about a hundred boys home because he had decided that their hair was too long. This news soon reached the media, and television cameras arrived in school to make as much of it as they could. The Headmaster appeared on the National News broadcast by BBC TV and made his case. In due course all pupils returned to school sporting haircuts acceptable to the Headmaster. The next September a small number tested the Head once more. He suspended three boys for long hair and one for having a moustache. All bowed to the rules and were soon back in school. These problems with grammar school pupils did not augur well for the comprehensive era, but perhaps it was a shrewd move on behalf of the Head for he was laying down what he would accept and what he would not, and he had shown that he did not make idle threats.

Lunchtime
In January 1972, due to a severe coal shortage, pupils from Lower and Middle school were not in attendance. Because of the smaller numbers the dining hall staff experimented with a cafeteria system. The system worked well, so well, that when all the pupils were back in school more options were tried. By September 1973, there were 536 pupils at Pengam on the Cafeteria system for lunch and 370 dining in Lower School on the old system. By way of comparison with today the cost of a school meal then was 12p for a pupil, 14p for a member of staff.

Magazine
There was still a *Ludovican* magazine when the decade opened but the longer term prospects were not good. In fact the last *Ludovican*, with twenty fewer pages than in the previous year, appeared in July 1974, with teachers S I Jones and Bob Francis overseeing its production. Members of the Parents' Association typed it, *Chron. Peng.* and *Form Notes* were included again for the first time in four years, and it was printed in school. Many people worked extremely hard but there was no way the finished article could compare with a professionally produced magazine.

Decimal Currency

The country changed from pounds, shillings and pence (£.s.d.) to decimal currency on 17 February 1971. From that date on 6d, 3d and 1d coins were not accepted by the banks except in multiples of 5p (or old shillings). The school's final banking of the old currency took place on the tenth.

Music

Since the 1950s the school had supplied members to several orchestras on a regular basis. In 1972 Adrian Eales belonged to the National Youth Orchestra and Robert Lewis to the Glamorgan Youth Orchestra. There were also seven boys in the Glamorgan Youth Choir.

A feast of Music and Drama entertained parents and friends on the evenings of Thursday, 12 April and Tuesday, 17 April 1973. The first evening's entertainment was chaired by Kerry O'Connor, the Head Boy. It consisted of items given by fifteen soloists, the small choir and the school choir. The second evening, chaired by S I Jones BA, began with eighteen items selected from the Eisteddfod winners followed by a scene from the winning play, *The Long, The Short and The Tall* by Willis Hall. The evening concluded with a further eight items.

Non-teaching staff

The decade did not start well. The Head, Glyn Rees, had quite a challenging time, for the caretaker was away sick and the assistant caretaker was seriously ill. Added to this, during the year 1971-72 there were strikes, go-slows and industrial stoppages but the Head was most appreciative of the support he received from the non-teaching staff. The school, he reported, operated fairly well. The caretakers, Mr & Mrs Dwyer, saw that the school was clean and warm; assistant caretaker Mr Morgan organised things until Mr & Mrs Gibson took over, while Mrs David and Mrs Chappell kept the canteen going well. Others included in his list of thank-you's were Mrs Stevens and Mrs Barbara Laye the clerical staff, the Welfare Officers, D W Davies, the Director and the Inspectors. He also thanked the three members of the Youth Employment Service, Mr Pask, Mr Thomas and Mrs Pugh.

Numbers on roll

The number of pupils on the register for the three years up to the time of the change to comprehensive education oscillated around the 600 mark.

The projected numbers for September 1971, including those from Caerphilly and Llanbradach, were:

	Caerphilly	Llanbradach	Gelligaer	Total
Form 1	22	9	69	100
Form 2	13	10	88	111
Form 3	16	11	77	104
Form 4	21	10	69	100

In Upper School it was anticipated that there would be 104 in the Fifth form, 36 in Lower Sixth and 49 in Upper.

Parents' Association
In September 1972, in preparation for the change to a comprehensive school in 1973, every parent or guardian automatically became a member of the Parents' Association without payment of a fee. Over the years the Association organised numerous social and money-making events including a Dinner Dance at Nelson, a Jumble Sale at the Workman's Hall, Ystrad Mynach, a Summer Dance and a Safari Treasure Hunt. In compliance with the Taylor Report parents also served on the school's governing body with representatives of the local education authority, staff and the local community. This change was implemented by the 1986 Education Act, which also declared that there must be Annual Parents' Meetings.

School Rules applicable to the early 1970s
The lower half of windows, particularly in Rooms 9, 10, 11 and 12, should never be opened.

Only prefects, sub-prefects and those with permission can leave the school grounds during lunchtime.

Boys bringing sandwiches for lunch are to use Rooms 1 and 5. There is to be no eating while walking around. Chips purchased in the village are not allowed on school premises.

A Form Master can cancel Cs at the end of term. Prefects cannot give Cs.

Miscellaneous
The sudden death of T Dilwyn Jones BA, Head of French occurred on 11 October 1970. He had been on the staff for 22 years.

The Head Boy, Teifion Davies, was awarded a McLoughlin Scholarship by the Royal College of Surgeons in 1970. This was the second time for this national award to come to the school.

Christopher Rhys Williams went up to Cambridge University as a student in 1972.

The Education Committee waived the penalty clause (this was a fine) for premature leaving in 1970.

The new Secretary of State for Wales became responsible for Primary and Secondary Education in Wales in 1970.

John Hayter, a fifth form pupil, was Victor Ludorum in 1970. This was the first time for a fifth form boy to take the honour.

School tendered for, and agreed to buy, a bus from Gelligaer Omnibus Board in November 1970. The problem they then had was where to keep it.

The speaker at Prize Day in 1970 was former member of staff W H (Bill) John BA.

The first reference to a County Psychologist coming to the school was in November 1972.

Angelika Scholz, the German Assistant was surprised to find when she arrived that the boys wore blazers and the staff wore gowns.

The School Day
The time-table when Glyn Rees was Head was:

> 9 am Registration,
> 9.10 Assembly (except Monday when dinner money was collected),
> First lesson 9.25 - 10.15.
> Second lesson 10.15 - 10.55.
> Break 10.55 - 11.07.
> Third lessons 11.10 - 11.55.
> Fourth lesson 11.55 - 12.40.
> Lunch break 12.40 - 13.30.
> 13.30 ('The Dirty Bell' - this was intended to give boys time to clean up and be ready for lessons.)
> 13.40 Registration,
> Fifth lesson 13.50 - 14.30.
> Sixth lesson 14.30 - 15.10.
> Seventh lesson 15.10 - 15.50.

The teacher in Room 5 (the bell room) was responsible for ringing the bell at 10.15, 10.55, 11.55, 12.40, 2.30, 3.10, 3.50. The duty master was responsible for the bell at all other times. On Friday afternoon there was an extra 10 minutes for checking diaries, etc.

Sport

During the 1970-71 season school ran seven rugby and two soccer teams; in the summer there were cricket and tennis teams though these never reached the popularity of the winter sports. The following table gives a measure of the success of the school at sport.

	Played	W	D	L	pts for	pts agst.
First XV	26	23	0	3	456	144
Second XV	18	12	0	6	341	97
Under 15	8	2	0	6	67	99
Under 14	8	5	0	3	104	5
Under 13 A	8	7	0	1		
Under 13 B	4	2	1	1		
Under 12	3	2	-	1		

					Goals	
					F	A
Soccer						
First XI	13	4	2	7	26	35
Under 15	9	7	1	1		
Tennis	2	1		1		
Cricket	6	3				

The highlights of the time were: Gareth Morgan became Welsh Junior, Welsh Youth and Welsh Schools Senior Champion cross-country runner, Chris Williams was Welsh AAA, Welsh Schoolboys and Glamorgan AAA 400 metre champion and Stephen Maynard Welsh AAA shot put champion. Stephen was also the last Monmouthshire pupil to bring schoolboy international rugby honours to the school. He scored a try in the last match against France.

For the 1972-73 season the First XV were still a major force to be reckoned with, winning 23 of the 27 games played, scoring 616 points with only 170 scored against them. Likewise the Second XV won 16 of their 22 games and the Under 14s 18 of their 20. However, things changed the following season for the First XV won only half of the 24 games played (all the first team members except four had left) while the Second XV won just 6 of the fifteen matches played. In January 1973 A Lewis (VI2) played rugby for Welsh Secondary Schools against Yorkshire.

Golf continued to be popular. As a consequence the golf professional from Caerphilly G C was engaged to come to school to coach pupils. Outdoor pursuits was another relatively new extra-curricular activity but for it to become successful there was a need to acquire a Field Centre away from the locality of the school. Accordingly enquiries located a building belonging to the Red Lion Hotel at Pontrhydfendigaid (Tregaron). In March 1972 this building was passed as being satisfactory and later in the year planning permission was sought for a change of use into a field centre for the school. The idea was that groups of about fifteen pupils with staff would go there for a week during term time. On one occasion a group did a walk, referred to as a Star Trek, from Aberystwyth to Merthyr. It took seven days. How long the use of Pontrhydfendigaid lasted is not recorded other than to say that its use lapsed.

Staff

W H Hughes (Taffy) and Mrs Simmonds, both of whom had come to the school in the 1940s, retired at the end of the spring term 1970. Taffy made a very amusing comment about a mistake he had made on a mathematics paper: *Any fool can see that that + should be a -*. Ma Simms came with the Borden boys, stayed when they returned to Kent, stood in until H G Hoof returned from the war and came back when he moved on. For all that time and for many years thereafter she was not on the permanent staff.

S I Jones BA agreed to act as the new librarian in 1971; he also agreed to collect the staff dinner money.

Mr W Gray BA came as Head of French in the summer term of 1971 as replacement for Dilwyn Jones BA who sadly had died. In February 1972 Bryn Jones was appointed Second Deputy Head. There were now 29 staff apart from the Head.

The staff cricket XI in 1973 must have been very talented for they defeated Bargoed RFC, the staff of a primary school, the Parents' Association XI and the school XI.

P J Davies (senior physics) always had the chair to the right of the fireplace in the staffroom and woe-betide anyone who sat in it. He also used the coat hook immediately on the right of the door in the cloakroom half-way up the stairs.

Miss R K Thomas and Mr W Gray, who ran the Dancing Class together, organised a formal evening with a three-course meal in 1974. The evening included a great performance by Rahli the French assistant.

Some readers might be interested as to why W J Griffiths got the name 'Buck'? Apparently he told a boy named Len Evans that he didn't want any of his buck. How easily a nickname can be born. On another occasion W J G said he would like to see a large school hall but the chapel was unique in south Wales.

Comments from Vernon Davies who taught craft subjects: *The most significant changes have been in rugby, particularly the John Dawes era. Cricket never got its place. It's a selfish sort of pastime. 'Tennis is a "softies" game!'*

Trips
The first recorded trip of 1970 was that three staff took 23 boys on a visit to the Houses of Parliament where Fred Evans MP, former Headmaster, met them. Unfortunately the coach broke down on the way and there was a two-hour delay on the motorway. They eventually got to Parliament at 1 pm and not at noon as arranged. How they could have done with mobile phones then! Other visits were made to the National Theatre for a performance of *Richard III* and to the British Museum, London.

Trips abroad were made by three staff and 34 boys to Paris and to the Loire Valley at Easter 1970; Geraint Morgan took twelve boys skiing to Austria in January 1972, while 25 boys plus one member of staff joined Ogmore, Beddau and Maesteg schools to make one group for a skiing trip to Austria in 1974. Later that year the German department organised a visit to Brussels, Heidelberg and Bonn.

Berwyn Price
In the late 1960s Berwyn Price was a sixth form pupil who passionately wanted to play first team rugby. Politely he was told by his PE teachers, Bryn Iones and D B Davies, that he was too small to make the grade and the best thing he could do would be to turn to athletics. This turned out to be the best advice he could have been given for it led to his introduction to hurdling and in particular to specialising in the 110 metres hurdles. His subsequent achievements say it all. He represented Great Britain twice in the Olympic Games - Munich 1972 and Montreal 1976 (when he was Captain of the Great Britain Athletics Team); three times in the European Championships - Helsinki 1971, Rome 1974 and Prague 1978; and Wales four times in the Commonwealth Games - Edinburgh 1970, Christchurch 1974; Edmonton 1978 (where he was Commonwealth Games Champion and Captain of the overall Welsh Team) and Brisbane 1982. How important a word of sound advice can be at an impressionable age.

Comprehensive Education becomes a Reality

The new comprehensive school opened in the September 1973 with 1104 pupils on the register. There were 429 in Lower School and 675 in Upper School. Lower School was located in Ystrad Mynach; facilities for remedial pupils and craft were established in Tiryberth Primary School where the school had been allocated four classrooms, and the Upper School was at Pengam. Suitable furniture for Tiryberth was moved from Bedlinog school but one unforeseen setback was that the craft and woodwork rooms were not ready as the furniture intended for them was too heavy to move from Bedlinog.

At the new school there would be thirty-nine forms divided into three bands of instruction: Examination, General and Remedial. To service these needs the staff complement was set at fifty-seven. The school began operating with three posts unfilled.

The Head was pleased with the start, commenting that only a small number came to school in unsuitable clothing. The name of the new school became Lewis Boys' Comprehensive. This, at least, was something that everybody was happy with. Nomenclature is often a problem with a new school. What system should be used to refer to forms in the different year groups? A, B, C, ... is hardly suitable. After much discussion it was decided to use the letters L U D O V I C A.

The following article was written in 1973 by the Headmaster Glyn Rees. It generates great hope for the future.

DEAR LUDOVICANS

From time to time in my teaching career I've been asked by vocationally-minded pupils, 'Sir, what is the use of teaching History?' In my more philosophical moments, I used to reply, 'Boy! You do not use History, you live it, and make it!' I then would add that all our individual and collective day-to-day experiences would provide the historical facts for tomorrow's pupils. But even among our modest day-to-day experiences we feel there are certain ones of greater significance than others and therefore worthy of recording.

The pupils, Staff, and I are passing through such a period now. We are living out the end of an era. At the end of Term we shall close Lewis' School, Pengam, and in September, open Lewis Boys' Comprehensive School. Ninety-nine years ago, Lewis' Endowed School closed. It had been rendered redundant in the Elementary Education sphere of its work by the establishment of Board Schools under the Compulsory Education Act of 1870.

It closed therefore in 1874, and reopened in 1876 as Lewis Boys' Grammar School, and then began almost a century of wonderful achievement in scholarship, athletics and contribution to the social life of our country. Almost immediately our present Honours Board opened with our first pupil to the then newly-opened University of Aberystwyth. The corridor walls are now covered with them. There will be more, but the future ones will be creating a new image which will deserve the right to be judged on its own merits, free from comparison with the glorious past. Our prayer is that it will be a worthy successor. The new change, at least, saves me one great headache; where could I place the next one. In 1875, too, the Lewis' School, Pengam, ceased to be co-educational. Our sister establishment is going through the same changes as we.

Lewis' School, Pengam closes its records in a splendid manner. Despite the changes in the nature of our intake, we can claim that the year 1972-1973 was as representative as any year in its history. I G B Morgan upheld the tradition of Head and Deputy Head Boys; he goes up to Cambridge next year. Adrian Lewis represented Wales in Rugby; Raymond Bishop gained his Boys Clubs' international caps in the other code; John Thomas and Roderick Edmunds represented Wales in Public Speaking organised by the Young Farmers' Clubs. Donald Brown and John Moorman were awarded their 'Wings' in Gliding; Donald Brown won an R A F International Cadet Award worth £1,000; Our Five-a-Side soccer team won the Bargoed Rotary Shield; and in the Northern Area AAA Schools' Sports the school won the Senior and Junior Shields and was Runner-up in the Middle School, in short, a record of which to be very proud.

Another good item to report, after official sanction was given, was that we began work on our Field and Outdoor Activities Centre. Mention must be made of the very splendid effort in collecting money through the sponsored swim. Almost every boy took part. The R W Jones organ was completed, handed over and put into immediate use. The Eisteddfod was even better than last year's, and we thought that was the best. We bought a school bus, which has proved an enormous success.

Among the Staff changes, we began the year welcoming Mr H J Murray, BSc. (Careers) and Mr A R Thomas BSc. (PE and Physics, another old boy). We, very sadly indeed, lost Mrs Hiscock MA (French); Mr E G Morgan BSc. (Chemistry), Mr D B Davies BSc. (Physics); Mrs Hiscock resigned for family reasons. Mr Morgan was appointed Head of Chemistry in Caerphilly Grammar School, and Mr D B Davies Deputy Headmaster of the St Cenydd Comprehensive School in Caerphilly. We are about to say 'Goodbye' to Mr W Jones, BA (History) who has been appointed to a similar post in

Pembrokeshire, and Mr K M Horner, MA (English) who has been appointed Lecturer in the Hywel Harris College of Further Education, Brecon. We are grateful for the privilege of having known and served with all these colleagues for all the manifold services they have given us and we wish them well in their future careers.

Dr Roger Hacker, Ph.D., another Old Boy joined us in May as a replacement for Mr Morgan, Mrs Caroline Davies for French and Mr S D Edge, BSc., for Physics. They've all started well and we wish them a happy stay with us. Much preparation work has already been done preparing for the Comprehensive School. Mr Peter Jones' Staff in Graddfa and Mr Maddox's Staff in Bedlinog have co-operated wholeheartedly in the hard and heavy 'spadework'. We welcome them as colleagues and we are convinced that our combined enthusiastic efforts are a happy augury for the future.

Historically the school may be said to have contradicted its own motto 'Ni ddychwel doe', in that yesterday would seem to have returned in the sense that whereas in 1729, the only qualification for entry was to be poor, in 1974 the only qualification will be that of residence in our catchment area. Surely 250 years of tradition will give us a flying start in our new era.

Yours sincerely,
GLYN REES
Headmaster

Early Problems
During the first year of such a radical re-structuring it was inevitable that there would be problems. In the first instance there was the amount of wasted time as staff commuted, often more than twice a day, between buildings four miles apart. Another major problem was that the promised facilities were not ready when it was claimed they would be. The new block which would contain classrooms, craft rooms and a Sixth Form Common room, was not ready until January 1974. In the meantime some classes were held in Tiryberth Junior School, a mile away.

Debating Society
Slads, during 1973-74, was as popular as ever. Twenty-one meetings were held including two mixed debates with the girls' school. The society now operated, with attendances of the order of eighty, without any members of staff officially present. This says much for the organising abilities and discipline of the boys.

The Prefects 1960-61. Back row, extreme right: Neil Kinnock.

The Long and the Short, 1962.

The choir, conducted by John Williams, at the Parents' Evening, 1964.

School First XI, 1964.

The School Choir, 1965. Acting Headmaster Leslie Alden BSc. on the left, John Williams B Mus. ARCO on right.

Tennis Team, 1965. Acting Head Leslie Alden BSc. on left, D B Davies BSc. on right.

Tennis Team, 1966. Headmaster Fred Evans BA, on left, D B Davies BSc. on right.

A unique gathering: the Thomas brothers. Jeffrey (IL), James (IIP), Terence (IVS), Leslie (VI(i)B).

The bridge linking Upper and Lower School. The wall on the left was to shield the Headmaster's residence from traffic noise when the road was cut through the school grounds in the early 1920s.

The school showing the eleven buildings that made up the campus before the new comprehensive school was built.

The east end of the chapel in its latter days. It shows the memorial to Humphrey Owen Jones FRS on the extreme left with the lectern, pulpit, organ and the eisteddfod and memorial chairs in the centre. The pews have long since gone. The lectern, panels from the pulpit with the names of those old boys who fell during the Second World War, and the four chairs are now in the foyer of the new school.

The new Lewis Boys' Comprehensive School in 2013 together with one of the school's minibuses, as viewed from the east. Note the trees behind which shield the buildings from the main road.

The paintings: above, the property that was the original school; below, the new school as it appeared in 1848. See page 248 for article.

Postscript

In spite of having to battle against unremitting material poverty the school recorded great academic distinction. It enjoyed no independent endowments apart from that of its founder, and its buildings were in constant need of repair due to the mining operations beneath it. Every penny mattered. No one can read this account of the school's history without feeling inspired by the way in which the governors and so many long-serving staff faced these challenges, and overcame them for relatively little financial reward. The teachers were remarkable examples of unselfish people who were dedicated to their vocation.

The 'new' school provides a much wider choice of subjects than the 'old' which focussed, almost exclusively, on high academic attainment. A spacious and well-equipped new school, financed and maintained using a Private Finance Initiative, was opened in 2002. To compare the Grammar School of yesteryear with the Comprehensive School of today would be invidious: they are completely different animals. In the first instance instead of selecting entrants from a wide geographical area exclusively on academic potential, the modern Lewis' School enrols all the pupils from a relatively small catchment area, except for those who choose to go to the Welsh school. The result is a vibrant school with all kinds of clubs and activities unheard of fifty years ago. They include a Robotics and Astronomy Club, a Young Vision Sixth Form group capable of creating an EP from scratch, a group capable of making an original, highly technically competent film with no copyrighted music, a Welsh group linked with pupils in a 'Welsh' community in Puerto Madryn, Argentina, Science clubs linked with schools in Italy and Germany, a Boxing Club with a former professional coach, their own Radio Station which broadcasts during break-time and the luncheon period, a Model car/train club and a WiFi computer games club. The school even has boys who are members of the *Only Boys Aloud* choir.

The school of today is structured in quite a different way from the old grammar school. Approximately fifty full-time staff, plus support assistants equivalent to almost forty full-time staff, look after more than 1000 pupils. There are roughly 190 students in the Sixth Form including up to thirty pupils (mainly girls) from other schools. The time-table operates on a two-week cycle with five one-hour lessons daily. School begins at 8.30 a.m. and concludes at 2.50 p.m., with a fifteen minute morning break, and forty-five minutes for lunch. Pupils attend morning assembly twice a week but there is no religious service. The school motto has changed from *Ni Ddwchwel Doe* (Yesterday Never Returns) to *Every Pupil in the School Matters* - a statement that rings true for anyone who visits the school with their eyes and ears open, and walks the corridors emblazoned with its colourful home-produced murals. There is no Prefect system and staff do not wear gowns. *The Ludovican*, the former school magazine has been replaced by a termly *Newsletter* of sixteen A4 pages in full colour. This incorporates numerous photographs of school events.

Another significant difference compared with days long past is the extent to which the school is integrated into the local community. There is a thriving Inter-generational Club: local pensioners gather for lunch on the school premises and the pupils mix with them; some pupils have accompanied groups of pensioners on day-trips, even as far as London. There is a *Get It Together* group that helps older people to understand and operate the internet, and a St John Cymru Wales group that organises Emergency First Aid courses in the school. Pensioners also attend for indoor bowls and bingo with pupils. At the Christmas lunch the numbers exceed two hundred.

In earlier decades all pupils sat examinations set by the Welsh Joint Education Committee. Today each subject/department can choose from any of the Examining Boards operating within the UK. In consequence they choose the curriculum most suitable to their wishes and thereby hope to maximise their examination results. At Sixth Form level the school belongs to a consortium that includes Bargoed C S, Lewis Girls' C S, Rhymney C S, Ysgol Gyfun Cwm Rhymni and the College at Ystrad Mynach. This gives an enormous range of subjects for all the pupils within the consortium.

In conclusion it is very pleasing to be able to write that the most recent Estyn School Inspection (February 2012) states that the performance of the school in every aspect is *Good*. May Lewis' School aim to give the best possible start in life to all the young people within its catchment area.

Appendix I

How good it would be to gain a glimpse of what life was like for a pupil in Pengam in the 1880s. Fortunately that is possible through an article written by Edgar Jenkins of Pontypridd which appeared in *The Ludovican* in the Summer of 1951.

Lewis' School - 1882.

In 1882 a small boy of tender years was admitted into the Old School at Pengam as a day scholar. I was that nine year old small boy and I had heard a great deal about the School from an older brother who is still alive and who had been a pupil at the School two years before me. It is remarkable how vividly events of seventy years ago come to mind in one's old age, and my memories of the Old School are much clearer than events of recent years.

The School building comprised (1) a large assembly room approached from the entrance through a dark ante-room, which contained the library, (2) a class-room, and (3) the old church. The house for boarders, occupied by the assistant-master, was approached along a long cloistered passage to the right of the entrance. There were three classes in the School - junior, middle and senior, and I well remember being placed at the bottom of the junior class the day I was admitted, but by annual promotion I soon reached the senior class, where I had to take my place with boys of sixteen and seventeen years of age.

The Headmaster was the Rev. David Evans, MA, a towering giant to my eyes - he was well over six feet in height and proportionately built. He always wore a clerical hat and a frock coat, in the back tail pocket of which he always carried his cudgel, fashioned from a map roller, about 18 inches in length and tapering to a blunt point at one end. This cudgel was very much in evidence daily and became very smooth through constant use. It was the ambition of most of the boys to obtain possession of this cudgel, but, unless my memory fails me, the only one who achieved this distinction was a Ferndale boy (still living, in Porthcawl) who had felt its quality only to a little lesser degree than myself. Rumour had it that later in life he had it silver-mounted in a glass case, but I cannot vouch for the truth of this! I was the youngest boy in the senior class, but the Head expected as much from me as from boys of greater ages. For instance, I was once punished severely for not being able to prove on the blackboard that a quadratic equation had two roots!

The Headmaster lived in the Lower House and we often scanned his features as he walked up to School in majestic fashion, to try to forecast what was before us that day. Mr Evans was a preacher with the Calvinistic Methodists; and on Sunday morning all the boarders were marched to Bargoed for the morning service, along the upper and only road past the old Gilfach Farm, the only building between the School and the village.

The sole assistant master was Mr Roger Jones, BA, who, in 1886, I think, succeeded Mr Evans as the School's Head. Mr Jones spent most of his time in the large room attempting to teach two classes at the same time. He was cool, calm, deliberate, a fine disciplinarian; and one whose influence must still be felt in hundreds of lives of men who in their young days passed through his hands. We all feared him, in the sense that we would hesitate to do anything contrary to School law and order where he was concerned. He could enforce discipline where necessary; but his cane was always locked up in the library cupboard from which the delinquent had to fetch it, and wait in the ante-room for his punishment. This was a very rare procedure.

To Mr Evans I was always 'little boy Jenkins', while my brother was 'big boy Jenkins', but Mr Jones always addressed us by our Christian names. During the reign of Mr Evans the up-train to the Rhymney Valley, by which many boys travelled daily, reached Pengam station about 5 p.m. If any investigation had to be made into any wrong doing (and there were many), we would all be assembled in the large room to be catechised. The culprit would be asked to come forward; but there would be no response; and, of course, no one ever split on his friends. After several attempts, the Head would give it up and proceed to the entrance and look towards Hengoed for signs of the train. It was only when he saw steam from the approaching train that he would hurry back to dismiss us. What a rush those Rhymney boys would have to the station! However, engine drivers of those days were very accommodating and would hold up the train until the last panting boy arrived.

I recently repeated the names of about 60 boys who were my contemporaries. The Old School had a great reputation in those days and many of my school companions reached positions of honour in later life. Contingents of boys came daily from Blackwood, Ystrad, Bargoed, Pontlottyn and Rhymney. Most of us walked to School; and the weather was never allowed to deter us, although it meant a walk of 3½ miles each way. I remember distinctly the fiery hair of Harry Price, the slow manner of George Howells, who are both still alive and the shuffling gait of Henry Gethin Lewis. There may be others still with us whom I have forgotten. The Old School bred a tough lot of youngsters. We had none of the molly-coddling of to-day, no bus to carry us a mile to school, no school canteens, no sports-grounds and organised games. We were supplied with boxing gloves and had to learn to take hard knocks in good spirit. The only test games were Boarders v. Day Scholars and the excitement these games produced would outdo that of Twickenham.

In conclusion, I would like to thank the Editor for allowing me to write this short account for the Magazine. I should also like to say that any little success I achieved as Headmaster of a large boys' school, I attribute to the influence of one man whose name is ever fresh in the memories of Old Boys - Roger Jones.

Appendix 2

This essay won first prize in the 1931 School Eisteddfod.

Ysgol Lewis, Pengam, yn y Flwyddyn 2000

Dyma ni yn cyrraedd Pengam, mangre ysgol fyd-enwog Lewis. Edrychwn i lawr o'r awyr ar yr adeilad llwyd ac eang o'n'hawyrlong, a chanfyddwn y ffenestri dirif a'r tir bras a rydd ffordd glir i'r goleuni naturiol i'r gwahanol ystafelloedd. Tynnir ein sylw ar unwaith at y tir a ddefnyddir gan awyrlongau y meistriaid, a gerllaw, gwelir llecyn arall a ddefnyddir gan awyrlongau'r myfyrwyr. Gwelir amryw o awyr longau wedi cyrraedd, ond mae yn eglur bod llawer heb lanio eto.

Sylfaenwyd yr ysgol hon dri chan mlynedd yn ol, ac oddeutu can mlynedd yn ol dechreuodd wneud enw iddi ei hun fel canolfan addysg y rhan hon o'r Dywysogaeth. Pan ddaeth teithio'r awyr yn gyffredin, cafodd yr ysgol le amlycach ym mywyd y Genedl gan i'r cyfleusterau ddyfod i gyrraedd bechgyn o bellteroedd, a gallant yn awr ddyfod o'u cartrefi bob dydd i fanteisio ar yr addysg uwchraddol a gyfrennir ynddi. O dipyn i beth, daeth yr ysgol i'r sefyllfa y cawn hi ynddi yn awr. A gadael allan y brifysgol, dyma ganolfan addysg Cymru a pha ryfedd y ceir ar ei llyfrau enwau meibion prif-drigolion ein gwlad. Yma ymgymysga, fel yn yr hen ddyddiau, feibion prif golofnau diwylliant yn ogystal a phlant y gweithwyr. Erbyn hyn nid oes ond y nesaf peth i ddim i wahaniaethu rhwng y ddau ddosbarth. Ac y mae hyn i'w briodoli i helaethrwydd y gyfundrefn a ddilynwyd gan oruchwylwyr ac athrawon yr ysgol.

Ymhyfryda'r ysgol mewn adeilad gwych a adeiladwyd hanner can mlynedd yn ôl, wedi i'r hen adeilad syrthio o herwydd gweithio'r glo yn y tir odditano. Adeilad o faen ydyw, a saif ar ei ben ei hun fel enghraifft wych mewn celfyddyd. Gwelir y gellir agor rhan uchaf yr adeilad yn gyfangwbl fel y gellir manteisio ar awyr iach sydd yn anhepgorol angenrheidiol i gadw'r corff yn iach ac felly i roddi'r cyfle gorau i ddatblygu meddyliau'r ieuainc yn yr adeg bwysicaf ar eu hoes. Llenwir yr ysgol ag ystafelloedd eang, a chawn ynddynt bopeth angenrheidiol at y gwaith a wneir ynddynt. Mor wahanol ydyw pethau i'r hyn a welwyd yma yn yr hen ddyddiau! Gwelwn welliannau ymhob cyfeiriad fel yr awn ymlaen. Erbyn hyn gwelwn ysmotiau ymhob cyfeiriad a daw'r bechgyn yn lluoedd i'r ddaear. Dyma'r bechgyn yn ymddiosg eu dillad cynnes ar ol teithio drwy'r awyr lem. Parhânt i ddewis awyrlongau agored er y gallent wrth gwrs, eu cuddio eu hunain, pe dewisent, yng nghrombil yr awyrlong. Er yr holl gyfnewidiadau yn yr adeilad, nid oes gyfnewidiad yn natur y llanc. Erys yn fachgen ac yn anturiaethwr drwy'r oesoedd. Sylwn gyda phleser fod rheol a threfn yn parhau mewn

227

grym ac i brofi hyn, gwelwn bob bachgen yn glanhau ei beiriant, ac yn trwsio ei long cyn myned at ei lyfrau - defnyddir y rhain hyd yn hyn. Nid oes berygl o gwbl oddiwrth yr awyrlongau, gan eu bod yn codi ac yn disgyn yn syth ac nid oes arnynt eisiau llawer o le, felly, fel yn y dyddiau gynt.

Awn i'r adeilad a gwelwn bopeth yno'n gryno a thrwsiadus ac awn yn gyntaf i swyddfa'r prif athro. Efe yn unig a gawn yn yr ystafell. Gwna ei waith i gyd drwy beiriannau. Llefara i fewn i beiriant a dyna'r cwbl sydd arno eisiau yn ysgrifenedig ac yn barod iddo. Cynhesir yr ystafell â pheiriant y gellir ei reoli fel y mynnir. Mewn un gongl gwelir blwch mawr o wydr i'r hwn yr â pibell ar un ochr. Terfyna'r bibell y tu allan mewn peiriant hynod, a weithir â thrydan. Cysylltir y bibell a phâr o bethau tebig i 'headphones' a orweddant ar ddesg y prifathro. Deffroir ein cywreinrwydd gan y rhain a gofynnwn i'r prif-athro beth yw eu defnydd. Dywed ef wrthym mai amcan y blwch ydyw ei gynorthwyo i benderfynu materion dyryslyd. Pan fydd angen arno amau un o'r bechgyn, rhoddir ef yn y blwch a chwestiynnir ef. Nid ydyw'r bachgen yn ateb ond dyry'r prif-athro'r peiriant ar waith a daw'r atebion iddo o feddwl y bachgen yn dawel. Nid all y bachgen guddio ei feddyliau, a daw'r gwir allan yn eglur. Pan gyfeiriwn at absenoldeb y teliffon, gwena'r prif-athro a dywed mai yn yr Amgueddfa'n unig y gwelir hwynt yn awr. Cymerir ei le yn awr gan beiriant diwifr, ac er mwyn dangos i ni y modd ei defnyddir, dywed y prif-athro y geilw i fyny gyfaill iddo ysgolfeistr yn yr Alban. A at ei ddesg a chwilio llyfr y teliffon. Dywed wrthym y rhennir y wlad yn barthau. Y mae gan bob rhanbarth gyfnewidfa arbennig, yn ol cryfder y derbyniad. Ceir pob cryfder yn gwahaniaethu ac ni dderbyn un peiriant neges ond yn ol cryfder y derbyniad yr adeiladwyd y peiriant erddo. Wedi dyfod o hyd i gryfder cyfnewidfa y rhanbarth y trig ei gyfaill ynddo, newidia gryfder ei drosglwyddiad nes y daw'r ateb. Cymer y gyfnewidfa yr alwad i fyny a chenir cloch. Y mae gan bob peiriant yn y rhanbarth gryfder derbyniad amrywiol a derbynia negeseuon yn y cryfder neilltuol yn unig, ac nid effeithir arno gan unrhyw gryfder arall. Eglurir i'r gyfnewidfa y cryfder angenrheidiol a rhoddir y prif athro mewn cysylltiad â'i gyfaill. Gwelir yn eglur ragoriaethau y gyfundrefn hon. Nid oes wifrau i'w torri, gellir symud y peiriant fel y bydd angen, gellir galw i fyny unrhyw le yn y byd a gwneir i ffwrdd â rhwystrau o bob math. Dyma rai o'r dyfeisiau a welsom yn yr ystafell.

Gwahoddwyd ni i fyned i wasanaeth boreol yr ysgol a da oedd gennym ddeall ei fod yn parhau mewn grym ac yn hen ysbryd y Cymry. Awn gyda'r prif-athro i'r Neuadd fawr a lenwir gan y myfyrwyr a'r athrawon. Wedi i ni gyrraedd, dyma'r organ fawr yn cychwyn a'r holl ysgol yn ymuno yn y weddi agoriadol. Yna cafwyd emyn a dilynid ef gan ddarlleniad o'r Ysgrythur a Gweddi'r Arglwydd. Parhâ'r gwasanaeth yn syml ac adeiladol. Diddorol iawn ydoedd rhai o'r cyhoeddiadau. Yn gyntaf cafwyd proffwydoliaeth o'r tywydd am y dydd ac yr oedd hyn o fantais fawr, gan fod gan y tywydd lawer i'w wneud â'r trwsio angenrheidiol ynglyn â'r awyrlongau yn ystod y dydd. Cyfeiriodd y prif-athro at y ffaith iddo weled, ychydig dyddiau yn ol, rai o'r bechgyn lleiaf ar y glas wellt yn ystod yr awr ginio. Difyrrwyd ni gan y syniad fod deng mlynedd a thrigain heb adael yr un effaith o gwbl yn y cyfeiriad hwn. Synnwyd ni fod pob un o'r bechgyn a'r athrawon yn gwisgobathodyn Urdd Gobaith Cymru, a'u bod yn ymhyfrydu yn y ffaith. Deallwn y byddai cyfarfod o'r Urdd yn ystod y dydd. Penderfynasom fyned yno i weled a oedd yr hen ysbryd, yr hen frwdfrydedd, yn parhau. Wedi ychydig yn rhagor o gyhoeddiadau, gwasgarodd yr ysgolheigion i'w hystafelloedd. Cyn myned i'r ystafell, aeth pob bachgen i'w neuadd fechan ei hun lle y cadwai ei ddillad, ei lyfrau a'r offer perthynol i'w awyrlong.

Yr oedd ystafell arbennig i bob testun a phob un ohonynt wedi ei threfnu i roddi'r awyrgylch angenrheidiol i waith llwyddiannus yn y testun hwnnw. Rhennir pob ystafell yn ddwy ran a llenwir y rhan flaenaf â byrddau bychain a chadeiriau. Yn y rhan arall ceir ystafelloedd bychain o furiau gwydr, un ystafell i bob disgybl a dyma'r lle a ddefnyddir i ysgrifennu pan na byddai'r athro eisiau presenoldeb y dosbarth yn gyfan. Cysylltir pob un or ystafelloedd bychain hyn yn uniongyrchol â desg yr athro. Rheola pob bachgen gynhesrwydd ei ystafell fel y mynno. Cyfrennir yr addysg yn dra gwahanol i'r hyn y cefais i'r fraint o'i derbyn. Gwelais yn awr wir ddefnydd yr ystafell-oedd bychain. Gwneir llawer mwy o waith unigol nag yn yr hen amser. Gwneir llawer llai o waith gan y dosbarth fel cyfangorff a llawer mwy o waith gan y bechgyn eu hunain. Ymhob un o'r ystafelloedd mawr ceir llyfrgell gymwys i'r dosbarth. Hawdd credu, fel y clywais, mai yn yr ysgol hon y ceir y casgliad gorau yn y wlad o lyfrau ar bob testun. Arwydd eto o weithgarwch yr ysgol.

Ychydig iawn o lafur ofer a wneir gan y bechgyn. Dengys pob gwers gysylltiad trwyadl ac ymarferol â rhyw orchwyl a all fod o ddefnydd i'r bechgyn yn y dyfodol. Wedi myned drwy rai o'r ystafelloedd dangoswyd i mi nodlyfrau rhai o'r bechgyn. Synnwyd fi wrth weled eu bod i gyd yn ysgrifenedig mewn llawfer. Wedi datgan fy syndod, dywedwyd wrthyf fod y byd yn awr yn llawer mwy masnachol ac yn llawer llai llenyddol nag ydoedd yn y dyddiau gynt.

Rhwber oedd defnydd y llawr ac felly ni chlywid swn traed y bechgyn pan symudent o un lle i'r llall. Daeth adeg seibiant. Treuliwyd yr adeg seibiant yng nghyfarfod yr Urdd yn y Neuadd Fawr. Cymraeg pur ydoedd, bob gair, a melys oedd clywed y telynau yn seinio. Melys oedd clywed y bechgyn, y meistriaid a'r telynau yn ymuno mewn hwyl i ganu yr hen alawon. Hawdd gweled fod y Gymraeg yn cynyddu yn llenyddol fel y cynydda'r Saesneg yn fasnachol. Orig felys iawn a dreuliais yma.

Euthum ar ol hyn i ystafell y gwyddonwyr. Dychrynwyd fi gan yr olygfa. Yma eto gweithia pob bachgen ar ei ben ei hun, a chanddo gyflenwad o gyffur ac offer at ei wasanaeth ei hun. Yn ystod fy ymgom â'r athro gwenai wrth glywed fy hen syniadau am wirioneddau sylfaenol gwyddoniaeth a chanfûm fod yr hyn a ddysgais yn fy ieuenctid yn hollol gyfeiliornus a diwerth. Er i mi glywed aml i broffwydoliaeth a minnau yn fachgen, synnwyd fi gan y cyfnewidiadau a'r darganfyddiadau ym myd gwyddoniaeth. Rhaid i mi gyfaddef mai ychydig iawn o ddiddordeb a gymerais mewn fferylliaeth ar ôl fy nyddiau ysgol.

Paratoir ymborth i'r bechgyn mewn neuadd eang i'r pwrpas ac yma ceir pob math o ddodrefn angenrheidiol a'r bwyd wedi ei baratoi gan goginwyr profiadol. Yn un pen i'r neuadd yr oedd dwsin o fechgyn yn canu eu telynau i seiniau 'Sospan Fach,' a ddigwyddai fod ar y rhaglen am y tro.

Wedi cinio euthum i weled y meysydd chware. Cawsom faes y bel droed wedi ei barotoi ar gyfer ymgyrch rhwng Urdd y Ffradydd, Bangor, ag Urdd Ysgol Pengam. Gallwn feddwl mai ychydig iawn o ddefnydd a wneir o gwrt y bel-law ac nid ydyw hyn yn syndod pan welir y cyfleusterau a geir yn yr ymarferle eang a geir yn yr ysgol.

Wrth ymadael â'r ysgol sylwais ar hysbysiad tarawiadol iawn mewn llythrennau breision coch, fel y canlyn :-
Ysgol Lewis.
Gwyl Ddewi 2000 A.D.
Disgwylir i'r Wledd eleni:
BRIFWEINIDOG CYMRU
Y Gwir Anrhydeddus IOLO GRUFFYDD (Iolo Ddu).
Hefyd
Y Gweinidog Addysg- Y Bonwr Huw RHYDDERCH (Ap Llên),
A
SYR MOSTYN JONES (Heddfab) Cynrychiolwr Cymru ar Gynghrair y Cenhedloedd).
Pan glywais mai tri o hen blant Ysgol Pengam oeddynt, llawen-ychodd fy nghalon a gwaeddais -
'Yr Hen Ysgol am Byth !'

For those of us who do not understand what had been written Mrs Hetty Watkins has been kind enough to provide a translation which is given below.

Lewis' School Pengam, in the Year 2,000

Here we are arriving at Pengam the location of the world famous Lewis' School. We look down from the sky onto the grey and extensive building from our airship and we perceive the innumerable windows and the open landscape allowing the natural light to reach the different rooms. Our attention is drawn immediately to the land that is used by the airships of the masters and nearby we see another spot used by the airships of the students. Several airships have arrived but it is obvious that many have not yet landed.

This school was established 300 years ago, and around 100 years ago it started making a name for itself as the centre of education for this area of the Principality. When airtravel became commonplace the school gained a more prominent place in the life of the nation as opportunities became available to boys from a wider area, and they can now come from their homes every day to take advantage of the superior education given here. Over time the school achieved its present status. Apart from the university, this is the education centre of Wales and no wonder we are able to see on its books the names of the prominent people of our country. Here, mixing together, as in the old days, are the sons of the main pillars of industry together with the children of the working class. Now there is next to nothing separating the two classes, and this can be attributed to the wide reaching organisation followed by the school governors and teachers.

The school enjoys the advantages of a fine building - built fifty years ago, after the old building collapsed because of the mining underneath. It's a stone building standing on its own as an excellent example of architecture. We see that it is possible to open the top section of the building completely so that advantage can be taken of the fresh air that is indispensably necessary to keep the body healthy, and thereby giving the best chance to develop the minds of the young during the most important stage of their lives. The school is full of spacious rooms and equipped with everything necessary for the work to be done. Everything we see is so different from the old days. We see improvements in every direction as we proceed. By this time we see dots in the sky in every direction and the boys land in droves. Now the boys take off their warm clothes after travelling through the chilly air. They opt for open airships even though they could shelter if they so wished within the airship. In spite of all the changes to the building, there is no change in the nature of the boy. Throughout the ages boys remain boys and adventurers. It is a pleasure to see that order and discipline are maintained, and to prove this we see each boy cleaning his machine and tidying his airship before going to his books - which are still used. There is no danger at all from the airships as they rise and drop vertically and so they don't need much space as in earlier days.

We enter the building and we see everything there neat and tidy and firstly we go to the Headmaster's office. We find him alone in the room. He uses machines to do all his work. He speaks into a machine and that is all he needs to do. It is written and ready for him. The room is heated by a machine that he can control as he wishes. In one corner we can see a big glass box and into this goes a tube on one side. The tube ends outside in a strange machine powered by electricity. The tube is connected to a pair of what looks like 'headphones' lying on the Headmaster's desk. Our curiosity is aroused by these and we ask the headmaster what is their use. He tells us that the purpose of the box is to help him decide complicated matters. When he has an altercation with one of the boys he puts him in the box and questions him. The boy doesn't answer but the Head starts up the machine and the answers come to him quietly from the boy's mind. The boy can't hide his thoughts and the truth comes out clearly. When we refer to the absence of the telephone the Head smiles and says that one only sees 'phones in the museum these days. Its place has been taken by a wireless machine and in order to show us how it's used the Head says that he will call up a friend of his - a School Master in Scotland. He goes to his desk and consults his telephone book. He tells us the country is divided into areas. Each area has a specific exchange according to the strength of the reception. The strength varies and no machine receives a message that the machine is not built for. After working out the power of the exchange in the area in which his friend lives, he changes the power of his transmission until he gets a reply. The exchange takes up the call and the bell sounds. Every device in the area has a varying receiving power and receives messages in one particular power only; it is not affected by any other power. The exchange receives the signal at the required power and the Head is put in touch with his friend. One can see clearly the excellence of this arrangement. There are no wires to break, the machines can be moved when necessary, any place in the world can be called up, and all other hindrances are done away with. These are some of the devices we saw in the rooms.

We were invited to go to the school's morning service and it was good to see that it was continuing and in the old spirit of the Welsh people. We go with the Head to the large hall filled with students and teachers. After we arrived the large organ started and the whole school joined in the opening prayer. Then we had a hymn which was followed by the scripture reading and the Lord's Prayer. The service continues simply and in a dignified manner. Some of the announcements were very interesting. First we had a weather forecast for the day and this was useful as the weather had a lot to do with the necessary repairing and preparing of the airships during the day. The Head referred to the fact that a few days previously he'd seen some of the youngest boys on the grass in the lunch hour. We were amused by the fact that 70 years had not changed this. We were surprised to see that each boy and teacher wore the badge of the Welsh League of Youth, and that they took great pride in this. We understood that there would be a meeting of the league during the day and decided to go there to see if the old spirit, the old enthusiasm, were still present. After more announcements the pupils went to their rooms. Before going to their rooms every boy went to his own locker where he kept his clothes, his books, and the tools belonging to his airship.

232

There was a specific room for each subject and each one was arranged to give the ambience needed for successful work in that subject. Each room was divided into two sections and the front section was full of small tables and chairs. In the other section were booths with glass walls, one booth for each pupil and this is where the pupils write when the teacher does not need to have the whole class together. These booths are all connected directly to the teacher's desk. Each boy regulates the temperature of his own booth as he wishes. The teaching is delivered in a very different way from the way in which I had the privilege of being taught. I saw now the true use of the booths. Much more individual work being taught than in the old days. Much less work is done by the class as a whole and more work by the boys on their own. In each large room is a library relevant to the class. It is hard to believe, as I heard, that in this school there is the best collection of books on every country in the world. Another sign of the school's excellence.

The boys do not waste much time. In each lesson there is a thorough and practical link to some task that will be of use to them in the future. After going through some of the rooms I saw some of the boys' notebooks. I was surprised to see that they were all written in shorthand. After expressing my surprise I was told that the world was now more commercial and much less literary than in former days.

The floor was made of rubber and so there was no sound when the boys moved from one place to another. The break came and was spent in a meeting of the Urdd in the large hall. Every word was pure Welsh and it was pleasant to hear the harps playing. It was pleasant to hear the boys, the teachers and the harps joining together with gusto to sing the old tunes. It was easy to see that the Welsh was growing literally as the English was growing commercially. I spent a very pleasant hour here.

We went back to the science room. I was taken aback by the scene. Here again each boy worked on his own and had a supply of substances and instruments for his own use. During my chat with the teacher he smiled when he heard my old ideas about the basic truths of science and I discovered that what I had learned in my youth was quite heretical and worthless. Even though I learned many a prophecy when I was a boy I was surprised by the changes and discoveries in the field of science. I must admit that I only had a little interest in chemistry after my school days.

A meal is prepared for the boys in a large hall - purpose built - and here we find every kind of functional furniture and the food prepared by experienced cooks. In one corner of the hall there were a dozen boys playing their harps to the notes of 'Sospan Fach' which was on the programme at the time.

After dinner we went to see the playing fields. We saw the football field prepared for a match between the Friars' School, Bangor, and the team from Pengam school. I think little use is made of the court for handball and this is

233

not surprising when one sees the facilities in the large practice ground that the school has. Leaving the school I noticed a very striking announcement in large red letters as follows:

Lewis School
St David's Day 2000 AD.
We are expecting to the festival this year
The PRIME MINISTER OF WALES
The Rt. Hon. IOLO GRUFFYDD (Black Iolo)
Also
The Education Minister - Peer Huw Rhydderch (Son of Llên)
and
Sir Mostyn Jones (Son of peace)
The Welsh representative on the League of Nations.

When I heard that these three were Old Boys of Pengam my heart rejoiced and I shouted 'The Old School Forever'.

Appendix 3

Some impressions of an 'Old Boy'
upon visiting his Alma Mater in 1933

It was with some repressed emotion that I entered the portals of Lewis' Endowed School one fine morning in November; for had I not been a scholar there some fifty years ago. What memories it recalled.

The building is quite different from what it was at that time. I was sorry when the old building was demolished, but I understand that it was necessary as it was getting unsafe. The old spire was a land-mark, built as it was on an eminence. Those were happy days when I imbibed the knowledge given there.

The masters at that time were the Rev. David Evans, MA, and Mr Roger W Jones, BA. Mr Evans was generally known among the boys as Ianto. I fancy I can see him now with his hat, tilted somewhat in front, and with his frock coat from the pocket of which protruded his cudgel (I can assure you it was not an exotic product). This he used rather frequently upon those of us who needed it most, but I am afraid it had little or no effect. He was keen in Latin on the 'ablative absolute' and the 'accusative and the infinitive.' In the teaching of Mechanics, he had some original methods of his own; for instance, he demonstrated the force of gravity by letting his cudgel drop on the floor, which caused much merriment among the boys. Peace be to his soul! Mr R W Jones - Roger we used to call him as a term of endearment - was quite a different type of man. His lessons in English were extremely good, but what was more important he instilled into us the love for learning. The fact that I am still a student in the pursuit of knowledge, I ascribe to him, and I humbly pay this tribute to his memory.

He was a fine disciplinarian in the true sense, using the wand only on very rare occasions. We loved him too much to cause him any uneasiness. At that time (1882-1884) we numbered about 60 boys. Among my contemporaries were Mr James Evans, Barrister-at-Law, who has just retired after being General Inspector for Wales in the Ministry of Health; Dr Tom Jones, CH, Under-Secretary to the Cabinet; and the late Mr I H Davies, sometime Principal of Aberystwyth University College, and brother- in-law to Mr Tom Ellis, Chief Liberal Whip.

Prize-Day was a great event; it was held in the Church. On that day all the parents of the boys congregated to hear the speeches of some of the Governors, and the reports of the Headmaster and the Examiner. The boys contributed their part by performing a portion of a play from Shakespeare.

I found on my visit that the atmosphere and the spirit of the school are not only being maintained but enhanced. The governors are fortunate in having Mr L S Knight as headmaster; he is a man - apart from his scholarship - of outstanding personality, possessing great kindliness of heart, a worthy successor of R W Jones.

He is an ardent Welshman, proud of his nationality, although his name would lead one to think otherwise.

I arrived at the school early as I thought, but Mr Knight was there and he received me with great cordiality. After a few minutes' conversation, he asked one of the masters to take me to the morning service. The boys, between four and five hundred in number, were already assembled. I was taken to the dais and was given a seat. I was impressed with the discipline and the demeanour of the boys. There was not a sound, not even a whisper, yet they were not listless. To one like myself who has been a schoolmaster, it was striking. I felt honoured by being given a seat to the right of the Headmaster, as though I was a very distinguished person.

After the service, I was escorted around the various class-rooms; and I noticed the same quiet behaviour on the part of the boys, even though the masters would possibly be engaged in conversation with me.

In going into the Junior School, I noticed 3 or 4 of the older boys sitting down by themselves in a small room; upon enquiry I was informed that they had been seeking a haven of peace where they could devote themselves to study without any prompting from anyone.

The teaching is of a very high order. In one room, I listened for a brief period to a master who was taking a subject of which I have some acquaintance. The boys were deeply interested in spite of the matter being abstruse.

I am pleased to find that the name of the school, though officially the Gellygaer County School, is still 'Lewis' School' in ordinary usage, and that its original designation still preserves its continuity and tradition.

Altogether I was delighted with what I saw, for I realised that the Pengam spirit is more vital to-day than ever. I shall not forget my visit to my old School.

FLOREAT LUDOVICA!

E.J.D. *The Ludovican*, Autumn 1933.

Appendix 4

Taken from an article written by E J Davies which appeared in *The Ludovican*, Lent 1934.

The Value of the Study of Mathematics

The reason that so few take up the study of Mathematics is quite apparent to any psychologist. A limited number of people possesses those faculties that are essential to the study of this subject.

In the first place, what are those faculties with which one must be endowed in order to understand its principles and to solve the many and varied problems with which the subject abounds? They are Reason, Concentration and Observation. How few persons there are, who are able to reason logically! Most people have derived their knowledge through the process of memory alone. The information they have imbibed has been acquired without any criticism whatsoever as to whether that Knowledge is true or not. It is useful, and that is all that concerns them. They do not make any effort to understand; they are simply taking what is presented to them without any question as to its truth. They have swallowed their mental food without masticating it; it is not to be wondered at that their mental digestion is deranged. The assimilation of knowledge is thus hindered owing to this method of acquisition. This manner of absorption produces a sluggish inert mentality. Knowledge procured by this process is mere lumber; we cannot even designate it as ballast, because that serves a useful purpose in steadying the ship in ploughing its way through the ocean.

The chief objective in Education - in fact the only true one - is to cultivate the intellect, to train the faculties; not to store the mind with facts which are accessible in a well-selected library. The problems of life are so complex and varied that it is useless for us to have recourse to any book to find a solution, for much has to be left to the individual to make the necessary adjustments in the proper conduct of his life. The important factor in education is to train the mind so that it will readily act in dealing with any problem with which we are confronted. This can only be done by exercising the mind, just as the soldier is drilled so that he can perform certain movements automatically.

Mathematics, par excellence, serves this purpose, for incidentally it trains all the faculties, viz., Memory, Observation, Reason, Concentration and Intuition; furthermore, it creates a habit of mind which is of immense value in the exercise of human thought. It is characterised as being an exact science-which cannot be said of most sciences. It has few conventions. Its conclusions are not particular, but of universal application.

Mathematics too has its ethical value; for who, after its rigorous training, could give the consent of his mind to commit a wrong deed unless he is utterly, devoid of moral sense? At any rate, he realises the consequences of his misdeeds. This influence will undoubtedly serve as a deterrent to wrong- doing.

In the higher branches of the subject even that subtle faculty of the human mind - Imagination - is cultivated; in fact, imagination, as we find in poetry, is already delineated by means of the words of the poem; whereas in Mathematics it is evolved from the nature of the problem under consideration.

The uses of Mathematics which have been already described are by no means its only uses. Doubtless on account of its multilateral nature, Mathematics presents many difficulties to the average individual. Arduous application to the subject is compensated by that wonderful mental agility which results there from, but it needs intense concentration, persistent effort, and unity of purpose, which, it is to be feared, few persons are capable of employing.

Most people characterise mathematics as simply a process of calculation, and assert that a mathematician is nothing other than a mechanician; those who think in that way, oddly enough, are incapable of sustained thought.

Mathematics forms the substructure of almost every science; it also serves as a frame-work for many others.

What little advance would have been made in Magnetism, Electricity, Engineering, Chemistry, Thermo-dynamics, Light and even in Wireless, were it not for Mathematics!

The important point to be considered in the future is the interpretation of the various results, that is to find the corresponding facts in reality which those results represent. This field of philosophical research is full of immense possibilities and untold utility to every phase of human life. There is actually to be seen in some problems the adumbration of the biological evolution of the human species.

There is also another very important value in mathematical training - the Law of Induction - the educing of a principle which is common to several things. Most people look upon each fact as a separate entity, whereas a mathematician is ever seeking for a universal law which may permeate those facts, thus reducing mental effort considerably in subsequent practice. The physical world is full of inter-related phenomena and it is our object to discover that relationship.

Some subjects to a certain extent are only apologies for Mathematics, such as Logic and Philosophy. The only study comparable to it is that of Latin Prose, but even there memory plays by far the major part.

Avowedly, a mathematician must not neglect other studies, especially English, because he must express his ideas clearly, for ever choosing the right word and the correct expression.

The object of this article is to bring to the notice of those who question the value of Mathematics and the utility of its study, the loss suffered by its neglect.

Did not Macaulay in his later years deplore his ignorance of Mathematics, against which subject he had often fulminated with many a diatribe?

We cannot all be geniuses like Einstein, but we can force our way into the fastnesses of this fascinating subject. A lazy thinker will make no progress, but the patient student will have his reward by delving for that quartz which contains the gold hidden among its particles.

All subjects have their particular values, yet the one that stands out pre-eminently as the Matterhorn of knowledge is Mathematics, and like that huge and imposing physical feature it needs ingenuity and effort to scale its heights. We shall be amply repaid by the commanding view we get of life's environments.

Appendix 5

Assistant teachers from abroad

It has been the custom for decades for grammar schools to engage a student teacher from Europe on a one-year contract - the pay in 1936 was £100 p.a. The advantage is mutual - pupils in school are able to learn a language from a native speaker while the student teacher is immersed in a country whose language they are attempting to master. As early as 1932 a French Assistant wrote of her impressions as she arrived:

'On leaving Cardiff the scenery changes completely. Here is the county of Glamorgan more hollowed-out than a mole hill, undulating, dotted here and there with coal tips which resemble miniature mountains. Of this land which was to be mine for one year I saw at first nothing but ugliness, still increased by the melancholy of the early autumn. The sky was threatening, heavy with rain, the river was black, the houses formed long monotonous rows, the smoke from the stacks seemed to add to the hostility of the sky, and Bargoed seems to arouse such dark ideas as only coal can give.'

Many assistants contributed to local culture. In October 1952 Jacques Detain gave a talk to Bargoed Literary and Debating Society entitled *Some aspects of France, Britain and Spain* and in 1957 Simone Picot observed that *'every Sunday, the friendly homely Welsh put on their best clothes and go to chapel whereas the French play football. Perhaps times have changed.'* In 1954 E. Tahmizam commented that *'the double-decker bus was a thrilling but frightening experience'*. His principal complaint was the weather. He was from Provence and missed the sun. A Mathieu spent the following year with us. He was *'bewitched by the great charm of the country - Wye Valley, Brecon Beacons and the Vale of Glamorgan.'* He couldn't understand *'why Lewis' School was in Glamorgan but that the address was Monmouthshire'*. The people were *'exuberant and disciplined, home-loving and genuinely hospitable. Sometimes I wish the French would leave politics to play rugby instead but that game is pretty tough too'*. Simone Picot, from Joan of Arc country, found *'much hospitality and friendliness in Wales. The civic buildings in Cardiff are beautiful, but Welsh people babble a lot on the trains.'* The assistant in 1964 could not have had a happy time for *'the British are a cold race and the cooking is revolting.'*

A. Hoffman, a German assistant, gives advice to the senior boys *'If you can afford it, leave your home; go and see the world before you get rusty.'* He also comments that *'teachers look like blackbirds in their gowns (the wings are formed by the sleeves); you have cosy open fire-places!! and have a hot face and a cold back'*. On some of the trains he could not understand a word - it was all in Welsh. *'You are not reserved but are open-hearted, very friendly and make us all feel at home.'* Werner Bleyehl says that people are very friendly and fair. He'd never expected such a mild winter but, because our heating systems are so inefficient and our houses so poorly insulated, he'd never frozen so much in any winter. We hate uniformity. We turn our forks upside-down to eat peas. We have total liberty - to join a union or association. Everybody fits neatly into his exact social classification. So much unites the British and the Germans. W Butt, the assistant in 1962-63, had a different take. We have an inferiority complex. We are insular and lazy, with very inefficient fire-sides, draughty windows and wide open spaces indoors, we make fun of ourselves. We think Germans are all hardworking. German police never fail to impress their importance on you, they are always alert to catch you out. They give instruction rather than help to people in need. British police have an air of dignity; they're interested in your welfare. Germans distrust uniforms especially in the young.'

The impressions of Genevieve Moliner as she was about to leave after spending a year as French Assistant.

Have you already been to France? Do you know it very well? I expect that some of you have visited Paris and after that you judge France from what you read and from what you hear. The result of all this is that in general you have got a queer idea of France - and false!

I had the same mixed ideas of England - sorry! Great Britain. It was the first time - oh! what a shame! - that I had been to Great Britain. My idea of the typical English man was an odd mixture of what I had read and of what I had heard from people who know nothing about it. The result was that for me the Englishman was very tall (at least six feet tall), skinny, with short fair hair, blue eyes and glasses. During the week he would wear a black jacket, striped trousers, a bowler hat and carry a briefcase - with his lunch in it - and during the weekend wear his oldest golf trousers to mow the lawn. He was very cold and reserved, never spoke to a person unless introduced and when he happened to like a foreigner, he would say: *'What a pity he does not speak English!'* His main topic of conversation was the weather.

I thought that the morals were still the same as in Victorian days when - so they say - they used to wrap the piano's legs in cloth because it was shocking for them to be shown. All that in spite of some more modern information by which we were told of the existence of 'some' mods and rockers.

As for the food, some persons - who had never come to England - had warned me very much by telling me that English people mix everything on their plate: sugar, salt, jam, all kinds of sauces, forgetting of course, that we almost do the same.

As for the fashions I still thought the girls were wearing dresses down to the ankles. I found they wore them ... a little shorter.

But there was a very important thing my professors had forgotten to tell me: Wales was different from England. Had they done so, I would not have been so surprised. I had been told to answer: *'How do you do?'* when asked: *'How do you do?'* and never to shake hands. Unfortunately for me nothing happened as I expected. I have never been asked: *'How do you do?'* and the first thing people did when I was introduced was to shake hands with me in such a way that I could have screamed out of pain.

I belong to a people who have a reputation for being talkative and liking gossip. But I think that Welsh people are even better in that respect with the result that I felt almost at home in this atmosphere.

I found that, in general, Welsh people had that disrespect for English people we southerners have for people from the north of the River Loire. So I have been able to find that, in many respects we are alike.

The only important fault I could find in Welsh people was that they did not speak French.

The Ludovican, Summer 1966.

Another German assistant's View

Stefan Lodes, the German student who was to spend a year at the school relates how he found himself in Blackwood but did not know how to get from there to Pengam.

Some young fellows took pity on me and took me over to school. But I could not understand a word of their conversation. What had I been studying English for? He goes on *The headmaster gave me a very hearty welcome and showed me around the school, which I would have mistaken for a church without further knowledge. The Monday after, when I first appeared at school, I could hardly believe my eyes, when I saw the teachers moving around in black gowns which was a completely new sight to me. The next new thing which amazed me rather more was the morning-assembly and the service. Perhaps Welsh people are more religious than continental ones, the impression of which was confirmed by the disciplined and devoted homage to God.*

Another point which I find worth mentioning is the classification of boys into subprefects, prefects, deputy head boy and head boy. On the one hand, it may be very useful to entrust them with certain rights and duties from a relatively early age to relieve the teachers from organisation and supervision work and, in addition to that, give them a certain feeling of responsibility, on the other hand, however, it involves the danger of imposing on them an unwanted hierarchic system which society may not require. Perhaps there are some other reasons I have not yet discovered.

As to wearing school uniforms (which is also unknown on the continent), there is one strong argument justifying it, namely social equality by uniform appearance. Yet one cannot achieve this goal by creating a restriction of personal freedom and possible suppression of individualism and thus doing more harm than good. To keep things up only for the sake of tradition, which might be another reason in favour, is in this case not very convincing as there is no compelling evidence to do so.

It is not my concern, however, to criticise institutions which, applied to British standards, have served you well. There are quite a few things we can learn from them. The wide range of subjects which are offered to pupils is amazing and insofar different from ours as you can choose the subjects you are inclined to and by that reach a very high standard. Another thing which caught my eye right from the beginning is the amount of time and effort spent on sport. Apparently, British schools have the right attitude towards physical education and pay the tribute it deserves in contrast to Germany. The great variety of games, in which Rugby obviously enjoys absolute priority, provides the necessary compensation to brain work as well as it creates a feeling of solidarity and pride when competing with other schools.

Furthermore, I appreciate the general atmosphere in Lewis' School. The relation between teachers and boys is far more personal than in German schools and the relatively small groups and streams allow a more individual education adequate to one's standard.

I think, if the school goes on like that, it will maintain its reputation throughout South Wales.

The Ludovican, Summer 1971.

Appendix 6

Three talented former pupils

Legion are the boys who have been educated at Lewis' School, many of whom have been mentioned in the pages of this book. As an adjunct I have chosen to expand on the lives of three boys who went on to make their marks in the world: cousins Henry Gethin Lewis and David George Hall, both of Pontlottyn, and Lewis Boddington of Brithdir.

Henry Gethin Lewis, born 1872, was one of the most successful old boys in the field of business in the early part of the last century. In 1911 he, together with his cousin David, founded a company of Wagon Contractors, a company that grew to be the largest private Wagon Company in the whole of Britain. During World War I, the company was responsible for transporting coal from the collieries to His Majesty's ships. By the 1920s Henry had reached the zenith of his success and influence. In 1927 he bought Wernfawr at Harlech, and presented it to the founders of Coleg Harlech, the principal founder being Thomas Jones CH,

Henry Gethin Lewis and Dr. Thomas Jones CH.

another Pengam old boy. Henry Gethin also bought and gave to the National Library of Wales the E C Quiggin Celtic Collection, was High Sheriff of Glamorgan 1920-21, a governor and treasurer of University College, Cardiff, a governor and councillor of the National Library, and treasurer of the National Eisteddfod.

Henry Gethin's cousin **David George Hall**, who was affectionately known as 'D G', was born of a humble family in Pontlottyn. At that time industrial depression overshadowed the country and his father travelled twenty miles to work at Celynen Colliery, Abercarn. Tragically, when 'D G' was still young, his father was killed in a colliery explosion. However, in due course he won an entrance scholarship to Lewis' School. Having matriculated, he ventured into the busy world of commerce, being employed by Tredegar Iron Company before joining his cousin and setting up their wagon company. Following in the footsteps of his cousin D G was appointed High Sheriff of Glamorgan in 1935. Not forgetting his old School, in token of this great honour and realising how Lewis' School had prepared him for his future life, he presented a beautiful ornate, brass lectern which still stands in the school foyer. David G Hall, JP, will always be remembered as a man of remarkably gentlemanly disposition. He was known for his generosity, and was always ready to help anyone in need.

Lewis Boddington was a native of Brithdir, who attended Pengam School from 1919 until 1924. After five years at School he entered the University and Technical College at Cardiff, to study Engineering; here he obtained a joint Diploma of both Colleges and was awarded the Edward Nicholl Scholarship. In 1936, he entered the Royal Aircraft Establishment at Farnborough as a technical assistant to P Salmon, the father of Naval Aircraft Operations. On Mr Salmon's retirement in 1942, his place was taken by Lewis Boddington. In these war years the demands were great on this aspect of the Navy, the well-worn techniques of the time being literally shattered. Tremendous credit is thus due to Lewis's contribution to the development of aircraft carriers especially the techniques of taking off and landing. The name of Lewis Boddington will always be remembered when such terms as 'flexible deck' and 'angled deck' are mentioned.

However, the activities of Lewis were not confined to engineering. He was largely responsible for the re-organisation of all the Drawing Offices of the Royal Aircraft Establishment to comply with war-time needs. He had strong associations with the RAF Technical College and was justly proud to be a member of the Board of Governors of Farnborough Grammar School. In 1951, after fifteen years at Farnborough, Lewis was transferred to the Ministry of Supply, to the post of Deputy-Director of Research and Development of Aircraft for the Royal Navy. Two years later he became its Director. In 1953 he was awarded the Bronze Medal of the Royal Aeronautical Society and in January 1955 the Government made a significant grant to enable his work on 'angled' flight decks for aircraft carriers to continue.

The achievements of these three former pupils who, apparently, were ordinary valley men, remain an example to us all.

Appendix 7

Two shining stars - P J S and J D F

Philip James Stradling Williams was Head boy for the school year 1956-57. The classics master, W J Morris, stated that he was the brightest boy he had ever taught. In later years many claimed that, as a Welshman, he possessed the most piercing intellect of his generation. P J S, as he was always referred to in school, was to become a world renowned scientist but his all round ability is epitomised by his success in the 1957 school eisteddfod. He won Senior Lyric, Senior Short Story, Senior Recitation and English Essay, and scored more points than any other pupil that year. Thereby he was awarded the silver cup which had been donated by his parents to be awarded annually to the boy with the most points at the School Eisteddfod.

Phil Williams

P J S was also secretary of the Scientific, Literary and Debating Society (SLADS), the most important society in the school. A State Scholar, Phil, as he became known out of school, was offered an Open Scholarship to Clare College, Cambridge, an Open Scholarship to Gonville and Caius College, Cambridge, and a Meyricke Scholarship to Jesus College, Oxford. He chose Clare following his brother David who had gone up to Clare a few years earlier. Have you ever wondered if good health and academic ability are significantly correlated? For the record, in fourteen years in school before going up to Cambridge P J S never missed a day.

As a student at Clare he was awarded a First, then a PhD for post-graduate research at the Mullard Radio Astronomy Observatory at Cambridge. Although a Fellow of Clare, for most of the remainder of his career Phil was based at Aberystwyth where he was appointed Professor of Solar-Terrestrial Physics in 1991. He was a Fellow of the Royal Astronomical Society and served on their Council for three years. Apart from his scientific career politics played a very important part in his life. For several years he was Vice-President of Plaid Cymru. He stood unsuccessfully for the Westminster Parliament and for the European Parliament before being elected to the Welsh Assembly in 1999. Phil Williams died in 2003. He had so much still to offer.

John David Francis Jones, known in school and to his work colleagues as J D F, followed P J S as Head boy. His literary skills were apparent to all while he was still in school, contributing numerous articles, poems, short stories and reports of events, to *The Ludovican* of which he became editor. In his last year he, like P J S, scored more points than any other boy in the school eisteddfod. His wins included Senior Short Story, History Essay and the Crown Poem.

Showing yet more versatility J D F won second prize in a National Exhibition of Children's Art in Wales.

J D F won a State Scholarship and went up to Balliol College, Oxford, in 1959 where he read history. As a journalist he began work at the *Merthyr Express*, then moved to South Africa where he was employed on the *Pretoria News*, followed by a short spell with *Reuters*, before joining the staff at the *Financial Times* as launch editor of Weekend F T in 1985. At the F T he progressed first to foreign editor, then managing editor and finally weekend editor. He revolutionised the international reporting of the newspaper by setting up a network of correspondents second only to that of the *New York Times*. He succeeded in his aim to convert a commercially languid Saturday newspaper into a genuine competitor for the Sunday press. J D F retired from the F T in 1993 to become a full-time writer publishing several novels about Africa where he had been a foreign correspondent from 1981 to 1985. He, like P J S, failed to reach his three-score-years-and-ten leaving, when he died in 2009, an unfinished biography of Jan Smuts, the South African statesman.

P J S and J D F are but two of the former pupils who passed through the portals of Lewis' School, who showed great promise while there and would go on to make their mark in the world. These two contributed significantly to our understanding of the world and its peoples and to solving some of the associated problems.

Appendix 8

Unveiling of the pictures

Copies of the two pictures are shown in colour on page 222.

This ceremony was held in the School Chapel at 2.30 p.m. on Friday, 26th February, 1971.

After the processional hymn the Rev. D Parry, Rector of Gelligaer, offered the opening prayer. This was followed by a speech from the Chairman Mr W E Park, who was deputising for County Councillor D Williams. He expressed his regret at the absence of the latter but at the same time said that he was delighted to have the opportunity of attending the service. Following this speech Mr B Parry, the music master, gave an excellent rendering of a variation on Crimond on the organ. After a short speech by Dr A Trevor Jones, provost of the Welsh National School of Medicine, in which he outlined the history of the school up to the present day and commented on its high standard, the unveiling took place.

The first picture to be unveiled was that of the original Lewis' School at Gelligaer in 1729, while the second was a picture of the present school as it was when it first opened in 1848. Both pictures were skilfully painted by an old boy of the school Mr J Coslett Jones.

We then had a dedication prayer by the Rector. After this the School Choir sang the Russian Hymn, in which P Edmunds, a member of the junior school, was the soloist. Mr W T Jones, the donor of the pictures, then gave a short speech in which he talked of the artist and congratulated him on his fine work.

The Headmaster conveyed his thanks to all the distinguished people present and remarked that this was a memorable day in the history of the school.

On behalf of the pupils, Tony Andrews, one of the Deputy Head Boys thanked all concerned who made this presentation possible. The service was concluded by a Benediction from the Rev. D Parry.

G. A. KITCHER, S. PHILLIPS *Ludovican* 1971

Note. The original school house at Gelligaer opened in August 1762. The outside staircase was added in 1815.

Bibliography

DAVIES, IOLO, 'A Certaine School', Cowbridge, 1967.

GLOVER, E P, *Newport High School for Boys, The First Sixty Years 1896-1956*, R H Johns, Newport 1957.

GUY, John R, *The Diocese of Llandaff in 1763*, Cardiff: South Wales Record Society 1991.

HARRISON, Wilfred, *Greenhill School Tenby 1896-1964. An Educational and Social History*, Cardiff, 1979.

JENKINS, J Geraint, *Getting Yesterday Right*, Amberley Publishing 2009.

JONES, Gareth Elwyn. *Controls and Conflicts in Welsh Secondary Schools 1889-1944*, Cardiff 1982.

JONES, Gareth Elwyn. *Which Nation's Schools, Direction and Devolution in Welsh Education in the Twentieth Century*, Cardiff 1990.

JONES, G E and G W RODERICK *History of Education in Wales*, University of Wales Press 2003.

KNIGHT, L Stanley. *Welsh Cathedral Schools to 1600AD*. Hon. Society of Cymmrodorion, 1919.

LEECH, Barbara. *Full Circle, City of Cardiff High School for Girls 1950-70*. Printed by The Starling Press Ltd, Risca 1986.

O'BRIEN, A Mór, *The County School for Boys Pontypridd 1896-1973*. Published 1989.

SAUNDERS, E John and others, *The Gelligaer Story*. Gelligaer U D C 1959.

SEABOURNE, Malcolm. *Schools in Wales 1500-1900, A social and Architectural History*, Gee & Son Ltd, Denbigh 1992.

THOMAS, Jan, *Our Heritage, Memories of Lewis Girls' School 1729-1998*, published by the school.

WILLIAMS, James. *Give Me Yesterday*, Country Book Club, 1973

WRIGHT, Arthur. *The History of Lewis' School, Pengam*, published by the author 1929.

Newspapers and magazines.
Caerphilly Local History Society,
Journal of Gelligaer History Society
South Wales Echo
Western Mail

Glamorgan Record Office
Copies of *The Ludovican* and various papers

Winding House, New Tredegar, various, including:
Admission and Progress Registers.
Annual reports.
Collection of Arthur Wright's photographs
Headprefects' diaries
The Ludovican, 1931 to 1973, published by the school
Minutes of Governors Meetings.
Minutes of Staff Meetings, 1928-1936
Outward correspondence 1964-65
Dr J A Pate's collection of newspaper cuttings 1926-1963.
Punishment Book
School log books 1943-1966
Speech Day programmes

Index

262